VIETNAM, 1965

The whine of the chopper engines and shouts of "Saddle up" awoke me at dawn. I grabbed my harness and rifle and ran beside Johnson toward a waiting line of four slicks. The Blues were already there, standing in a ragged circle and playing rifles and machine guns like imaginary guitars. They were shouting lyrics of "Rockin' Robin" above the beat of the chopper blades, swaying and stomping their feet in cadence. "Rockin' Robin . . . bop, bop, bop." That gyrating circle of men, black and white, with mustaches and sideburns, hung all over with belts of ammunition and grenades, was like a scene from a psycho ward. A few minutes later, these same men would be stepping over muddy bodies many miles away . . .

"Vividly written and appallingly graphic . . . Brennan describes with sympathy and understanding the heroes, the cowards, those who enjoyed the killing and those who went to war to be killed themselves."

—*Publishers Weekly*

Matthew Brennan

BRENNAN'S WAR

VIETNAM 1965-1969

POCKET BOOKS

New York   London   Toronto   Sydney   Tokyo

Artwork on page vii by Sally Oliver

POCKET BOOKS, a division of Simon & Schuster Inc.
1230 Avenue of the Americas, New York, NY 10020

Cover photo courtesy of UPI/Bettmann Newsphoto

Published by arrangement with Presidio Press
Library of Congress Catalog Card Number: 85-518

ISBN: 0-671-70595-4

First Pocket Books printing September 1986

10 9 8 7 6 5 4

POCKET and colophon are registered trademarks of
Simon & Schuster Inc.

Printed in the U.S.A.

FOR THE PILOTS AND HELICOPTER CREWS
OF THE 9TH CAVALRY.
THEY WERE BRAVE BEYOND
HUMAN UNDERSTANDING.

HAPPINESS AND SADNESS
I WILL REMEMBER FOREVER.

NVA *soldier's diary*
Suoi Ca Mountains
February, 1967

Contents

"If all men were just,
   there would be no need for valor."

AGESILUS
444–400 B.C.

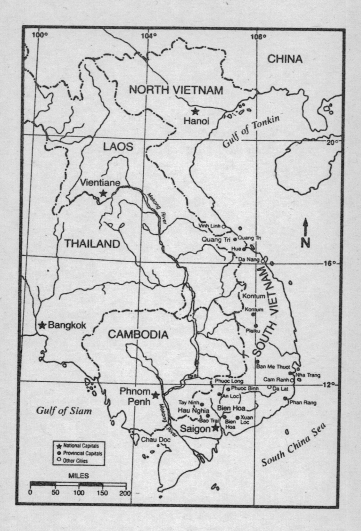

Prologue

Most of this book is about life in an air cavalry troop. Each of these company-sized outfits served as the reconnaissance unit for an entire brigade. An air cavalry troop had ten gunships, ten small scout helicopters, an understrength infantry platoon, the Blue platoon, and six slicks to carry the Blues into battle. The number of engagements started by these troops was far out of proportion to their size. A month in one could be equal to a year in combat in many line outfits. Whatever personalities we had before coming to the 9th Cav Blues were soon submerged by the endless cycle of helicopter landings and violence. Men were changed forever. Our rule of thumb was that the typical new recruit had about six months before he was killed, wounded, or pushed to the edge of insanity.

We learned not to get close to many people because it was always harder to see your friends die. We seldom cared what day of the week it was. It was only March or May or August, and the only events anyone ever recalled were those that held some special meaning in our special world. Our reference points to life were "the ambush on December first" or "the day Arthur died" or "the night Doc got drunk in Chu Lai." Our loyalties were only to each other.

Vietnam was a place of contrasts. Beauty and devastation often coexisted in such a peaceful way that it seemed to be almost natural. Once I found a delicately painted porcelain teacup in the mud of a wrecked jungle bunker. A fire set by helicopter rockets raged all around us, but the teacup seemed as natural in the mud as it would have been on the altar of a Vietnamese family shrine.

There was another day when we had spent the entire afternoon stalking through a destroyed village. Artillery shells had sheared the top from every palm tree and left the few huts still standing without roofs. Nothing stirred in that smoldering hellhole. Even the Viet Cong had abandoned it. Then we saw her. A young woman sat on a low stool at the edge of the village, nursing a baby. It was such a strange thing to walk through all that destruction and then to find her. We brave children went into the groves at the edge of the jungle and brought back the few undamaged bananas and coconuts as gifts. The woman smiled and the baby nursed and the place was transformed. She was our Vietnamese Madonna. In that particular region her husband had to be a Viet Cong fighter, but it just didn't matter at the moment.

The brutality of Vietnam was commonplace and endless. Once we found a seventy-year-old woman who had been shot through the head by a Viet Cong political officer. She had refused to share one half of her meager rice hoard with the local guerrilla squad. There was a teenage girl from the same area who was killed by us as she defended a large rice storehouse in the hills. She had been firing a captured American rifle. I remember her well—a soldier dragged her body into the burning hooch to serve as a warning to others. Today the Vietnamese Communists will probably tell you that the old woman was useful as a lesson for the other villagers and that the young girl was a heroine. I don't know.

I never understood why America was in Vietnam or what motivated the Viet Cong and North Vietnamese soldiers to fight so bitterly. My understanding was only that I was among the small fraction of Americans in Vietnam who were actually involved in the fighting. I had wanted to be a "combat" soldier, and I wore the blue Combat Infantry Badge with pride. After all, the badge always got such respectful stares from rear echelon supply clerks and truck drivers. Our collective future, the time of being a Vietnam veteran and of being afraid or ashamed to mention it, was still light-years in the future.

CHAPTER 1

Decisions

In early 1965 I was a teenage private in Germany. News of America's war in Asia could be found mostly in latrines and beer halls in those days, and the Army's rumor mill was going full tilt. The Marines were at Da Nang. The paratroopers were in War Zone C. Men with certain special skills were being suddenly transferred back to the United States. We listened to an ex-helicopter gunner from another unit tell the same stories about "hunting dinks" over and over again. Something big had to be brewing, and many of us volunteered for Vietnam. We were all turned down. The artillery units in Europe were too understrength as it was.

I returned to the United States in September 1965 to attend the United States Military Academy Prep School at Fort Belvoir, Virginia. It was there that I first read of the bloody battles being fought by the 1st Air Cavalry Division in the Ia Drang Valley. I was sure the war would end while I was stuck in a classroom. I resigned from the prep school over the protests of my tactical NCO, a man who proudly displayed a captured Viet Cong flag and wore two rows of decorations. He told me not to be so eager, that the war would still be there in 1970 when I graduated from West Point. But I couldn't imagine the war lasting for five more years.

Soon I was in Oakland, California, waiting for a flight across the Pacific. The replacement depot was a beehive of activity.

Artillery and infantry units in the United States were being cannibalized to supply new blood to the units already in Vietnam. Always there were the endless lists of men being called for shipment to the war zone, and always new faces were arriving from a stream of cabs and military buses.

Many of the replacements were from the 82d Airborne Division, the All-American division of World War II fame, recently returned from a police action in the Dominican Republic. Those loud, swaggering soldiers would sit on the bunks until the early hours of the morning, sharpening their assorted trench knives, boot knives, and bayonets and bragging about how they were going to stop the dinks in nothing flat. They cleaned and oiled their "unauthorized" pistols, some of which had accompanied fathers and older brothers to other wars in other places.

The replacements at Oakland felt and acted like part of a conquering army. Most of us didn't understand what was really happening in Vietnam. We believed that the war had reached its final stages and that we might arrive after the last big battles were won. All of us were proud of America's strength and her ability to end guerrilla wars quickly. We were too naive to be afraid.

My group left for Vietnam in mid-December 1965. Twenty-two hours after the flight began, the plane was taxiing up to a wooden terminal building at the Tan Son Nhut Air Base outside Saigon. We walked onto a steaming and unhurried airfield that might have been a large civilian airport, except for the uniforms that most people wore. We scrambled for shade to stop the sweat that was already staining our uniforms. We had expected the battle lines to be drawn right on the edge of the field, but instead of being issued combat gear and hustled off to waiting units, a short, wiry lieutenant from the transportation corps, wearing a freshly starched khaki uniform and a single row of ribbons, herded us into the rear of several two-and-a-half-ton trucks that brought us to a place called Camp Alpha.

At Camp Alpha, Vietnam's Army replacement depot, we went through the tedium of processing once again—paperwork, more shots, standing in long lines. We stayed in brown army squad tents and slept on cots or on the ground between cots. Later, Alpha would be outfitted with bunks and mattresses, supply rooms, wooden buildings, and an extensive public address system. The additions would include game rooms, shops, and paved roads. But back then it was only a field of mud and brown canvas tents.

Before we left Alpha, the Army treated us to the standard briefing for new arrivals. A grim lieutenant warned us that the U.S. military personnel were guests in this country and that we were to treat every Vietnamese with the utmost respect. This was an ironic touch because up to this point, we had seen the Vietnamese only from a distance. The officer gave us a verbal horror show on the various types of poisonous snakes, scorpions, and spiders in the country and the equally numerous varieties of venereal disease. The only danger not mentioned was the Viet Cong. From that lecture I learned two things—always shake out your boots before putting them on and always wear a rubber.

An Air Force C-130 transport took the replacements for the 1st Cav hundreds of miles north and west to Pleiku, a provincial capital and military headquarters in the Central Highlands. We were stowed aboard alongside Vietnamese families carrying large bundles of clothes and wicker cages full of chickens and young pigs. We bounced along in the roaring plane, moisture condensing on the ceiling and falling on our backs and necks. I wasn't near a window, but I managed to lean over a couple of chicken cages and an ancient Vietnamese woman to catch a view of Vietnam. I had imagined that we were flying above rice paddies and irrigation canals. What I saw was a confusion of high mountains reflecting a kaleidoscope of green, purple, and brown hues.

An Army Caribou transport was waiting for us at Pleiku. Our group was off the C-130 and filing aboard the banana-shaped Caribou within minutes of landing. Then we were flown east toward the sprawling 1st Air Cavalry base camp at An Khe. I spent the flight watching row after row of truly rugged mountain peaks glide beneath us. The tangled trees and mat of green jungle canopy made the highlands look like a scene from another planet. The Caribou landed at An Khe in late afternoon, and we waited, resting in the shade of trees and a single tent beside the airstrip.

It was almost dark before two battered Army dump trucks, each with a sandbagged bed, arrived for us. The drivers laughed when they told us that the sandbags were for protection against mines. My truck moved slowly through the sleepy town of An Khe, which was little more than a string of houses and shops along both sides of French Colonial Route 19. Then the driver stopped for a hitchhiker, a muscular black soldier with white chest bandages showing under the green of his jungle uniform. He flashed a big grin, probably at the thought of riding with a bunch of "fresh meat" just in from the United States. I managed to catch his eye, hoping that he would say something.

"Replacements, huh?"

"Yeah. We've just been here a couple of days. What happened to your chest?"

"Got hit by a mortar in the Ia Drang. Bad shit. Gave me a chance to get out of the field for a while." His carefree attitude caught the attention of every man in the truck.

"That must have been some fight. Could you tell me what the division is like?"

He grinned again before answering. "Wait and see, man."

"Has there been much fighting lately or was the Ia Drang the last of it?"

He was getting bored. Obviously, new dudes weren't worth spending time on. "Man, you sure do ask questions. Listen, my buddies been beating the bush around Pleiku for weeks and ain't seen nuthin'. I think it's 'bout over. We might all be home in a couple of months." He turned away from us and stared toward the mountains in the distance.

I thought that I had come too late after all and had blown my chance to go to West Point. The dump trucks drove under an arch woven from branches with the division's horse head symbol and its motto, The First Team. The soldier wanted off, and we shouted for the driver to slow down. A quick thumbs-up signal and the truck left him in a cloud of dust.

The trucks ground to a halt at the replacement center, located at the foot of a big jungle hill crowned by a wooden sentry tower. Its name on the maps was Hon Con, but everyone called it Hong Kong Mountain. There were no tents for replacements, so a loud supply sergeant gave a green wool blanket to each man and pointed to a field of elephant grass. I made a nest in the tall grass and began a losing battle with the insects I had disturbed. I had never seen such a variety of insect life. My nest became a highway for at least three types of ants and several long black cockroaches. Mosquitoes and small biting flies were drawn to the field in swarms.

The tropical night arrived with its usual suddenness, along with a Donald Duck cartoon, being shown on white sheets somewhere inside the camp. Twelve thousand miles from America and here was Donald Duck in full, living color. Then it started to rain and didn't quit until morning. Of all the frightened, miserable nights I was to spend in Indochina, this was probably the worst. I was wet and alone and wondering what in the hell I was doing in that field.

At dawn a sleepy cook woke us for a meal of stale bread and powdered eggs that had already turned green. There would be times when the green eggs were a welcome substitute for C-rations, but that morning I could only eat the bread. Clerks gathered our papers and ushered us to a large tent for a briefing. We sat in the heat of the tent for an hour, watching a GI taunt a rhinoceros beetle with a stick. The huge black beetle would rear up on its back legs, hiss, and grab the stick between two enormous pincers. The soldier would lift him off the ground, shake him loose, and start over again. It never occurred to the aggressive beetle to retreat from the stick. A tough-looking sergeant major stepped into the tent, and the games and laughter ceased. The rhinoceros beetle disappeared under the soldier's boot with a final hiss and a loud pop.

"Teng Hut!"

We jumped to our feet like a bunch of puppets and stood more or less at rigid attention. A man behind the sergeant major walked

7

in, a real one-star general. He glanced briefly around the tent, then began his presentation.

"At ease, men. Please be seated. Could some of you men roll up the tent flaps and get some air in here? Gentlemen, I'm General Wright, the assistant division commander. The division commander couldn't make the briefing today, so I'm filling in.

"On behalf of the officers and men of the First Cav, I welcome you to the best damned division in Vietnam. Many of you have already read about some of the things we've accomplished since arriving here. We cut this base out of the bush and built the biggest helipad in the world, mainly with axes, saws, and machetes. This is a hard-working bunch of men with a tremendous spirit, and we expect the same from you.

"A couple of months ago, everyone was working at clearing bush when a couple of black pajama boys stepped out on that rock ledge up on Hon Con and took a few pot shots at the camp. The whole division must have grabbed rifles and opened up on them. It must have scared them half to death, because we haven't had any trouble from up there since. That's the kind of spirit we have.

"We've met and defeated the enemy every time they've shown themselves. Our biggest problem is finding enough of them to fight. We can go anywhere at any time. The division has over four hundred helicopters and is completely airmobile. Contrary to what you may have heard, our small arms are proving themselves to be superb. In the Ia Drang Valley, the M-16s had such a flat trajectory that the enemy simply couldn't crawl in under them.

"We all have a hard job to do, and all we ask is that when you get to your units, you do your part. Thank you."

The sergeant major stepped forward, bellowed a "Teng Hut!" and it was over. They left and then we left. We stood around in the intense heat, waiting for assignments.

I had an artillery specialty called fire direction control. This training would allow me to either compute the trajectories of rockets and cannon or be a member of a forward observer team. I wanted to be a forward observer with an infantry company, but when my name was called, I was assigned to Division Artillery Headquarters. I didn't know what the job entailed, but I knew I wouldn't like it.

A jeep delivered me to my new home in a steaming squad tent. Across a dirt road was the giant helipad with its rows of olive drab helicopters. The helipad had been a stretch of heavy jungle only three months before. Now the division had cleared it so well that they called it the "golf course." It was enormous enough to hold the division's entire arsenal of 435 helicopters.

I was sitting on my empty cot when the headquarters first sergeant poked his head through the doorway of the tent.

"You the new FDC man they sent us?"

"Yeah."

"Good. I'm First Sergeant Barley. Glad to have you aboard." He gave me an unexpectedly warm handshake. "Unpack your duffel bag, and then go over to the supply tent and draw field gear. Get some sleep and report to the orderly room tent tomorrow at seven sharp. We have a lot of sandbags that want filling."

So my new duty was to fill sandbags. This seemed like a good time to bring up the subject of a transfer. "Sergeant, I may not be here long. I'd like to request a transfer to an artillery battalion."

He stepped away as if stung. "Any particular reason?"

"Yeah. I want to be a forward observer."

He shook his head. "Boy, that's crazy talk. Anybody who wants to be an FO must be dumber than the headlight on my jeep. It's not so bad here. You'll be doing a lot more than filling sandbags. It's just to keep you out of trouble until the forward CP returns to pick you up."

"Sergeant, I'd like to try anyway."

He adopted the patient, impatient attitude of a teacher trying to reason with a wayward student. "Look, boy, the life expectancy of a forward observer can be measured in days, sometimes minutes. They live in the bush like animals, and they're begging for a chance at a safe job like you'll have."

"Maybe we could arrange a swap."

9

He looked me square in the eye. "If you apply for a transfer, it'll be refused. We're short of men the way it is, and the replacement center has been waiting for someone with your scores for weeks now. Report to the orderly room tent tomorrow at seven." He disappeared through the doorway of the tent.

I sat on my cot and cursed the air. Sergeant Barley was trying to help me, but I was too angry to care. I finally fell asleep to the booming of cannon, the perpetual thunder of Vietnam.

CHAPTER 2

The Secondhand War

For the next two days I piled sandbags around the house-sized bunker that held the An Khe artillery headquarters. Over the next months, anytime the forward command post was at the base camp, if only for a few hours, the enlisted men were ordered to repair and expand the bunker. It became the object of our hate and scorn. Before the year was through, it had a lawn, beds of flowers to please the colonel, neat gravel sidewalks bordered with crimson-painted artillery shell cases, and God knows how many sandbags.

I have a vision of that bunker as it was in March 1969. The cavalry was gone then, far to the south among the lowland jungles west of Saigon. I was returning to the 9th Cav from the hospital in Japan and had made a special trip to see the bunker. The flowers had died soon after our colonel left for home, and the grass was about two feet high all around. The rain was rotting the timber supports, and the sandbags were pouring their contents into the damp interior. A large rat and I crawled around on top of the decaying heap; then the rat scurried away through a hole in the roof, and I was left alone with my thoughts. I couldn't escape the feeling that the bunker was going the same way as the war. A lot of sweat and suffering had gone into building an illusion, and now everything was crumbling.

I joined the forward command post when it returned from an operation in a mountain valley to the east. My main job would

11

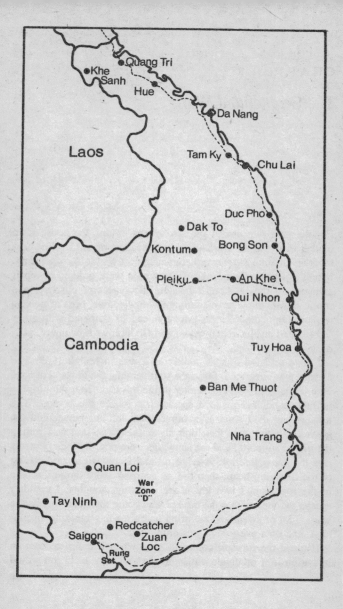

be communications—giving targets to the artillery batteries, making sure no "friendlies" would be shelled by mistake, coding messages and authorizing the movement of artillery pieces to new positions. It wasn't a bad life by Vietnam standards, except that we worked twelve-hour shifts and usually manned defensive bunkers or dug holes during the twelve hours we were supposedly off-duty. The command post was really airmobile in those days. Everything and everybody could be loaded in two jeeps with trailers and several three-quarter-ton trucks with trailers. In 1966 we could dismantle our equipment and move in a matter of minutes, and we often did.

My first ground's-eye view of Vietnam came when the command post traveled west to Pleiku along old Colonial Route 19. The convoy rolled through the desolate country around Mang Yang Pass with the vehicles, each carrying a machine gun, spaced widely apart. All the jeeps and trucks carried one or more layers of sandbags to protect the riders from mine blasts. The sheer wildness of the terrain we were passing was unlike anything I had ever experienced. In some places the fields of elephant grass stretched from the road to the first line of neighboring hills; in other places there were sharp drop-offs beside the winding road; in still others, a tangled wall of trees came within a few feet of the crumbling pavement.

The convoy inched around wrecked bridges and passed a cluster of fire-gutted armored personnel carriers (APCs). I realized for the first time just how nervous everyone was, especially the officers. Every officer rode with a pistol or an automatic rifle across his lap. They frequently signaled for the trucks and jeeps to stay a good distance apart. Soldiers in each vehicle were constantly sweeping the countryside with their eyes and weapons. Single troop-carrying helicopters, the "slicks," roared over at regular intervals and set down infantry squads in the tall grass beside the road. Gunships of the 9th Cav, with the crossed sabers insignia painted on their noses, patrolled the surrounding jungle.

I asked the machine gunner in our truck what was going on. "What's all the fuss about? Are all convoys like this?"

He relaxed his grip on the trigger, but his eyes never left the jungle trees we were passing. "They're supposed to be, but here it's for real. The One-Oh-First Airborne got their asses kicked up through here right before the Cav arrived. Everybody's afraid of ambush going through Mang Yang. The major back there"—he pointed to an officer in the jeep behind us—"looks like he's going to have a baby." The major was staring into the distance with bloodshot eyes and jerking his head back and forth like a mechanical doll.

The 101st Airborne Brigade had arrived to clear the area around An Khe in August of 1965, and one company had taken a severe beating at Mang Yang Pass. Of all the Army and Marine outfits that served in Vietnam, the men of this elite airborne brigade were the most respected by the Air Cav. They were like us, a fire brigade that never stayed long in one place. The fact that those tough paratroopers had been bloodied there gave Mang Yang a special aura of evil.

Our convoy continued down the road toward Pleiku, passing a stone marker about the size of a graveyard headstone, almost hidden by weeds. The machine gunner told me that a French convoy had been wiped out here and that the stone was a memorial to them. Later I learned what had really happened to the French in 1954. An entire French mobile group, a battalion on wheels, had been shattered by a series of Viet Minh ambushes. The stone memorial was the only monument to the brave soldiers of that lost battalion. I now understand why the officers were so nervous that day at Mang Yang Pass. Perhaps the major was a student of military history.

The command post was set up at a place called Monument Hill, which was crowned by a large statue of the Virgin Mary. She gazed down Colonial Route 19 toward the mountain jungles along the Cambodian border. There was evidence of the French war there as well. When mortar rounds explode, they leave their tail fins embedded in the ground. As I climbed the hill to the statue, I stumbled over many badly rusted 60mm and 81mm mortar tail fins. That they were lying so thickly on the surface of the hill indicated that someone had taken quite a pounding there at one time. More tail fins turned up every time we erected a tent or dug a trench, and the men of the command post began to feel sorry for the forgotten defenders of that hill. A French unit had been surrounded and overrun there by the Viet Minh at about the same time as Mobile Groupe 100 was being destroyed at Mang Yang Pass.

My days at Monument Hill were uneventful. I remember them as long shifts spent transceiving coded messages inside a busy operations tent and long hours digging trenches in the rocky soil. Our jobs required the same mental agility the young staff officers needed, but they at least had twelve hours off-duty between shifts.

The operation we were supporting was taking place miles to the west along the Cambodian border. It was largely a failure in military terms. The biggest day was when an observation chopper spotted about a hundred Viet Cong carrying huge sacks of rice through a region of elephant grass. All guns within range hit the target. The artillery took the porters by surprise; many of them just stumbled around through the shell bursts. Others ran to their spider holes in Cambodia, but couldn't get into them with the big sacks of rice strapped to their backs. Many of the shells were the air-burst type and the result was a slaughter. As I listened to the pilot describe the carnage, I tried to imagine how men could be so frightened that they would forget to throw off their packs.

The Army changed its name for the enemy during this operation. The U.S. military had been calling them PAVN (People's Army of Vietnam), which is what they called themselves. Someone decided that calling them PAVN would sanction the Communist cause and give the North Vietnamese troops recognition as the people's army. Now they would be known as NVA (North Vietnamese Army). I never understood what difference the change could have made.

After three weeks at Monument Hill, the command post returned through Mang Yang Pass with the usual heavy gunship and infantry protection. We passed the town of An Khe and descended toward the sea, through Deo Mang Pass on the opposite side of the An Khe Plateau. Here the countryside was even more rugged than at Mang Yang, but mining incidents and ambushes were rare. The reason was obvious.

The commanding hills along the pass were occupied by South Korean platoons and companies, and the Vietnamese had great respect for the fighting ability of their fellow Asians. Stories about the Korean ferocity and cruelty in battle were told throughout the Central Highlands. The Koreans did not make a habit of taking prisoners. So we passed the lonely hilltop outposts in the morning mists and watched the Koreans practicing Tae-Kwon-Do in their shorts and T-shirts. The Sang Vao, Yellow Star Division, that had controlled the Deo Mang Pass before the Koreans arrived, had retreated deeper into the mountains and left them to their martial arts exercises.

The convoy reached the sandy coastal plains and headed north along Colonial Route 1, until we reached the little town of Bong Son. Foreign soldiers were still a rarity in coastal Binh Dinh Province in those days, so the citizens filed out of their shops and homes and silently watched our convoy rumble down the muddy main street. Some of them gave us looks of pure hatred, and only the children displayed any positive emotion.

This had been a Communist slice of paradise. The area around Bong Son is among the most beautiful regions anywhere. Mountains stand in the distance, gradually giving way to sloping countryside covered with coconut palms, these yielding in turn to the white sands and the blue water of the South China Sea. In later days, when helicopters took the Blue platoons above the palms on the way to landings, even the hardest men could appreciate the view. Purple mountains, green fronds, white sand, blue ocean, thatched roofs, and the occasional green and brown of paddy fields. The Bong Son Plains is a place for living in communion with nature, provided there isn't a war going on.

The command post was set up outside the wire of a little Special Forces camp, and again there was evidence of another war. I was trying to dig a trench as protection against incoming shells, but the entrenching tool kept striking jagged pieces of metal embedded in the upper foot or so of earth. Then I uncovered the unexploded half of an old artillery round, which started steaming when I knocked the mud away. A young Special Forces sergeant saw the smoking chunk of metal and strolled over.

"That's Willy Peter. This place is littered with old pieces of junk like that. This was Commie Country back in the French war and they shelled it a lot from offshore."

"Oh. What's Willy Peter?"

The sergeant gave me a condescending look. "You must be new, partner. You know, white phosphorus."

Every foxhole and trench produced more scrap metal, but all the digging proved unnecessary. The only incoming shells during the operation were a string of eighteen 82mm mortar rounds. The explosions had two immediate effects. They put an Air Force spotter plane out of action for a few days, and they put the fear of God into me for a few hours. I would one day be able to hear a mortar round as it left the tube, but that skill takes practice. This time none of us heard the shells until they were "walking" past us.

We were part of a bloody Army-Marine operation that sported names like Masher and Eagle Claw before it ended. Binh Dinh Province had been a Communist stronghold since 1946 and targets were everywhere. All the dying was still secondhand to me, so I spent my free hours swinging in a hammock stretched between two palm trees and watching the enormous tropical moon. That little pleasure made up for the monotonous work and rations and made the days seem worth living.

The war did touch us indirectly at times. Once the CP orchestrated a division TOT (time on target). This was an artillery method in which all available guns are aimed at a certain target and the firing is timed so that all the first shells land simultaneously. The target was a factory village, dug into a hill and camouflaged, and everything that could reach it was used. Guns of all sizes, high explosive and white phosphorus rounds, and instant, delayed, and air-burst fuses. The barrage continued for about half an hour, and the Air Force observer who was watching the fireworks was thrilled.

"That's beautiful, just beautiful! The whole place is going up! Keep it coming! Keep it coming!"

We crowded outside the tent to see the flashes of light and the better to hear the muffled detonations. Something must have been hit, because explosions shook the hill for hours afterward. It was a good night for Division Artillery.

One day a baby-faced major joined me in the shade of the palm tree where I usually ate my C-rations. He was the artillery liaison officer with the 9th Cav, the division's reconnaissance squadron, and although he had often smiled and nodded, we had never talked. His rank made me nervous, and I was sure he had come to talk to me about some mistake I had made on the radios.

"Is something wrong over at the CP, sir?"

He gave me a troubled look, then began. "No. Not at the CP. We lost our first FO today. Strickland. A boy of about your age. He was humping a radio with one of the Blue platoons of the Ninth Cav. I just can't seem to get it out of my mind. I've known him since the States."

"How'd it happen?"

"They were in the Crow's Foot walking some ridges and he was on point, radio and all. I told him not to walk point, and I thought we had an understanding about that. He came over the crest of a hill and they shot him. The rest of the platoon hightailed it down the trail. Just left him there. When they got their nerve back, he was dead. The VC took everything—his radio, his rifle, even his belt and boots."

I didn't know what to say. I mumbled that it was a shame and that I was sorry. The major sat there for a while longer, looking dejected and tired, and then left for the CP. I seldom saw him smile after that day. Whatever the bond had been between him and Strickland, it must have been deeply felt.

There were other aspects of the war at Bong Son. Air Force spotter planes would fly from the Special Forces airstrip twice a day to drop surrender leaflets along the ridges and trails. I collected those leaflets for a while and then gave it up. There were too many of them. One that was dropped in large numbers proclaimed 1966 to be the Year of the Horse, referring to the 1st Air Cav and not the Chinese lunar calendar, and urged the enemy to save themselves by surrendering. Another simply had a picture of a B-52 dropping its bombs and told the Vietnamese how many bombs each jet carried and how many were likely to fall in a single strike.

And then there was graves registration. Those boys had a tent across the road from the command post and were always in the village getting drunk or hunting for whores. Most men with their jobs would have done the same. The graves registration team had to meet each chopper with its load of carrion and transport the bodies on their bouncing "mules," little four-wheel-drive vehicles that looked like platforms on wheels, back to the processing tent. The bodies often arrived neatly sacked in regulation body bags, but if things were really rough somewhere, the GR helipad could be a horror of bloody corpses. I never believed anything like that could happen to me, but I went out of my way not to look in the direction of the GR helipad or walk down the narrow road beside it.

The command post returned to An Khe in early March. We continued a pattern that varied little over the entire time I was with them. The CP convoyed over the crumbling French Colonial roads in support of operations taking place all across central Vietnam. Later in March we were in Pleiku, across the road from the newly built prisoner-of-war camp. The inmates were there mostly through the efforts of the 1st Air Cav.

In early April the command post left Pleiku and journeyed north to the mountain city of Kontum, a town heavy with the brown stucco architecture of the French era. It was famous for an open-air market where the various nations of hill tribesmen sold their beautiful brasswork, multicolored cloths, and woven baskets. We were billeted in old French army barracks, and for the first time in Vietnam I had a real roof over my head, even if it did leak like a sieve. Beside the compound was a narrow dirt road. It was used by the Montagnards as a trade route between the city and their mountain homes, and we never tired of watching the steady trickle of loin-clothed men and bare-breasted women.

That road is also associated with my worst memories of Kontum. One evening at dusk, a jeep driver from a neighboring unit was decapitated by a wire stretched across the road at neck level. I had often raced a jeep down this very road with the windshield folded down. It was the only way to get cooled off in the stifling heat. Our behavior had evidently not been lost on the local Communist cell, and now one of us was dead. An official order was given to drive all jeeps with windshields raised. No one had to tell us.

The command post returned to An Khe in late April. In line with some new duties, I was a courier on helicopters traveling from An Khe to artillery positions in the field. One of those missions was more than routine and took me closer to the fighting than I had been before.

A battle was raging on a jungle ridge above the Crow's Foot War Zone, near an artillery base called Bird. Artillery shells were bursting on top of wooded hills—flashes, and then tree limbs and trunks hurtling into the air before crashing down into the black smoke from the explosions. The reason for the shooting was on display at Bird. Outside the artillery battalion's command post tent were three Chinese 12.7mm heavy machine guns on wheels, with a major standing proudly beside them. He saw me step out of the chopper with my document pouch and called me over. He was beaming like a new father as he pointed to the trophies.

"They're really something, aren't they?"

"Yes sir, they sure are."

"You know what's happening out there? The Seventh Cav is having a field day. A scout ship from the Ninth Cav flies over and draws fire from these guns, and we pound them with our one-oh-fives. All the infantry has to do is go and police them up. There's another one on the way in now. You tell those rear echelon bastards back at Divarty what you saw here."

The battle wasn't as simple as the major's version. The first scout helicopter that day had not only found a 12.7mm, it had been shot down. What had begun as a rescue mission had become a gun-hunting operation, tempered only by certain infantry losses that the major may not have known about. A chopper returning to An Khe just ahead of mine was hit by one of the remaining machine guns. An NVA antiaircraft unit had probably moved onto the ridges and been drawn into a fight before it was dug in and ready to defend itself.

20

Heavy machine guns are devastating to helicopters. There were so many times in Vietnam when choppers were caught in cross fire from those guns placed atop hills and ridges. I helped rescue the crews of dozens of those downed helicopters. On sadder occasions, we would collect their bodies. The thought of the few times when I came under 12.7mm fire still makes me shudder. There are few things more frightening than to be in a thin-skinned helicopter and to hear or see those big .51 caliber bullets rattling past. There is no more helpless feeling.

Our next operation was in the Vinh Thanh Valley, or Happy Valley. We made our camp at a place called Cobra, about halfway down the valley beside a mud road leading to a Special Forces camp. It was this camp that the 1st Cav hoped to save from an expected North Vietnamese assault. Happy Valley was brutally hot and full of malaria. It was May now, and the air was heavy with humidity from the monsoon rains. The surrounding upland jungles choked off any breezes that might have cooled us.

We located a wrecked building that had been built by the French Colonial administrators of the valley. Its roof had been destroyed long before, and the walls were pitted with bullet holes and other war scars. We cleared away the rubble and erected the communications tent in one of the open rooms. Ponchos were strung between the naked walls of a smaller room to protect the supplies and rations from the constant rain. The command post was soon business as usual, an endless cycle of duty, digging, and sleep.

I carried daily intelligence dispatches between Cobra and the Special Forces camp. It was a good opportunity to escape the routine of Cobra and rest in the shade of the trees beside the underground bunker in the center of the camp. The trips also gave me the chance to listen to the Green Berets' war stories. There was one balding sergeant who shook all over when he talked about the war. He loved to squint his hard blue eyes and tell his favorite story.

"We set up a claymore ambush beside this little footbridge and were waiting for something to happen. Then this squad of dinks started crossing the bridge, real slow-like. When the first one reaches the other side, we blow the mines on the ones that hadn't

21

crossed and get the swinging dinks on the bridge with machine guns. It was bee-u-ti-ful! Blood everywhere! I've never seen so much blood at one time! Not one of those little fuckers got away!'' The sergeant always ended the story shouting. The battle at the footbridge had taken its toll on more than the Vietnamese.

At Happy Valley I learned to recognize the peculiar clacking sound of Chinese 7.62mm bullets. The initiation tore holes in my pup tent just above ground level and made me appreciate the recent order that all soldiers were to dig in and sleep below ground level. At Happy Valley I saw my first North Vietnamese at close range and had the sad experience of standing by helplessly while other NVA overran an American platoon on a nearby hill. The valley was a pest-hole, full of heat and insects and harassing NVA attacks. We were glad when the operation ended.

The command post traveled far to the south for another operation with the 101st Airborne Brigade. I remained for a summer in the An Khe artillery bunker that I had helped build. My job was to plot H&I (harassing and interdiction) targets and develop countermortar plans for the base defense artillery. The H&Is were designed to keep the enemy off balance and constantly on the move by random shelling of the areas where they were most active. We had a variety of high-technology gadgets to catch the Vietnamese cooking, sweating, or just walking around, but most of the shells only busted empty jungle or killed birds and snakes.

The countermortar plan was our response to the periodic Viet Cong mortar attacks. We tried to guess where the next mortars would fire from and have a howitzer trained on the spot. When we guessed wrong—and we always did—the artillery bunker was supposed to coordinate efforts to locate and destroy the mortars. That usually didn't work either. The rapid ''walking'' mortar barrages of 1966 ended too quickly. Long after the tubes were reburied and camouflaged, our howitzers were firing at radar echoes from their own shells, while gunships rocketed fires started by the artillery.

The part of my job that I liked best was the box seat that the daily intelligence reports gave me on the war. The 1st Cav was conducting simultaneous operations from the Cambodian border to the South China Sea. Its units stretched along two hundred miles of coast, patrolling provinces where the French had never dared to set foot after 1946. I had a teenager's pride at being a part of something so enormous.

My An Khe vacation ended in early September, and I returned to the endless CP operations. The Cav was now fighting in an open region south of Bong Son, called the Fertile Crescent because of its half-moon shape on the maps. Several moves brought us to Hammond, the principal Air Cav base in the Crescent. When the CP first moved to Hammond, I wanted to be anyplace in Vietnam but there. I had previously been sent to the base to report on the effects of an unusually heavy Viet Cong attack.

Eight-inch howitzers had been slamming 200-pound shells into enemy base camps and mountain rest areas since the Cav's arrival in the Crescent. The Viet Cong had come down from the mountains to destroy the big howitzers. The artillery camp had been blanketed by mortar and recoilless rifle rounds, and every truck, jeep, armored personnel carrier, and howitzer had been hit. When I arrived to assess the damage, the gunners were still stumbling around like drunks. What impressed me most deeply was a brown paper shopping bag and two boots. They had been placed to one side in a field littered with broken glass, metal shards, pieces of muddy canvas, and many black mortar craters. The boots were still laced around feet, and the bag held part of a rib cage. That was all that was left of the first man killed in the attack. When the CP suddenly began packing for the convoy to Hammond, I remembered the shopping bag and the boots.

But soon my days at Hammond were almost routine. What made them unusual was a unit stationed nearby. Helicopters with the crossed sabers of the 9th Cav took off and returned within easy view of the CP tent where I worked. If a particular mission had resulted in dead NVA somewhere, the gunships would roar over Hammond at treetop level, trailing long streamers of red smoke. The Blues walked by our tent wearing captured NVA belts and carrying souvenir rifles, and I envied them. They didn't spend their days talking into a damned radio.

The 9th Cav was already a legend in the division. They had

23

started the battles in the Ia Drang Valley and every other major Cav battle since that time. They were noted for going after the enemy like bloodhounds, and soldiers in other units called their Blues the Headhunters. A new artillery liaison officer with the 9th Cav had been coming by the CP tent daily, asking if any radio jockeys wanted to see the war firsthand. I followed him out of the tent one day and asked if he was serious about wanting forward observers. He was serious. He told me that he could have me transferred immediately.

I had only a few weeks left in Vietnam, but I wasn't proud of my easy tour. The bullets and mortars had come close more than a few times, but I had never felt a part of it. Now I had the chance to be a soldier. It was easy for me to forget the baby-faced major who had grieved so for his lost FO at Bong Son. Nothing like that would happen to me.

A few days later I joined C Troop's Blue platoon—the men whose lives I had envied. Their radio call sign was Brave Fighter. It was a fitting name.

CHAPTER 3

Brave Fighter Blues

Shirtless men with blue bandannas tied around their necks were cleaning their weapons when I arrived at the Blue's pup tent compound. They sat on the low sandbag walls around the tents with pieces of rifles and machine guns spread on oilcloth rags at their feet. Some were sneaking looks at me, sizing up the new FO. I reported to the platoon sergeant, Samuel, who shook my hand warmly and welcomed me to the platoon. He was a handsome, athletic black man with a quiet air of authority, and I liked him instinctively.

The sergeant sat with me on the sandbag wall around his tent and explained the unit I had chosen. He told me that our mission was to provide intelligence for a brigade of three infantry battalions. The Blue platoon's part of this effort involved taking prisoners, capturing documents, and patrolling through areas where the enemy had been seen. The entire troop often killed more NVA in a month than the individual battalions did, and in some months the troop would destroy more enemy soldiers than a brigade that was about thirteen times its combat strength. The Blues would see only a fraction of the troop's total effort because the gunships and scout helicopters often fought battles in remote areas or places completely inaccessible to helicopter landings. In other cases, the choppers would land long enough to collect the weapons and documents themselves.

Sergeant Sam pointed out that this was one of the few combat platoons in the Army authorized to have a captain as platoon leader. Although our total landing force was only twenty to twenty-five men, it included two medics, two artillery forward observers with a radio, and six infantry radios. Each squad could act as a separate recon element and always be in radio contact with Sam. Sam had two radiomen, one for talking with the squads and one for communications with our helicopters. This small platoon carried four machine guns and four grenade launchers. Everyone else had automatic rifles.

When he had finished the briefing, Sergeant Sam gave me a quick tour of the barbed wire and the machine gun bunkers along its edge, pointing out fields of fire. Then he showed me to my new home. It was a makeshift tent thrown together from four tent halves and barely large enough for me and the team radioman. The edges were held down by a single row of sandbags all around, and the floor had been dug down about two feet into the sand for more room and protection. As I dragged my field gear into the cramped space, Johnson, my radioman, appeared out of nowhere. He stuck his head through the small entrance way, forced a smile, and crawled in beside me.

"Hi. I'm Greg Johnson. I'll be carrying your radio." He started shaking when he said the last part of the sentence.

"Matt Brennan. I hope you know what's happening around here. I'll need a little help getting started."

He nodded and waited a second for effect. "No sweat, but I'll only be around for a couple of days. Just got a radio job over at squadron. Did you just get in from the States?"

This would be my first admission of the greatest sin in Vietnam. "No. I extended my tour."

He gave me a look of pure shock. "Oh. Well, I'm glad to be leaving." It was obvious that this pale little man had seen enough. He looked away in embarrassed silence while his body twitched and jerked.

Three weeks before, the Blues had landed in a quiet place called the 506 Valley. They ran into unexpected trouble and had spent the night pinned down by two machine guns firing from the edge of a wood. After that experience, Johnson decided the Blues were not his line of work. He found excuses not to go on landings, and several times this had left the platoon without an FO when they needed one. Sergeant Sam had requested that Johnson be taken off his hands.

I spent the early evening assembling the heavy field gear of the infantry. Twenty magazines of bullets, a smoke grenade, four hand grenades, two first aid pouches, and two canteens. The harness felt like it weighed a hundred pounds when I first fitted it over my shoulders. I had almost finished cleaning my battered rifle when a tall black medic walked silently over. He sat beside me on the sandbags, threw a hunting knife into the sand at our feet, and slowly grinned. He was there to check me out for the others.

"Hi, FO. I'm Doc Hansen. What do you think of this bunch of clowns?" He indicated the low profiles of tents where those Blues not manning the bunkers were now sleeping.

"I don't know them yet, Doc. They seem all right to me."

He nodded his head. "They're a good bunch of men, and they're damned happy to have an FO again." He winked like a fellow conspirator. "Gives them a sense of security, you know."

"Yeah. I guess it does. How do you medics work it on missions?" The landings were called "missions" here.

He hesitated. I must have hit a painful nerve. "Well, me and the other Doc used to switch off, before he got hit on December first. That way we only had to go out every other day. If there's some deep shit, only one gets hit. For a couple of weeks I've been the only medic, and that gets a bit hairy." He brightened for a moment. "One thing's a fact, you do get a lot of good souvenirs around here."

Doc pulled three leather belts with stars on their brass buckles from one of his leg pockets. He dangled the buckles so the stars would reflect the moonlight. "If you'd like, I'll give you one. They're all the same."

If I told him how much I coveted a belt, he'd laugh. "Thanks anyway. I'll get one myself sooner or later." One day I would have a collection of eleven different styles of those damned Communist belts, each representing the death of a "liberation fighter."

Doc shrugged his shoulders and flashed another grin. "If that's how you want it." He dug his big knife out of the sand and disappeared into the night like a silent jungle cat. I hoped that I had been approved.

The whine of chopper engines and shouts of "Saddle up" awoke me at dawn. I grabbed my harness and rifle and ran beside Johnson toward a waiting line of four slicks. The Blues were already there, standing in a ragged circle and playing rifles and machine guns like imaginary guitars. They were shouting the lyrics of "Rockin' Robin" above the beat of the chopper blades, swaying and stomping their feet in cadence. "Rockin' Robin . . . bop, bop, bop." That gyrating circle of men, black and white, with mustaches and sideburns, hung all over with belts of ammunition and grenades, was like a scene from a psycho ward. A few minutes later, these same men would be stepping over muddy bodies many miles away.

The choppers lifted off in a cloud of swirling sand, and we were flown to the west, over rice paddies and peaceful villages with clumps of trees beside irrigation streams. We would spend the day somewhere among the abandoned rice valleys and jungled ridges of the Crow's Foot War Zone.

Someone had fired at a gunship. The slicks pulled away from the route toward the west and circled over a line of green foothills. Far below us, gunships rocketed a hill beside an overgrown rice valley. Black explosions sent tree limbs crashing down into the jungle. Our door gunner listened intently to a message coming over his earphones, then shouted excitedly over the roar of the chopper blades.

"We're going in. Two ships. The gunbirds took fire from that valley." He pointed down and waited for another message. "LZ is hot."

"Hot" meant that enemy fire was expected and that we would go in with all helicopter machine guns firing. Yellow smoke

28

marking a landing zone drifted over a clearing on
the hill. My ship and another made a tight turn awa
other choppers and dropped toward the smoke. We jun
the slicks as they hovered across the open space and ra
shin-high water to the bushes along its edge. My legs were

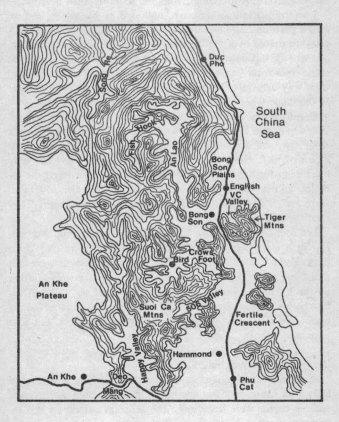

numb and my head still buzzed from the din of the chopper blades. It was happening too fast. I crouched behind a bush with Parga, a fat Hispanic grenadier, and he didn't like it.

He jabbed me with his elbow and looked me square in the eye. "Look, would you mind moving off a little? There's plenty of bushes on this hill, man. Hanging together ain't healthy."

I scrambled to another bush, bothered by his anger, and realized that the rain had already soaked through my uniform. A gunship roared over the clearing only inches above the bushes, and one of the door gunners tossed a red smoke grenade into some trees forty yards farther up the hillside. The Blues picked their way carefully through the tangled grass and muddy water to the place where red smoke floated among the branches.

Beside a smoking rocket crater were two mangled bodies. The whole one had fallen forward into the mud, with his neck somehow bent double beneath him. The other corpse was just a pair of legs, complete with belt and trousers. They had only been dead for minutes, but already flies buzzed around the remains and a sweet, heavy odor hung in the air. My mind screamed, "My God, those can't be men lying there. They aren't really dead."

We found two decaying huts under the trees behind the bodies. In a straw lean-to beside the second hut were two khaki packs and a jumble of cracked rice bowls. The bowls were still moist and warm from an early meal. Sam sent one squad farther up the hillside to search for anything of military value. They had barely disappeared up a trail when a rifle stuttered a long burst. We dived into the mud and crawled for cover, but Sam remained standing, frowning down at us.

"Let's go, Blue. That was a sixteen." Johnson and I were the last to pull ourselves out of the mud.

A squad leader walked down the trail, shoving a frightened little Viet Cong with the muzzle of his rifle. Both the prisoner and his captor were trembling. The sergeant gulped air and reported to Sam.

"I just killed a broad back there hiding in the bushes. I didn't know it was a woman. She had her hair rolled up under a VC bush hat. This one didn't move until she bled all over him."

The sergeant, a man from Indiana named Hobbs, had just killed his first human being. He looked confused and sick. Sam turned away from him, trying to ignore Hobbs's agony by directing questions to our interpreter.

"Okay, Minh, ask this one what they were doing here."

The two Vietnamese talked rapidly in their singsong voices, then Minh turned back to Sam. "He say they are farmers."

Sam pointed to the packs we had found. "How does he explain these?"

"He say they find them."

"Did they have weapons?"

"He say no weapons, only packs."

The last answer was accompanied by a violent shaking of the prisoner's head. Sam's face lost all expression for a moment, then he ran down the trail to the rocket crater. He stooped and pulled an SKS rifle from under the pair of legs. Apparently he was the only one who had seen it. He returned with the rifle and waved it slowly, about two inches in front of the prisoner's nose. The man's knees buckled and a Blue pulled him back to his feet.

Sam put the muzzle under his jaw and asked one more question. "Now that we know he's a liar, ask him who the woman was."

"He say they are farmers and she is his wife."

"Christ, loyalty unto death. She was more likely a damned nurse. Get this scum back to the LZ."

We burned the huts and the lean-to and threw the packs into the flames, saving only some papers and a few Chinese bullets. The belts were stripped from the crater bodies by a GI, but they didn't have stars on their brass buckles and that disappointed him. He wiped the blood off on his jungle trousers, carefully folded the belts and stuffed them into one of his leg pockets.

Two Blues ripped the cavalry horse head patches from their shirt sleeves and tossed them on the crater bodies. Another

31

Blue ran up the trail to the woman's body and put his patch on her forehead. The 9th Cav wanted them to know who had done this. I had seen the dark outlines of fabric on many of the Blues' jungle shirts, where patches had been worn and then taken off, but didn't know where the patches had gone. The platoon was keeping two local seamstresses busy sewing on new patches.

Soon the slicks came in again, machine guns firing all the way. There was a mad scramble for seats as they touched down in the clearing, and then we were away from that desolate place. Even our prisoner seemed happy to be leaving, especially when he realized that we weren't going to push him out the door. I had spent a year in Vietnam without getting as wet as I was then. As the choppers climbed through the downpour, I realized the true advantages of a helicopter. The blades keep out the rain and the wind dries your clothes.

That night they gave me a blue bandanna.

The Blue platoon spent the next two weeks on clearing operations in the Crow's Foot War Zone. This region was called the Kim Son, but its valleys looked like a bird's foot from the air. The Kim Son had once held numerous little farming villages; the people were mainly Roman Catholics who had fled from North Vietnam after the partition of 1954. The Catholics hated godless Communism, and this made it one of the potentially most loyal areas for any anti-Communist government. But the valleys were rich in rice and thus a tempting target for the undersupplied North Vietnamese units in the surrounding mountains. There had been heavy fighting here during the previous year, because the Communists needed that rice and the Americans were determined to keep it from them.

The solution to the problem of separating the enemy from the peaceful farmers, while denying this enemy the rice, was to declare the Kim Son a war zone. This would allow the Americans to kill the remaining rice with chemicals, to blanket everything with artillery fire, and to shoot on sight anything that moved. The war zone was not created without consideration for the people who lived there, that is, if you don't take into account the misery involved in tearing people away from their beloved villages and paddy fields.

Spotter planes spent weeks dropping millions of leaflets telling the people to leave within thirty days or face the full weight of American power. The leaflets got the word about the coming B-52 and artillery strikes to the bulk of those peasants who still lived in the Crow's Foot. Our job was to find the rest and get them out before it was too late.

We would land throughout the Crow's Foot War Zone, gathering little families, usually just women, children, and very old men, and taking them to resettlement villages on the coast. There was one ancient blind woman who had lived for weeks on the rice stored in her hut. She was alone in her dark world; everyone else in the village had left, and she wouldn't or couldn't follow. A gunship spotted her only because she had been frightened by the noise and had scuttled into her hut as the machine roared overhead. There were also the stubborn ones—old men, single women, or the occasional families who simply refused to leave their homes. We forcibly dragged them to the waiting helicopters.

All the empty huts and storehouses could never be destroyed with bombs and shells, so we had another task. The Blues would search deserted villages, many of which had beige stucco Catholic churches crowned by the one true cross, and burn every standing structure. Huts and haystacks were set aflame; rice caches were soaked with aviation fuel and burned. On some days we would burn so much rice and so many huts that in the evening our day's route would be marked by dozens of columns of rising white smoke, extending back across some silent valley or another.

The remaining livestock could not be left to feed the Communists, so the platoon shot pigs and chickens and machine-gunned water buffalo. Sometimes the grenadiers would use water buffalo as target practice for their 40mm grenades. The damage one of those grenades could do to a big animal was appalling. Imagine a cow with a grenade shot into its head or side. Having been

33

around farm animals for most of my life, I could never participate in the butchery.

I remember one day especially well. Blue followed a stream to the site where bombs had fallen several hours before. A trail led us to an NVA rest station about halfway up a wooded ridge. Among the damaged huts and broken trees was a small pen containing five fat little pigs. A soldier raised his rifle to shoot them, but Sergeant Hobbs had a better idea.

"Don't shoot those pigs; it'll alert every Charlie within miles."

The soldier spat in disgust. "Hell, Sarge, they're going to see the smoke anyway. 'Sides, we just bombed them."

"I don't care; don't shoot them. Those are my orders."

"Well what do you suggest, Sarge? Leave the porkers for Charlie?"

"No, kill them, but not with bullets."

The soldier grasped his meaning. He borrowed a bayonet from a friend and attached it to the end of his rifle. As I walked down the trail, the piglets began screaming.

That was how Blue cleared the Crow's Foot. It worked in the end. Eventually the region would become an uninhabited wasteland, abandoned even by the Communists. We walked through valleys where peaceful farmers had once lived and others that looked innocent enough from the distance, but were full of extensive bunker and trench systems. We left everything in ashes, blowing up the earthworks when there was time.

But you can't demolish a nation. Everyone dug in Vietnam, soldiers on both sides and civilians too. The reason is simple enough—explosions don't make distinctions. That digging had been going on at least since the French war, and in some cases, back to Chinese rule. Once, near a village alongside a shallow river, we found two old cannon balls embedded in a field. I wondered who had fired those and at whom.

Few of us liked the clearing operations. They only seemed to make the world a little more empty.

On the nights when we weren't in the field, we manned the bunker line at Hammond. Ex-soldiers know the tension of guard duty in a war zone, the straining to see something in a pitch black night, the monotonous ticking of a wristwatch that seems to be turning seconds into hours, the terror of trying to decide whether a sound is a man, an animal, or simply the rain. There was danger. Once a soldier heard a splash, which could have been one of a hundred things, and fired just to be sure. The next morning we found the body of a Viet Cong scout. He had maps of the positions, including the location of the bunker from which the shot had come.

During one of those first nights in the bunkers, I had a talk with a big Italian rifleman named Corda. He was just plain scared.

"FO, you don't know what you got yourself into. This outfit is a death trap. Man, right now we're rounding up civilians and burning hooches, but it ain't gonna last forever. Why in the livin' hell did you extend?"

That was the one question that I could never really answer. "I don't know. I guess it's because it was something I had to experience before I died. I wanted to experience war, not just read about it in books and have other people tell me about it."

He sadly shook his head. The FO is such a fool. "FO, before this is over you'll wish you had read about it. I got here three months ago, and I'm one of the last ones left. This outfit must have the highest casualty rate in the Army. They're givin' us an easy time right now because we got creamed on December first, lost ten goddamned men, but time's runnin' out, baby. Do you know about December first?"

"Yeah. Johnson said you lost the captain that day. But we've been in contact a couple of times since I got here and it turned out okay."

"Contact? Chasing a couple of scared gooks is not contact. You don't know what contact is. We're gonna be out in those hills again, and you're gonna be wishin' you'd gone home when you had the chance." I didn't know what to think. Surely he was only trying to frighten me.

We had reached the trail at last. I thought the climb up through the trees would never end. The path was wide, with many sandal prints in the mud, all heading in the direction that we were traveling. Blue had gone less than eighty yards and already we were finding black telephone wires hidden in the bushes. Someplace here were units big enough to have telephone hookups. Sam was obviously worried when he radioed the news about the telephone wires to the gunships. He told us not to cut the wire yet, because the NVA might not know we were on the trail.

The platoon was in single file, following the trail as it climbed over a ridge, when the point man fired a long burst. AK bullets clacked past my head, and I dived into the muddy grass beside the trail. Sam grabbed his radioman's handset and shouted that we were in contact, then Johnson tapped me on the shoulder and handed me his handset. The artillery lieutenant, circling above us in a gunship, said that shells would be landing around us within five minutes. When I gave Sam the message, he sent squads to the sides of our hill to form a circular defense.

The AK fire ended with a burst that splintered the bark of a tree beside Sam's head. The word was passed in whispers that the point had taken a prisoner. The captive was prodded back along the trail by our point man. He was a tough-looking man of about twenty, dressed in a khaki uniform and bleeding from a bullet wound in his side. His trousers were already soaked with blood. The point man shoved him to his knees while Doc pulled off his shirt and wrapped a field dressing around his waist. Then Sam questioned him.

"Minh, ask him what he's doing here."

A brief exchange gave a lot of answers. Minh began, "He say he is NVA corporal. He is in the South for eight months. He is point man for patrol of fourteen who come to check the American landing."

"Where is his weapon?"

"He doesn't carry weapon, just that." The NVA had pulled a few bloody rounds of Chinese rifle ammo from the pocket of his trousers and was holding them out to Sam. "He say if point man carry weapon and is killed, the weapon is lost."

36

"Minh, ask him how many of them are along this trail and what they are doing here."

Minh's question produced a long-winded reply from the NVA corporal. "He say he will not tell you his mission. He doesn't know how many they are, but they are many." He interrupted Minh's report with another comment, and the color drained from our interpreter's face. "He say they are very many."

Sam grimaced, then turned to Hobbs. "That's just fine. Cut the wire! Cut the damned commo wire!"

Our gunships had strafed the trail to our front with miniguns, rockets, cannon, and machine guns. Now they pulled away so the artillery could begin. I had to direct the shelling, but only if Johnson would come with me. His eyes jumped out of their sockets as I moved off in a crouch.

"Where you going, Sarge?"

"We've got to get up to the point and bring in some rounds."

"No. Not me. Let's do it from here."

"We can't, man, that would risk hitting our own men."

His eyes were pleading now. "Sarge, please. This is my last mission. We can bring it in just as well from here."

I turned back to Johnson, but saw the look on the NVA corporal's face. He was amused by our fear. "Come on, Johnson, I need the radio. You're gonna make it."

He started to follow, then stopped and pointed an accusing finger. "Okay, Sarge. But if I don't, it's on your head."

That pointed finger had unnerved me. Would it be my fault if he got hurt? As we moved down a prostrate file of Blues toward the contact point, I realized just how alone Johnson must feel among these men. Each soldier gave me a thumbs-up signal or a word of encouragement like "Get some, FO." The same men greeted my radioman with hostile stares or curses.

The first shells had exploded far up the trail. Now the lieutenant walked them back toward us as I tried to estimate how close they were bursting. When his chopper ran low on fuel, I was on my own. You know how far away shells are hitting in heavy jungle by watching the shrapnel. If it buzzes two or three feet over your head as you lie on your stomach, bring it in closer.

When the fragments start slapping into tree trunks a foot or so above your head, move it out a bit. I was learning these facts for the first time. My European-style FO training had been worthless. I worked the shells along the hillside to our front—each time two explosions and then two more. Whump whump! Whump whump! Metal whizzed through the air as I called corrections to the gun crews.

"Left five zero, drop two zero, repeat platoon two." Only rarely did we see the black smoke from the explosions.

When I stopped the artillery, we moved down the trail past a jumble of broken trees and smashed boulders. The prisoner had said nothing more, only that there were many of his friends here. Then we began finding the camps. We walked for hours along the trail, discovering so many spider holes, bunkers, and weapons pits that we grew indifferent to them.

The camps were spread out, about 100 to 150 yards apart, and each had held either a platoon or a company. In some camps, uniforms were drying on jungle vines or ropes woven from women's hair. The hair had been donated by village women as their personal sacrifice for the "liberation." In other camps were boxes of unfinished rations; in still others, a private's belt or a camouflaged bamboo helmet. The enemy was making a determined effort not to be seen. They had us outnumbered too many times over to worry much about a puny platoon of twenty men or the two gunships circling overhead.

The NVA corporal walked with us all the way because there were no clearings for helicopters to land in. He was smiling. He knew that at any moment his comrades would stop playing cat and mouse games and rescue him. We expected the same thing to happen. But now there was a clearing and we dared to hope that we had been spared. We passed through one last camp that had an interesting toy. On a vine rope above the bunkers was an accurately carved wooden model of a Skyraider fighter-bomber. It was fastened with a metal ring to slide along the slanted cord. The NVA had been getting lessons on tracking aircraft with rifles.

We broke into a clearing barely large enough for one chopper to hover down through the tall jungle trees. The slicks took us out of there, one load at a time. It was a perfect ambush site, but our strange enemy was letting us escape. No doubt we were being watched by hundreds of men. As our chopper skimmed the wooded ridges of the Crow's Foot War Zone, Johnson hopped up and down on the seat beside me. He shouted above the roar of the blades.

"We made it, Sarge! We made it! It's a-a-l-l over! A-a-l-l over!"

Back at Hammond, he was off the chopper before it touched down. He ran to the tent, and baggage was soon flying out of the doorway. Then he grabbed his few possessions and was gone, not stopping to say good-bye to anyone.

The day had been important for me as well. No forward observer was ever accepted by the infantry until he proved his ability to do his specialized job. It was an unspoken rite that I had to undergo with each new group of men I served with. I didn't realize how crucial the day had been to my credibility until a succession of tired, dirty Blues stopped by my pup tent. Each man told me in his own way how good the artillery protection had made him feel and, for the first time, really welcomed me to the platoon.

Johnson's replacement arrived later that evening. I had thought Johnson and I were different sorts, but that was before I met John Martin. He was a tall and incredibly thin Slovak from the mining country of Eastern Pennsylvania, with a long face and a shock of thick brown hair that he refused to cut to regulation military length. John was already a college graduate, a rarity in the Army in those days, and one of the finest people I have ever known. He would have a great effect on my thinking during the next hard months.

Martin introduced me to a world of literature and poetry I would never have discovered but for him. He showed me beauty where I had seen only terrain. But that was in the future. That first day there was only mutual suspicion. I was a sergeant, which indicated to John that I could not be trusted. I had also committed the crime of extending my tour of duty when I could have gone home. He was an outspoken nonconformist and a confirmed private, both of which made me equally wary of him. He would refuse rank and decoration until the day he left Vietnam. I eventually got him a promotion, a Combat Infantry Badge, and meritorious decoration, all behind his back. In exchange, he let me know I was interfering in his life.

John had spent time in the stockade in the United States for a unique offense. He had done so well in a basic course that the Army wanted to give him more specialized training in communications. He had declined the offer with too much zeal, and they jailed him. When he was released, he had to take the training anyway. Now he was capable of operating sophisticated electronics equipment, but would instead carry the simplest of all field radios. He was shipped to the 9th Cav because he was a thorn in the side of anyone in authority. It's an understatement to say we were mismatched.

Martin tossed his duffel bag through the door of my tent and offered his hand. "Well hi, Sarge. I'm John Martin."

"Sergeant Brennan. Why don't you call me Matt."

A grin. "I'll call you Sarge; you probably like that name better. You're a lifer aren't you?"

"I don't know. I never gave it much thought."

Another grin. "Aw, come on, Sarge. Did you really extend for this shit?"

I felt like I was branded with the devil's mark. "Yeah. Word travels fast around here."

"Johnson told me. That settles it. You're a lifer."

I mentally cursed whoever was responsible for sending this hellcat to C Troop. "We're going to have to work pretty close together. Why not try to get along?"

A derisive glare. "Well, anything you say, Sergeant." End of round one.

It was 3:00 A.M. and the rain was pouring down. The Christmas truce had been over for only three hours, but our commander was walking down the line of slicks, telling each miserable huddle of Blues that Bird was being overrun. Some of the 9th Cav infantry would be landed inside Bird to reinforce the defenses. We were waiting to be landed behind the attacking NVA. It had to be the soldiers who were hiding from us two days before.

I shivered in a chopper beside Sergeant Saito and tried to keep dry. Saito had only been back from leave for a few hours, and he looked exhausted. This was a man with a reputation. The men in his squad said they would follow him anywhere. General Westmoreland had personally handed him a Silver Star for his exploits with grenades on December first. The platoon had fought three NVA companies in a fortified village on that day. I wanted to meet Saito.

"How was your leave home, Sarge?"

He didn't look surprised that I knew him. He answered in his always gentle voice. "It was very good. I miss my family in Hawaii very much right now. I'm going home for good in six months. They tell me you were a fool and extended, too." So he already knew about me.

"Yeah, I extended. I'm thinking of home myself. Christmas was rough."

He put his hand on my shoulder and smiled. "Welcome to the platoon. I know why you had to stay and I understand." He was the only man who ever understood.

"What do you think we'll find at Bird?" I hoped he couldn't tell how nervous I was. I was sure that the jungle camps we had found had housed at least a thousand NVA.

"Don't worry. It won't be bad. If they wait until dawn to insert us, the VC will be gone. They can't stand up to our choppers in daylight." I hoped he was right. The slicks took off a few minutes later in total darkness.

Phantom jets had hit a low mountaintop with 500-pound bombs, and one of the big craters would be our LZ. Artillery and gunships had finished their fireworks, and dawn arrived as Go Go tore at the mountaintop. Go Go was a heavily armored Chinook helicopter with thirty-eight rockets, two miniguns, a 40mm automatic cannon, and several heavy machine guns. It looked and sounded like some giant prehistoric dragon, spitting

41

fire and death. Two of those monsters were trying to flatten the place.

After Go Go had blasted the jungle with rockets and cannon, the big choppers each made a final pass with miniguns ripping the silence. The heavy machine guns in their tails poured down a steady stream of bright red tracers. The tracers disappeared into the barely visible trees, then came bouncing back in all directions. The jungle was still echoing as Blue and a platoon from D Troop jumped into the muddy crater, one chopper load at a time. The D Troop soldiers used a captured 61mm Chinese mortar to lob shells down the mountainside. I walked 105mm artillery shells around us. It was very costly and dramatic, but it was all wasted. The only thing to greet us was a wilderness of broken trees.

It took our two platoons most of the morning to get off the mountain, then we began crossing scattered treelines and the deserted paddy fields of the Crow's Foot War Zone. Here we found the trail of the NVA retreating from the bloody attack on Bird. It was a muddy track, made by hundreds of Ho Chi Minh sandals, heading away from us, around the base of that damned mountain. All that was left of the attackers was a row of fresh graves holding bodies buried upright, shrouded in French camouflaged parachute silk. The graves had been dug before the attack. Some of them were empty.

The scout helicopters and gunships followed the trail and began killing stragglers. I listened to their dry reports over Martin's radio.

"White One-One. Engaged two NVA with packs and weapons. Two NVA KIA."

"Red Three-Three. Engaged NVA in khaki uniform. One NVA KIA. Area is open. Request permission to collect weapon."

"Red Three-Five. We're receiving AK fire from that streambed. Rolling in hot!"

We continued the patrol toward Bird. We searched a few battered villages and burned everything that had escaped our torches in the previous weeks. In the late afternoon, we passed a company campsite of the night before, complete with regulation NVA latrine hole, and took long-range shots at khaki figures running away in the distance. A short radio transmission brought two scout helicopters racing in for the kills. Then our little force passed the smoking wreckage of a gunship and reached the barbed wire defenses of Bird.

Inside the base were rows and piles of NVA bodies, killed by point-blank artillery fires as they swarmed toward the howitzers. The gunners had fired the Top Secret "Beehive" flechette rounds, and the NVA had literally been stopped in mid-stride by a buzzing wall of tiny metal arrows. The survivors of the 22d NVA Regiment turned and fled. Before their run was through, 266 North Vietnamese bodies littered Bird and the trails leading back into the mountains.

We ate C-rations as the slicks orbited above the wooded foothills of the Suoi Ca Mountains. That morning Blue had destroyed tons of salt farther to the west. The jungle doesn't provide salt, so each huge pile represented months of gathering and carrying. We poured aviation fuel on the piles and lit them with our Zippo cigarette lighters. Now we were waiting for an air strike.

Below us a spotter plane fired a white phosphorous rocket at something on a hillside. Thick white smoke bubbled up through the green canopy, then a Phantom jet dived through the clouds. The first jet released two bombs and pulled up sharply. Shock waves and black smoke marked where the bombs had hit. The second jet followed, releasing two bombs and climbing away. The Phantoms turned high above us, and then darted by at what seemed an incredible speed. Four more black explosions, and the pilots were on their way back to air conditioning and TV sets.

Gunships rocketed the streambed that would be our landing zone. I watched the tracer streams and white pinpoints of exploding 40mm cannon shells and hoped that the LZ would be cold. As the slicks dropped, Martin pointed to the smoking craters and uprooted trees that marked our objective. He folded his hands as if praying that no one would still be there.

We ran over slippery rocks in the streambed, stumbling through

43

the swift current at the base of the hill. A gunship roared over our heads, and red smoke blossomed from the hillside above. We were too close to see the bomb craters, but the water around us was littered with fresh leaves, huge clumps of red earth, and torn branches. A tough black sergeant, Hardy, a veteran of three wars, led the Blues up the hill. We found the place where there had once been a long mess hut and a cave. Now most of the hut was gone, and the roof of the cave had been collapsed by a bomb. Martin's prayers had been answered. The NVA were either buried or gone.

Blues made a bonfire of everything burnable that remained at the rest station. I was back at the streambed, watching the flames and jiggling a pin on one of the big Chinese land mines that we had captured, when I had a visitor. An old Blue from Boston, Shay, walked over, pointed to the brown disk in my hands, and wagged his finger.

"Say, Sarge, you ever handled mines before?"

"Yeah. Lots of times." I was ashamed to tell him that I had only been in the infantry for three weeks.

He didn't believe me. "Well, watch what you do or you'll get yourself blown away. That pin you're fooling with is the safety."

When Shay had strolled away, Martin looked at me with a cat-eyed squint. "Sarge, you haven't ever handled mines before, have you?"

I looked around to be sure that Shay was out of hearing distance. "That's right. But he doesn't have to know that."

"I'm curious, Sarge. Why did you tell him you had?"

"Hell, I don't know. Pride I guess."

John lowered his eyes. "Pride. All right. Ah, thanks, Sarge." Score one for John Martin.

We are in the high hills north of the Suoi Ca Mountains. Blue is patrolling through elephant grass toward a village hidden among the trees of a deep ravine. Below us is a small pond with a dead pig lying half in the water, and I leave the file to see how it died. I never find out, but glimpse a scene that is at once both primitive and ageless. A large freshwater crab sits in the shallow water beside the stinking carcass, pulling away chunks of rotting intestines with one of its claws. The crab doesn't mind if I watch.

The village is a Montagnard hamlet of plank houses standing on stilts. The hill tribesmen have fled so quickly that they spilled some of the gourds of foul-smelling rice wine they were drinking. We search about twenty huts, but find nothing except crude three-legged stools and stacks of curing animal hides. Perhaps we will spare this hamlet. But, no. Not this time. Hardy pulls two NVA canvas belts and a canteen from underneath a reeking pile of hides. More odd pieces of equipment are discovered under piles of rags. Sam decides in an instant.

"Burn it. Three squads back to the LZ for extraction. Hobbs's squad stay here and make sure all the hooches go up. Then get back there on the double."

Some Blues gather handfuls of straw and light the ends. Others pour rice wine on the plank floors and pile cloth and baskets in the corners of the huts. As the slicks lift us out, the ravine is filling with smoke, and the treetops crackle and blaze.

The slicks flew us north from Hammond in pitch darkness. Beside me was Saito, looking unconcerned as usual.

I cupped my hands and shouted, "Where are we going at this time of night?"

"All I know, FO, is that we're going to Bong Son for a mission!"

The choppers landed on that familiar airstrip at Bong Son, where I had once spent innocent nights swinging in a hammock and living the secondhand war. I walked down the parked row of scout helicopters, gunships, and slicks and wondered what they had in store for us this time. Saito rested with his back on a Vietnamese grave mound, with his ear pressed to a radio handset. He listened quietly for a moment, then waved me over.

"This could be something. A Lurp team just got overrun in the An Lao. We're supposed to go in and look for survivors. It's up in the mountains, and the commander's trying to get flares to light up an LZ.''

The thought of a night landing in the mountains chilled me. ''I'll contact the artillery. How do you rate our chances of going in?''

Saito thought for a moment, then shrugged his shoulders. ''Very slight. Less than fifty-fifty. Night assaults are tricky business. If they did get overrun, there's not much we could do until morning.''

Saito had been right again. A last minute conference decided that the risks of a night assault were too great. When an infantry company landed at dawn, it found the place where the long-range patrol had been strewn with empty cartridge cases and a few pieces of equipment, but no bodies. It was a double loss. The LRRPs (Long Range Reconnaissance Patrol) had been testing one of the new night vision devices. As far as I know, their fate was never determined.

When I told Martin about Saito's ability to guess right, he added a very personal view of the nisei. ''Sarge, Saito's a killer. His specialty is head shots.''

I considered Saito a brave man and a friend and tried to defend him. ''That just stands to reason. He figures each situation as it comes up. A man's not going to shoot back if he's hit in the head.''

Martin threw up his arms in disgust. ''That doesn't make it right, Sarge. Besides, I think he likes it.'' John ended all talk by walking away.

The New Year's truce arrived the next morning. We had hoped for a rest, but truce violations were a habit on both sides. One of our choppers was on a recon mission when the scout gunner discovered two unarmed NVA walking down a trail in the scrub country at the edge of the Suoi Ca Mountains. Hobbs's squad was launched on a one-ship raid. They landed behind the NVA, away from the mountains. When the Vietnamese tried to run toward the safety of the hills, the scout gunner dropped tear gas grenades in front of them.

46

Seven frightened Americans panted down the trail after them. A couple of flying tackles later, the NVA, still crying from the tear gas, were forced to surrender at gunpoint. No weapons had been fired, so technically the truce had not been violated. The prisoners were reported as "returnees" to the government cause. Several days later a visitor from the artillery command post asked me if I'd been along when the Blues had picked up "those two gooks who surrendered to a passing helicopter."

I wanted to laugh at his question and tell him why but only said, "No. I missed that one."

CHAPTER 4

Bait

(January–February 1967)

The New Year's truce had been over for about fifteen minutes, and the sky lightened as our armada of gunships and slicks circled over a mountain valley in the Suoi Ca. Door gunners had killed three NVA in a clearing only minutes before the truce started, and the troop commander wanted us to collect the weapons and search the bodies. We orbited in a clear sky above a solid blanket of white clouds. Mountain peaks jutted through, looking like green tropical islands in a white sea.

Beside me, Martin swept the scene with his hand. "What do you see down there, Sarge?"

"Cloud cover. If it doesn't break, we can't go in."

He hung his head. Not the answer he wanted. "No, Sarge. Isn't it beautiful down there? I hope the clouds stay there forever."

I hadn't expected that comment, but he was right. "Yes. Yes it is beautiful." We remained in the cold morning air for another thirty-five minutes, then the choppers returned to Bong Son.

It had rained all morning, and we were soaked to the skin. Most of the choppers had not been able to fly through the downpour, and we hoped that none would be able to leave. Now the skies were clearing. Sam listened to a pilot's message and threw on his harness.

"Saddle up, Blue! Saddle up!"

Within minutes, we were running through a silent village in the An Lao Valley, trying to burn wet haystacks and hooches. Only Sam knew our mission, and he was talking rapidly to the gunships roaring overhead. Lots of them. I joined Hobbs's squad as they passed a hut with a rack of NVA canvas belts, all hung with Chinese grenades. We followed a jungle trail behind the village, and almost stumbled over the reason for the landing.

Five NVA had been running down the trail when a door gunner shot them. They had died in a row, legs pumping even in death. Four were facedown in the mud, but the fifth had turned over to get one last look at his killer. The mud was littered with rifles, mess kits, a loose grenade, and magazines for AK-47s. It was neatly stitched with lines of bullet holes.

Spider holes lined a bank just above the trail. All were full of water from the heavy rains, and one had a green Chinese canteen floating in it. There were crashes behind us, and Hobbs grabbed his radio handset.

"Blue Mike, this is Blue Two-Six. What've you got, over." A long pause. "Oh. Thought you were in contact." Another pause. "Roger that."

I asked Hobbs what had happened and he answered slowly, fighting to control his anger. "Well, shit! Some shithead set fire to that hut without getting the grenades first. No one was hurt, but one of Sam's radiomen was shook up pretty bad. You know, we're liable to lose this war without the gooks' help."

Sam had told Hobbs to stop at a clearing at the base of a jungle hill. When we arrived there, I turned back toward Sam's command group. An explosion down the trail sent me scrambling for cover. Then I looked up. On the lip of a spider hole was a dead NVA, sprawled on his back, fish eyes bulging out of a shocked face. Shay stood over the body, shaking his head in disbelief.

"Where did he come from?"

"He was hiding in that hole, Sarge. I was walking up the trail and saw this canteen floating in the water. Then I looked again and it was movin' like somebody breathing down there. There wasn't any wind comin' through the trees. I chucked in a grenade

49

and out he came. Didn't have time to warn you. Just look at that!"

"Look at what?"

"That body, man. Not a mark on it. Concussion must have got him!" The man's canteen must have floated free as he hid under the water. Shay ripped the Cav patch from his shirt and slapped it on the dead man's face.

I reached Martin and Sam just as one of Hobbs's men walked down the trail with a prisoner. Sam questioned the rifleman.

"Where'd you get this one?"

"We set up at the edge of the clearing like you said, and I went into the grass to take a leak. I looked down, and I was almost pissing on this dude here. He started begging for mercy, so I brought him in." The soldier didn't tell Sam that he had left his rifle behind when he went to pee. Sam wouldn't have understood.

Sam went into high gear at the thought of six dead NVA and one prisoner. "This place must be crawling with Charlies. Get Minh over here." Minh hurried to Sam from his usual position—as far to the rear as he could get. Sam pointed to the muddy prisoner. "What's he doing here, Minh?"

"He say his squad is harvesting rice from the paddies. They don't expect helicopters because so much rain."

"What unit is he from?"

"He is from Twenty-Seventh Company of the Eighteenth Regiment."

"Where is his company now?"

"He say they are on the hill where the trail goes. They have bunkers and recoilless rifle."

"In that case, we leave the hill for an air strike." He turned to Hardy. "Get him out to the paddy so a chopper can pick him up."

We stayed for four more hours with the gunships flying crisscross patterns over our heads. It was here that the teenage girl died defending a rice storehouse. A trooper named Gould pulled off her black pajamas, asked if anyone wanted some pussy, and dragged her body into the flames. She had been very pretty.

Rice was hidden everywhere. We found it under floors, in walls, in huge clay pots that could hold a man, or sometimes just piled to the ceiling of a hut. Everything was torched. A soldier was lighting the roof of one hut when Sam received a message from the helicopters. He ran over and pulled off the burning straw.

"Don't light it yet. Scouts say they shot a man crawling under this hooch. Let's have a look-see."

He was there, somehow squeezed into a space a few inches high. It took long minutes of digging and all the strength of three Blues to drag him free. One arm clutched a battered American carbine. The face was twisted and frozen in terror. The woods reeked with the stench of violent death.

The slicks finally took us back to Hammond. We were glad to leave that deadly place.

We jumped into a shallow stream in the An Lao Valley as gunships blasted a ruined village with rockets and cannon. A bullet slapped the water in front of me. Another bullet careened off a flat rock just behind me. A high, cracking volley echoed down the streambed. The cracks sounded oddly familiar. They were coming from a high bank in front of the hooches. Sam was the only one still standing.

"We can't stay here! Let's go, Blue! Charge it! Charge it!" The platoon rose from the water in a single mass, shamed by Sam's bravery.

"We're in for it again, Sarge!" It was Martin, gasping as he ran with the weight of his heavy radio.

We stumbled in a yelling mob toward the village, with the ones in front spraying the bushes along the high bank. Then we scrambled up through the mud and slick grass and tumbled into the village, panting hard. Behind the bushes was a long trench. Beside it were three riddled, minced bodies, the work of a minigun. Even their weapons had been chopped to pieces.

Saito's squad set fire to a hut and tossed the three bodies through an open wall. This was supposed to strike fear in the hearts of the enemy. It struck fear in my heart. The burning roof collapsed in a shower of sparks.

One of Saito's men found a bunker at the end of the long trench. He looked inside—nobody there. Then he stood up, and the man inside fired a burst from his AK-47. Saito ran over and shoved the soldier away from the opening.

"Back! Get back!" He pulled the pin from a grenade and tossed it into the bunker. Silence. He threw in another, and again nothing happened. He calmly pulled the pin on a third grenade. "Hell, this one has to work." He lobbed it underhand, and it plopped back at his feet. The man inside had thrown the grenade back. "Grenade! Hit it!"

The charge exploded with a loud bang, blowing off the roof of a hooch but injuring no one. Saito held the fourth grenade for four seconds after he pulled the safety pin. It blew the bunker apart. He crawled into the dark hole and returned with the pieces of the dead man's rifle. The constant rain had damaged our grenade fuses.

We reached the end of the crumbling village without further incident. Jefferson, a black squad leader from the inner city of Chicago, was searching the last hut. He found nothing until he looked up, then his shouts rang through the village.

"Hey! Hey! Somebody give me a hand!"

A big NVA was hiding in the rafters. Three pointed rifles convinced him to come down and join us. He dropped from the rafters, folded his hands, and began bowing to Jefferson. The prisoner was well over six feet tall, and his undersized khaki uniform made him look like a clown. His sad face and spotty haircut added to the impression.

Sam needed some quick answers. "Okay, Minh. What's he doing here?"

"He say they are harvesting rice when the helicopters come."

"How many are with him?"

"He say about twenty before the helicopters come."

"Where is his unit?"

"He say his company is in Crow's Foot about twenty kilometers from here."

Sam started to walk away, then remembered something. "Where's his weapon?"

Our prisoner took a long time explaining something to Minh. Then our interpreter nodded and turned back to Sam. "He say he have no weapon. This man is medic and volunteered to come along in case some soldiers get sick. He say he never carry weapon because his job is not to hurt people. There is much malaria in his company."

We had found a pack in the bushes, stuffed with East German drugs and Vietnamese bandages, so his story was believed. Our mission was over. The village was burning, and we had a prisoner. Clack-clack. Someone was trying to kill one of Sam's radiomen. The sniper was in a palm grove behind the village. We crawled through the mud as helicopter rockets tore apart the palm trees. Then we ran in an exhausting half-crouch back through the woodsmoke and flames.

I was back at the long trench when a bush moved. A Blue emptied his rifle into it, and a branch-covered body pitched forward into the mud. Sam rolled the quivering body over with the toe of his boot. Then he saw the rifle.

"A sixteen. I thought that was a sixteen firing at us before. This must have been the Charlie who pinned us in the creek. Must have been waiting for another crack at us."

Blue was back at Hammond a few minutes later. Maybe the rest of January would be easier than the last two days. There were replacements waiting for us as we jumped from the moving slicks, and I swaggered by them, trying to look like a veteran infantryman. Martin spoiled my mood in an instant.

"You've got something in common with them. Only a year left. Huh, Sarge?"

On January fourth, Blue waited in the graveyard at Bong Son. It was a fitting place to be. Sam had called a meeting to tell us that we would be returning to the An Lao behind a B-52 strike. We had walked through B-52 strike zones before, and I considered them mainly useful as lessons on how to splinter trees and kill wildlife with big bombs. But today's strike would be directed at a known base area. There was no doubt that the 1st Cavalry was planning to return to the An Lao Valley in force and that we were being used as bait to see what was waiting there. Two days of bait was already enough for me.

The An Lao is a long rice valley running for miles parallel to the South China Sea, separated from the Bong Son Plains by a chain of mountains running south to north. It was a place with a different character. An Lao had been one of the areas longest under Viet Cong control. A major victory had been won there by the NLF when I was a junior in high school, four years before. It was a place with a reputation to uphold, and the Communists continued fighting for it long after the rice was gone and the villages were ruins.

The Cav had raided the valley in 1966. It would come for a longer stay in 1967, and after we were gone, the 173d Airborne would place the valley "off-limits"—too dangerous. To the soldiers of 1967, An Lao was a sinister place where death always threatened, where the Vietnamese fought on when normal men would have quit. There was never a routine mission to the valley. But all these impressions were formed much later, after we had begun to know the An Lao Valley on more familiar terms.

There's a saying that goes, "Some days you get the bear, and some days the bear gets you."

The slicks dropped toward the foothills on the western wall of the An Lao. Ahead was a small valley, an abandoned paddy field shaped like a horseshoe. Steaming B-52 craters stretched away into the mountains. We jumped into green, scummy water and weeds, triggering long bursts as we ran for cover behind low paddy dikes.

A machine gun clattered, and I wondered if Sam would tell the gunner to stop wasting ammunition. I looked around for him and saw a line of bullets kicking up water twenty feet behind me. As I dived back into the rotten water, hell broke loose. The NVA had waited through the bombs, guessing that someone would land here. Now they had us in a horseshoe ambush in a natural horseshoe. At least one machine gun fired from each side of the U— white tracers. AKs were at the bend and along both sides—green tracers.

54

I was terrified by the screams and noise and prayed for the first time in years. "Dear God! Please don't let them kill me!"

Slugs chewed away at the corner of the paddy dikes where Martin and I hid. Shay ran for a corner like ours and was chased by a string of white tracers and waterspouts. His legs were knocked out from under him as he reached the corner, and his head hit the dike with a loud thud. Parga was behind a tiny dead tree that had once grown from a paddy dike. He saw a machine gun inside one of the bomb craters and fired his grenades. The machine gunners spotted Parga. Bullets chopped the tree to pieces as Parga screamed.

"Mama! Mama! Oh, Mama, Mama!"

"Somebody help that man! Hold on, Parga!" It was Sam, shouting above the incredible racket.

Doc Hansen jumped across a paddy dike and was chased back by bullets. It was then that I saw the bravest act I can remember. Doc leaped over the dike and crawled through thirty yards of mud, bullets, and stinking water. He grabbed Parga's shirt and dragged him back through that hell. Every NVA weapon turned on them. For long seconds, the only targets in the horseshoe valley were a medic and a wounded grenadier. The paddy water boiled from bullet hits, but they made it. Doc Hansen was untouched.

Then they turned their guns toward the rest of us. I tried to fight back by shooting at flashes or at the crater gun that got Parga, but it seemed useless to be throwing bullets at all those trees. If I moved quickly, a machine gun started chopping down the mud dike. The dike was saving my life.

Our gunships roared over and rocketed the trees around the horseshoe. Then artillery shells began falling. They didn't even break holes in the thick canopy. I had the breath knocked out of me by a clump of hard earth thrown up by a shell, but it didn't matter; the Vietnamese suddenly stopped firing. We were saved. At least some of us were saved.

Shay had been shot through both hips and legs and was unconscious. He was dying. Shay would have gone home in two weeks. Parga had taken three bullets in the back. He had lost a lot of blood and was too weak to scream anymore. Two of last night's replacements were wounded. Another one was dead.

The commander pulled us out of the horseshoe valley and rewarded us. Blue got the rest of the day off duty. An infantry company took our place. They searched the hills and trails around the horseshoe, and found only three scared local force Viet Cong hiding in a cave. Our NVA attackers had escaped.

The platoon was on patrol in the Suoi Ca, hunting for the troops of an NVA regiment that had been driven out of the lowlands. The point was cutting a path with machetes over the rugged hills when it happened upon a gigantic pile of boulders. It would have been a scenic overlook in any American state park, and it gave me a rare view of the entire lowland plains. I stood on that wooded hilltop, somewhere in central Vietnam, and looked across the flat Crescent, all the way to the South China Sea. It was a magnificent sight, marred only by the distant specks of brown helicopters searching for prey.

The long patrol had rewarded us only with nests of biting red ants and thorns that tore our skin and uniforms, so the slicks were on the way to pick us up. Saito's squad cut a path downhill toward a clearing until they found a footpath heading back up the hill. Sam sent Jefferson's squad to investigate. Corda was on point.

Deep cracks from an M-16, rapid popping sounds from a carbine, more cracks. Jefferson's men raced down the footpath and threw themselves into the thorn bushes around us. Carbine shots popped through the thorns inches over my head as Corda shouted in a hysterical voice, "Gooks in a cave! Gooks in a cave! Gooks in a cave!"

Sam grabbed his shoulders and shook him back to sanity. "Slow down, boy. Take it easy. Now what have we got up there?"

Corda looked around with wild, bloodshot eyes, as if seeing the rest of us for the first time. "There was three VC standing in this cave and just staring at me. I shot one of them and the other two started shooting. One of them turned around to run and I shot him in the back. There's more up there!"

More carbine shots popped through the thorns. Sam grabbed his radio handset and talked excitedly to the gunship pilots covering us.

"Squad leaders, pop smoke! We're in too close for rockets. They're coming in with miniguns. Everybody keep your heads down!"

The beating of the chopper blades drew more carbine shots. My ears roared with the harsh buzzing of the minigun. Twigs, bark, and branches fell around us, then ricochets from the cave whined through the bushes. More smoke grenades, another minigun run, and the cave was silent.

We ran down the footpath toward the clearing. Saito's men stopped at the rock bunkers along the way just long enough to collect armloads of NVA equipment. They had left everything behind. Then we reached the clearing and a clattering flight of slicks landed to deliver us. As the choppers headed back to Hammond in the twilight, there was the beautiful orange blossom of a phosphorous marking rocket, and two jets dived for the hill. Another day, full of beauty and violence and a hundred different emotions, was through.

Corda had been getting more desperate each day. December first, the horseshoe valley, the VC in the cave, and the fights in other months had taken their toll. We talked that night at Hammond.

"I told you things would get worse," he began, wagging a finger in my face. "I'm never going to see the City again. They've got my number, Matt."

"That's nonsense. You can make it if you want to. Seven months from now, you'll be telling war stories on the street."

"Eight months. That can be forever in this death trap unit."

I was beginning to think he had a good point, but his paranoia didn't need more encouragement. "You'll get a job in the rear before that. Just don't give up yet."

He shook his head. "No! No jobs with my luck. You don't know how unlucky my life has been. Not with my luck."

"Why don't you try praying or something? That usually helps people."

His eyes were wild again. "Pray? Shit! I don't pray because the world is godless. Think about it. How can men with so much blood on their hands believe in a god?" He wandered off into the night air, pausing once to kick a wooden case of grenades.

I had bought a .38 caliber Smith and Wesson revolver from a gunship pilot. One day my rifle would jam like everyone else's. Corda often borrowed the revolver when he went on outpost duty. The evening after our talk, Jefferson woke me from a deep sleep. The outpost had Viet Cong moving all around them. The men on outpost were from his squad, and he needed volunteers for a relief mission.

The Blue volunteers threw on their equipment and ran to the barbed wire. From somewhere in the darkness ahead came the sounds of rifle and carbine shots. Eight of us crawled under the wire and ran toward the shooting. We found Corda behind a tree, groaning and bleeding from a leg wound. Jeff and I hoisted him in a fireman's carry and staggered toward the barbed wire. Corda weighed well over two hundred pounds and we couldn't carry him the entire distance, so we rested for a moment in the damp sand.

A man in black pajamas walked through a gap in the hedgerow right behind us. He was firing a carbine from the hip, spraying bullets in an arc. If we had been standing, we would have been hit. I fired a burst and he vanished, stepping backward through the hedgerow. It was like a scene from an old war movie. We picked up Corda again and got the hell out of there. Behind us, 40mm grenades exploded in spark showers along the hedgerow. We had reached the last ditch in front of the barbed wire when two American machine guns opened up on us.

Corda, the defeated man, lowered his head. "Jesus Christ. We're going to be killed by our own men."

Jeff and I shouted like devils. "Tell those bastards to stop firing! Cut the fire! It's Charlie Troop! It's Charlie Troop!"

Military Police on guard duty had mistaken us for Viet Cong. I suppose they thought VC always charged in little clusters of three men. For fifteen long minutes, we hid in the ditch while tracers zinged a foot over our heads. Then it was over. An MP sergeant was waiting by the barbed wire to apologize.

We learned the next day that an Army doctor was getting a Silver Star for our rescue. This brave medic had run all the way down to the barbed wire to wait for Corda. The rest of us were not even thanked. What we did was expected. It wasn't until later years, when the Blues rarely had the opportunity to fight, that they started receiving numerous medals.

A squadron aidman returned my revolver a few days later. He had a message from Corda. "Corda said to give you this. He said to tell you that he doesn't need it anymore." I checked the cylinder and found one bullet fired. After that, I often wondered how Corda had really been wounded.

It was January fourteenth, and we were on our way to the third landing in five hours. At dawn, we had searched a village in Happy Valley that was supposed to be a Viet Cong rest camp. The farmers had loaded us with coconuts and bananas, and our boots still stank from the manure of their American dairy cows. Later we were in the mountains. It was a beautiful place with a waterfall over huge boulders and jungle trees growing from rock ledges. The trails we searched had been made by barefoot mountain tribesmen herding their pigs. Now the slicks carried us north of the Special Forces camp in Happy Valley.

We leaped into a field of tall grass. The outlines of old rice fields could be seen from the air, but there was no trace here, only slight bumps that had once been paddy dikes. Red smoke rose beside a narrow stream. Ho Chi Minh sandals drifted in the slow current, and five packs were scattered along the muddy bank. Two bodies in black pajamas, a man and a woman, were sprawled facedown in the stream. Their blood mingled with the water running past them and made long pink streaks that flowed around the rocks. They had been carrying only rice and hand grenades.

Jefferson's squad patrolled down an embankment, probably an incomplete railroad bed, with jungle trees forming a curved canopy above us. I was the last in line, and when we had gone far enough, Jeff turned to me.

"FO, you're already there. How about taking the point on the way back?"

I walked along the embankment until I saw the man climbing toward me on a footpath. Our eyes met and we briefly nodded to each other. VC! In that long instant, his facial expression told the whole story. It was saying, "I just made a stupid mistake!" He reached for something on his belt and jumped soundlessly into the bushes beside the trail. I fired by instinct. When the bullets were gone, I dropped the empty magazine at my feet and forgot to reload the rifle. I was shaking from disbelief when Jefferson got to me.

"What were you shooting at, FO?"

"I saw a Charlie. He disappeared down there."

Jefferson walked down the footpath and quickly returned. He was holding a rusty American pineapple grenade. He slapped me hard on the back. "Dude didn't have a chance to pull the pin. I owe you a beer tonight, FO. Better reload that rifle." That was Jefferson's way of telling me that I had just killed a man and that he understood what I was feeling.

We waited for the slicks beside another corpse with a Cav patch plastered on its face. Martin stood to one side with a dark expression. I had a terrible feeling of guilt and disgust, but I had to talk to someone.

"What's bothering you, John?"

"You know these people didn't have a chance against gunships. They just killed another one. Blew his head off. Sounds like Saito's work."

"No, John. It was me." Martin stared away in silence.

Next were the landings in the Suoi Ca Mountains. This was the base area of the 18th NVA Regiment, the unit with the great misfortune of being battered by the 1st Air Cavalry time and again for fifteen months. These brave soldiers were hunted in the plains by helicopters and could find safety nowhere. We came across them often in the mountains—thin, tired, scared men. It was impossible to hate them.

We would fly through the mountain valleys with the winds buffeting the choppers as if they were toys, then land in the vast open spaces and walk into the hardwood forests. It was never a monotonous life. Blue would pass mountain caves and brooks or walk along cool trails where tall trees never let in the sunlight or the rain. It was a twilight world of deadly beauty. Sometimes we would find fresh bootprints on the trails and would suppose that other Americans had been there. Then one day we saw the new NVA jungle boots and realized that the pattern on the soles was very similar to our own. Those hills were magnificent, and even the seemingly deadly things were not really so deadly.

The elephant grass above the treelines was filled with thousands of bamboo punji stakes, but they weren't new, and they hadn't been made for us. Forests of trees had branches slit, in which punji stakes were placed at every possible angle. But the trees had grown around the stakes and mended themselves. Here was a glimpse of that other war. The French had access to this region only through paratroop drops, and these greeting cards were meant for them. The effort used to make, carry, and plant those rotting slivers of bamboo must have been enormous.

We often found crumbling bunker complexes, sides overgrown with moss, and one day we saw the granddaddy of them all. Blue walked for hours through a camp, many years old, on the scale of a city. Some of the bunkers could hold houses. A regiment had lived there once. I tried to picture the Viet Minh soldiers, sweating for weeks to carve the defenses out of those timeless hills. As the file walked down an ancient trail, someone broke through rotting planks covered with earth. He dug away the rest of the planks, and discovered four British Sten guns wrapped in decaying oilcloth. Who had buried those guns, and why had he never returned to claim them?

Once we landed in the open spaces and followed a forest trail beside a swift-flowing stream. It had been quiet, and our new lieutenant let us rest by some disintegrating huts on a hillside. They were soon burning. I wanted to get away from the smoke and found what had once been a trail. I followed the faint path up a steep rise and found yet another reminder of that other war—an old defensive position in a circle under the trees. It must have been French because the collapsed foxholes were big like ours, not small and round like spider holes. At one place was a rusting American-type helmet riddled with jagged holes. At another were the ruptured steel canisters of homemade grenades that had exploded unevenly. At yet another were the cartridge cases of French army bullets. As I leaned against a tree whose fragment wounds were so old they appeared as dark spots in the living bark around them, I wondered who had won the little fight and whether its outcome had mattered, except to the men who had fought there.

Patterson was on point. He was a new man, but those quiet mountains were a good place to learn the position. Crack. Patterson ran along our file yelling, "Gooks! Gooks! Gooks!" A low branch sent his helmet spinning off his head, and he stopped, staring at our surprised faces. He had walked into six Viet Cong munching rice balls in the middle of the trail. His rifle had jammed after a single shot, and he had thrown it at them.

One of the Viet Cong had lost his way. He splashed down the stream below the trail, fighting the strong current with all his strength. He wore soaked black pajamas, a scarf of camouflaged parachute silk, and a leaf-covered jungle hat. The water boiled around him as a dozen rifles fired at once. He looked up at us with a shocked expression on his face, then was flung back into the water. His body spun for a moment in the current and wedged between two boulders a little farther downstream.

Gunships chased the other Viet Cong into the steep hills along both sides of the stream. Hardy almost killed another one with grenades, but the man was too skilled at catching them and tossing them away before they exploded. We collected the abandoned equipment, halfheartedly searched the woods along the stream, and walked the short distance to a clearing. It had been a long day and we wanted to go home. The Viet Cong had been eating lunch almost on the edge of our pickup zone.

The slicks had left us in the vast open spaces of the High Suoi Ca. Since dawn, we had cut straight downslope through brush, thorns, and clinging vines. There was no trail this time. We finally rested in a place so steep that we had to brace our boots against trees to keep from sliding farther down the mountainside. I knew our commander didn't care how exhausted we were; he just wanted us out of the way while they shelled our objective with long-range cannon. I ate my canned beans and listened to the shells exploding in the trees along a stream below us. Sam was beside me, eating his beans. We always got the worst rations—Sam, because he let everyone else choose first, and me, because I wasn't fast enough. Sam wanted to talk.

"The scouts want us to check out a creek down there. Those are one-seventy-fives hitting it. Out of range of everything else. That's why we broke here. They're afraid of us getting closer in case one of the rounds gets off target."

"I didn't know the pilots cared so much."

He laughed softly. "Neither did I." Now his eyes grew solemn. "Hey, FO, be careful today. We're a long way into these mountains, and they aren't sure what's going on along that creek."

Sam was going home in a few weeks, but he was still putting the welfare of his platoon ahead of his own. "Thanks, Sam. I'll watch it."

It took us another hard hour to reach the stream. We forded it by clinging to a vine rope the Viet Cong had left there, and then crossed a series of hundred-foot-deep ravines on muddy logs. We had to shuffle sideways for forty feet or more, using our rifles like balancing sticks. One false step would have aborted our mission and caused an almost impossible rescue attempt through three hundred feet of jungle trees and rock walls. This was one of the wildest places I had ever experienced.

Hardy's squad was on point when they saw an SKS rifle leaning against a pile of rocks. An NVA had been sitting inside the rocks, probably an outpost for something, waiting for the artillery to stop. Maybe he was asleep. Hardy found a small opening in the pile and cupped his hands.

"Lai day! Lai day! [Come out! Come out!]"

Silence. He lobbed in a hand grenade, and when it exploded, we heard a man scrambling over loose rocks.

"Dammit! *Lai day! Lai day!*"

We tossed in another grenade, and the man inside groaned loudly for the few seconds before it went off. Hardy looked into the opening, and the man scrambled away for the second time. He turned to the Blue holding his M-16.

"Lousy fuckin' frags. Give me my sixteen."

He pointed the rifle into the rocks and fired the entire magazine. Then he pulled out the body of a man in his late thirties. It was hard to believe he could have been so thin and still lived. When Hardy ripped off his khaki shirt, I noticed that four bullets had entered the smooth skin of his back. The man must have been very sick, because the bullet holes were tiny and bloodless, as if he had been pricked several times by a big pin. We left him there, in a jumble beside his rock pile. When the rest of the platoon had walked on ahead, Martin returned to the body. He took the Cav patch from his face and covered the man's head with his khaki shirt.

A short distance down the trail, Hardy heard female voices. He walked around a large boulder and came face to face with two women in black and a man in khakis. The man smiled and put his hands in the air, then reached for something in his pocket. Hardy shot by reflex. By the time Sam's group had arrived, Hardy had big tears rolling down his cheeks as he stood over the man he had just killed. The man had been reaching into his pocket to show Hardy the bandages he was carrying there.

"If he had just not moved, he'd be alive right now."

Sam tried to comfort him. "Don't take it so hard. This is war and people get killed."

"That poor bastard. Why did he do it? Why the hell did he do it?" The rest of us were ready to cry along with him.

Sam tried to change the mood. "Okay, what's everyone standing around for? Get these women back to the trail!"

But Hardy remained by the body. "Why? Why? It was such a stupid thing to do."

Sam was on the other side of the boulder, questioning the women. "Minh, ask them who they are."

"They say they are nurses. This is the hospital area of the Eighteenth Regiment. They say for us to leave."

"How many people are there around here?"

"They say, yes, there are many. Most of them are sick."

Patterson had discovered two caves a few yards behind the medic's corpse. One of the caves was full of straw sleeping pallets, bamboo bunks, and boxes of East German medicines. When he looked in the other cave, he jumped away as if stung by a wasp. He saw me watching and jerked his thumb at the entrance.

"Man, I saw somebody moving in there. Let's frag it."

Hobbs didn't like that idea. "Better check with Sam first."

When Sam heard about the caves, he had the nurses brought over to him. "Minh, ask them if there is anyone in that cave back there."

"They say, 'what cave?' "

"Minh, explain to them that we don't want to kill unless we have to. Ask them if they had anyone else with them."

The Vietnamese talked for a moment, then one of the women spat at Sam. Minh was embarrassed. He blushed and said, "Sergeant. They say no more questions."

Sam stared at the women for a long instant, then looked away. "Frag it, Hobbs."

Patterson threw two grenades into the cave and went inside. Then he returned, dragging the body of a nurse by its long hair. One of the grenades had landed squarely on her back, exposing intestines and breaking her spine. As he pulled the body along the ground, it bounced like a jelly manikin. Patterson was shaking with anger. "They let their friend die. I'll kill those bitches for making me do this!"

As he headed for the trail, still dragging the corpse, Hobbs grabbed him roughly by the shoulder. "Forget it! There ain't no way Sam's gonna let you do that. Just forget it. Get rid of that gook and git your ass back up there and search those caves."

Patterson let go of the hair and stood there like a cornered animal. "I just hope they try to run!" He stroked his rifle for emphasis.

Our mission was over for today. We climbed uphill to a slanted, rocky one-ship clearing. The slicks that took us home left another platoon behind in ambush. The NVA were supposed to think that all of us had left, when there had really been a switch. I didn't want to stay and find out if it worked.

Martin had been impressed by the day's events as only he could be. We were becoming friends in the little tent during those days in the mountains and now we could talk. He broke a long silence that evening with a thought.

"Matt, those poor little guys. They haven't got anyplace left to hide."

"I know. The one by the rocks got to me. He was so thin."

John nodded. "Listen, I've been thinking. Let's propose a toast to them."

"Name it."

"To the Eighteenth NVA Regiment: may they sleep on firm straw pallets tonight, and may their rice rolls be full." We raised our imaginary glasses.

At dawn the next morning we were back, waiting among the boulders for the ambush platoon. A tired, dirty file of men slid down the trail toward us. They broke into smiles when they saw us. Their night had been hell. Campfires blazed on the mountainsides until the slicks arrived, and groups of NVA had walked along the trail throughout the night, laughing and playing transistor radios. Some of them were listening to rock music on Armed Forces Radio. The platoon's thoughts had turned from ambush to surviving until Blue arrived at dawn.

Blue led the way down yesterday's trail. The thin little man had been rolled on his side, but no attempt had been made to bury him. The bodies of the nurse and the medic were gone. We continued the patrol for an hour, passing unnaturally quiet caves that had to be full of people. When our force rested in an area crisscrossed by footpaths, the lieutenant sent patrols to investigate. What they found scared the hell out of us. The whole area was full of rock caves, walkways floored with woven bamboo mats, bamboo handrails, and bamboo arrows pointing in various directions at intersections. This was certainly the base area of a regiment, and our two platoons continued to exist only because of their goodwill or confusion.

Jefferson was curious. He was resting in front of a cave and had to know if there were people inside. He borrowed the lieutenant's .45 automatic and Sam's flashlight and disappeared into the dark hole. Seven muffled shots, then Jefferson scrambled out on his hands and knees.

Sam squatted down beside him. "What's in there, hotshot?"

"Two Charlies. They were sitting with their backs against the far wall. Their AKs were right beside them. When I flashed the light, they went for their guns and I shot them. I'm damned sure not going back down there!" He tossed the empty pistol to the lieutenant, who gave Jefferson an "I'm not going down there either" look.

Sam had the same thought. "Sir, if we get a man hurt in one of those caves, we're likely to pay the devil trying to get him out. That's Charlie's homestead down there."

The young officer was visibly shaken. "Right! Nobody goes into a cave." Jefferson breathed a loud sigh of relief.

Hobbs's squad led the way down the trail, with Gould on point. Gould was an unlikable braggart from a small town in the Midwest. He was an animal with a rare combination of survival instinct and bloodlust. He hated the Army, but he loved to kill VC. The first time I had seen him in action was the day he stripped the black pajamas from the young woman by the storehouse, leering all the while. I didn't like him, but he was a good man to have on the point.

Five minutes down the trail, Gould killed a North Vietnamese. He had ducked under a branch and stood up face to face with a surprised man in a khaki uniform. The NVA carried an M-16 rifle and a pouch of papers at his side. Incredibly, they still seemed unaware of our presence on the trail.

Minh shuffled through the papers and turned to the lieutenant. "Sir, he is messenger for Headquarters Company of the Eighteenth Regiment. He is carrying lists of rice rations for the battalions.'' The lieutenant's mouth dropped open, and he cautiously eyed the trees around us.

Eventually our two platoons took another break—strict silence, no smoking. As we sat in the mud of the trail, Gould heard laughter. The word was passed in whispers that Hobbs and Gould would take prisoners, but it didn't reach the other platoon fast enough. They had spotted an NVA in a tree platform. He was scanning the sky with binoculars, searching for helicopters. They shot him out of his tree. Now Hobbs and Gould would have to act quickly.

Rapid shots from the point, then the message—one enemy dead, one trapped, and two escaped. Hobbs had chased an NVA under a rock ledge and was shooting into the rocks above him, shouting for him to surrender. Then we had our prisoner. He was a pale teenage boy dressed in a filthy brown uniform. There were jungle rot sores on his face and neck. We walked up to a little waterfall, beside which the four NVA had been joking, while Minh questioned the prisoner. Unfortunately, there was a newsman with us that day, and Sam had been told to give him what he wanted. He wanted a human interest story.

He smiled at our prisoner and handed him a cigarette. Then he turned to Minh. ''Where's his home?''

''He say he live in farming village fifty kilometers south of Hanoi.''

''Did he join the army or was he drafted?''

''He say they come for him one day when he is in the rice paddy. He goes because he doesn't want to shame parents. He doesn't like the army very much. He say he want to go home.''

The newsman nodded. ''Me, too. This is my kind of guy. How long has he been in the South?''

''He say he gets here six months ago.''

''What's his job in the army?''

''He say he is rice-bearer for the Headquarters Company of the Eighteenth Regiment.''

Sam was seething. We weren't standing in smalltown America. ''Okay, that's enough. Let's see if we can find his buddies.''

Jefferson and I sat beside the trail, watching as Saito's squad fanned out to search the surrounding jungle. He couldn't understand how the other two NVA could have escaped so quickly. "Hey, FO, I wonder where they went. This is pretty solid brush."

I couldn't help him. "The only thing I can figure is they took off as soon as those guys opened up at the one in the tree." I happened to glance at the little waterfall, by which Saito's squad had just returned. An Asian face was peeking out of the bushes in my direction. Our eyes met, and the next instant he was up and jumping over the falls. "There went one!"

Jefferson had a suspicious look on his face. The FO is nuts, all right. "Stop kidding, FO."

"Have it your way, Jeff."

Blue was going home. Infantry companies would take our place and clean out the caves. The prisoner was enjoying a cigarette with his back against a tree, so I helped him to his feet. Then we trotted down the trail toward another one-ship clearing.

We landed in the rocky clearing at the other end of the caves one last time. Blues stayed only long enough to protect the place while a convoy of slicks brought in an infantry company. They all carried heavy pouches of dynamite and plastic explosives. The grunts looked around them at those wild mountains and deep gorges and stared down the narrow trail that led to the caves. They were already afraid. We left them while they waited for a second company to arrive.

The operation continued for days. I would sometimes read about the fight for a hospital and command complex southwest of Bong Son and would shudder at the thought of the casualties the grunts were suffering in those caves. The GI paper called them "moderate casualties," a military euphemism for "small units are taking heavy losses."

January ended with a fruitless overnight ambush high in the mountains. The only contact the previous day was with a haggard man who couldn't have eaten for days. He must have lost his way and then wandered aimlessly through those wild mountains. Our point man had seen only the khaki uniform and an Asian face. We left his thin body along a leaf-strewn trail. The platoon spent the night about two thousand yards from where he had died. When the sun rose, the slicks were clattering in, and it was February.

I was going home on leave on February twelfth. The remaining time was rather quiet, as we defined the word. Blue made landings in the Suoi Ca, Happy Valley, the An Lao, the Fertile Crescent, and Bong Son, but major clashes eluded us. The platoon continued to add prisoners and kills to our constant score, but there was nothing on the scale of January. Occasionally we would find fortified camps and jungle villages and destroy them with fire and plastic explosives. Once we almost captured an operating Viet Cong radio transmitter in the Suoi Ca. Through all these events, my thoughts were on home.

Our friend is dead. The slicks had flown us over this man's isolated hooch many times, and he always ran outside in his red swimming shorts to smile and wave to us. The scouts say he was counting our choppers and reporting where we were headed. The scouts had flown over unusually early this morning and found him returning from the mountains with his carbine and pack. The gunner took his red shorts for a souvenir. Now he lies beside a hedgerow with his naked ass shining in the morning sun. We had looked forward to seeing him this morning. The commander wants us to search the body again and burn his hut.

Scouts had chased five NVA into a cave. The slicks orbited to one side as high explosive and white phosphorous shells shattered rocks, churned the earth of an open slope, and set fire to brush and trees. Orange and black blossoms everywhere. Most of the slope above us was on fire by the time we jumped, and we raced between gaps in the hot brushfires to reach the cave at the top. It had been a storehouse for grenades and Chinese TNT. Five canvas packs were abandoned among the wooden crates.

One of the packs had been hit by artillery shrapnel and was coated with drying blood. A Blue dumped its contents in the mud outside the cave. Amid a pile of rice balls, extra uniforms, family photographs, loose bullets, and a toothbrush, was one of the common NVA soldier's diaries. Every North Vietnamese soldier we had searched had kept a detailed diary of his part in the war. It was against their army's orders, but they carried them anyway. Our intelligence teams loved the diaries, because they often told the entire history of units moving down the Ho Chi Minh Trail, the battles they had fought in the South, and a thousand details of everyday life.

This particular diary had taken a shell fragment through its center, which made turning the pages difficult, but Martin pried open the cover sheet. There was a neatly penned sentence. "I wonder what it says, Matt?"

"I don't know. Maybe the guy's name and address."

"No. Look. That's not an address. Let's find Minh and have him translate it."

Minh was crouched in an NVA spider hole, munching on a round C-ration cracker. It had to be the most protected place on the ridge. He took the diary, read the passage, and frowned.

"Come on, Minh. What does it say?"

I sensed that Minh didn't want to share it with us, but we asked him again. Something in his tone and manner told me that he was translating part of his culture for barbarians. "This is a very beautiful sentence, like something wise old man say. It say, 'Happiness and sadness I will remember forever.' It is good thing to write."

John solemnly nodded his head. "He was a sensitive man."

"Yeah, John. I guess he was at that."

The thing of importance that day was the line from a faceless soldier's diary. I hope he lived to write it again. His words will always be with me.

This was my last mission before going home. The platoon was searching a village near Bong Son, within sight of English, an American artillery base. It was the eve of Tet, and the scout choppers had buzzed a big civilian rally in a nearby field. They couldn't pick out the Viet Cong political officers who had to be there, so the scouts chased the whole mob away. Viet Cong flags were flying from all the villages of Binh Dinh Province, as they did every year at this time. Special cadres even hoisted them in

71

the middle of government controlled cities. Our door gunners had spent the day cutting down flags throughout the Crescent and the Bong Son Plains.

The village was deserted above ground. The women, children, and old men were hiding in family bunkers because they were afraid of the scouts and didn't know what our reaction would be to the propaganda leaflets the Viet Cong had pasted on each of the huts. There were paper VC flags, pictures of Ho Chi Minh, and many pamphlets, written in poor English. They told how the "People's Liberation forces" were beating "imperialist" and "puppet" units throughout the South. According to one of them, America had already lost more men and equipment than remained in Vietnam. I made a collection of the better ones to show to the folks back home.

We found the rally field, with a large Viet Cong flag flying in its center. The platoon formed a line and walked cautiously toward the flagpole, but I was greedy. I wanted to take that flag home with me. I ran to the pole and pulled down the red, yellow, and blue flag, then turned around in time to see most of the Blues scrambling for cover.

After a moment of silence, Hardy jumped up and ran over to me. "You all right, FO?"

What the hell was going on? "Yeah. I feel fine."

He started to say something, stopped himself, then exploded. "Boy, that was the dumbest thing I ever seen anybody do!"

"What do you mean by that?"

"You're lucky the damned thing wasn't booby-trapped. They expected someone to pull it down, you fucking idiot!"

"Why?"

"The English leaflets weren't for the benefit of the local yokels."

Now I felt like a fucking idiot. "Sorry. I didn't think about that. Sorry."

"You could have been a lot sorrier!" He kicked a clod of earth and walked back to his squad.

Now it was Martin's turn. "Still gung ho, huh, Sarge? What are you going to do with a homemade flag?"

"Take it home to Indiana."

He pointed at Hardy, who was standing in a little knot of men, gesturing in my direction. "He was looking out for your best interest. You did take a dumb chance."

"Yeah. I know."

I had a visitor later that same evening. The lieutenant, who had barely spoken a complete sentence to any of the enlisted men since his arrival, crawled through the doorway of our pup tent. He asked about my home and family, then we talked about the war, and somehow the subject got changed to the propaganda leaflets I had collected in the village. He was impressed by them.

"Those are nice leaflets. Wish I'd had the time to get some before everyone grabbed them."

"Yes, sir. I like them all right."

"I sure would like to have some, maybe one of each kind, to take home myself."

So that was why he was here. "Sir, I'd like to help you, but I only have one of each kind. Maybe we'll find some more."

He hung his head, so sadly. "I don't know. I have the platoon to keep track of. That's a full-time job. Maybe you could give me a few of yours . . . if you don't mind." That could be interpreted as a subtle order.

"I'd like to keep them, sir." He went away mad.

Martin had sat through the whole conversation with an amused look on his face. We discussed what I should do. We agreed that the lieutenant had no right to put pressure on me for my souvenirs. He had run from hut to hut, trying to grab some for himself, but all that were left had been glued too tightly and couldn't be ripped off the walls. We also decided that he was in a position to make my life miserable if he had a grudge. I reluctantly walked to his tent and rustled the flap. He was writing a letter by candlelight and threw me an annoyed look.

"It's Sergeant Brennan, sir. You might as well have these. I'd probably lose them, anyway." That was the "I'm just a dumb sergeant" act.

Now he was happy again. He grabbed the leaflets and inspected them to be sure they weren't damaged. "Thanks, Sergeant, I really do appreciate this. Ah, you wouldn't want to part with your flag, would you?'' The old ''foot in the door'' technique.

''No way, sir!'' The greedy bastard wanted it all.

The Blues left on a mission the next morning, and I hitched a ride on a courier chopper to An Khe. I had injured my ankle running after the flag and was wearing an ace bandage. When I walked into the 9th Cav orderly room to pick up my leave papers, a clerk saw the bandage. He pushed his typewriter to one side with a guilty look.

''Were you out with C Troop this morning?''

My mind made the connection. ''No. I'm going home on leave. What happened to them?''

''Charlie Blues got hit in the Suoi Ca. The lieutenant stopped a bullet in the back, and four other men caught grenade frags. Nobody was killed. They got the gooks that did it. I was just making out the casualty report.''

''Did the artillery radioman get hit?''

''No, they were all grunts.'' At least Martin was safe.

''What a waste of leaflets.''

He gave me a confused look. ''What did you say?''

''Oh, never mind. It wasn't very important.''

CHAPTER 5

Business as Usual

(March–April 1967)

The leave home was a time of disillusionment. It was snowing when I stepped off the plane in Evansville, and the flakes felt delicate and alien as they melted against my face. I had forgotten what snow was like. I showed my family the flag, which meant nothing to them, and when I tried to explain what had happened over the past fourteen months, I couldn't find the words.

The change from a hot world of danger to the lonely cold of an Indiana winter had been too abrupt. I cried when I tried to remember the naive boy who had left Evansville Airport in 1965. I now knew the jungle better than I had ever bothered to know the Indiana woods, and I missed my friends in the Blues. This world was dull and different. The things that other people of my age held important seemed so trivial. It didn't matter who your current lover was, or what model of car you drove; the only thing of importance was whether you lived or died.

I left home on a windy day in March, telling my family not to worry. I'd be home when the weather was warmer and the girls were home from college. I was glad to be returning to the Blues, but I couldn't say that to people who had already waited for such a long time, especially my loving mother. I grieve when I think of the long nights of pain she endured because of me.

* * *

The troop camp had been moved north, from Hammond to Bong Son. We were on the site where the graves registration tent had been twelve months before. The former GR helipad was now part of a parking lot for scout choppers. Martin had constructed a tent exactly like the one we had at Hammond, so finding it was easy. The Blues were on patrol when I arrived, but I found a door gunner cleaning his machine gun in the shade of a slick.

"Hi. What's Blue up to these days?"

He recognized me, but faces in the Blues changed too often for him to be sure. "You've been gone a while. Did you get hit or something?"

"No. I went home on leave. Just got back."

"Oh. We're going after the Blues in a few minutes. Want to ride along?"

"Sure. I'm looking forward to seeing everyone."

The four slicks touched down at a hillside clearing in the An Lao, and sweating, tired grunts rushed for the seats. I had forgotten just how tattered and filthy the platoon looked after a day on patrol. Most of the faces were new. I recognized only Hobbs, Gould, and Patterson. Patterson already looked much older than he did when I left. Hobbs had always looked worn around the edges. Gould looked like a choir boy. Martin was on another slick, riding with a new lieutenant, a new platoon sergeant, and Minh. Already, there was only a handful of men left from December. The choppers lifted out of the clearing and roared across the An Lao Valley floor at treetop level.

It was almost dark, the time when the Viet Cong returned to their villages after hiding all day in the mountains. As the slicks climbed over the An Lao Mountains, gunships spotted armed men running into a village on the edge of the Bong Son Plains. The slicks made a sudden turn and flew down the rocky slopes toward the village. I wasn't expecting a landing so soon.

We landed beside well-tended huts and palm groves. The village was populated, but the civilians were hiding in family bunkers, leaving the soldiers to fight it out above ground. Two bodies were sprawled in a courtyard, beside an enclosed Buddhist shrine.

They were the last Viet Cong entering the village and had been killed by a door gunner as they hid behind the shrine. Two Blues slung the dead men's Chinese carbines across their backs and decorated the bodies with Cav patches. A third Blue reached into the shrine and grabbed a stalk of bananas that had been left as an offering. Then he ran ahead, bananas in one hand and a rifle in the other.

Clacking bursts and scattered shots ripped by from deeper inside the village. We ran like Indians from palm tree to palm tree as the bullets ricocheted among the hooches. Then we reached a wide vegetable patch in the center of the village, with a hedgerow on the far side. Clack. A bullet from the hedgerow missed by inches. I ran for cover behind a large palm tree and saw Martin for the first time, hiding behind another tree.

"Hey, John! I couldn't find those poetry books for you. I even went to the Indiana University bookstore."

A horrified look. "My God! How can you talk about books at a time like this?" That ended the homecoming conversation.

The lieutenant was afraid to send us across the vegetable patch. They could catch us in the open and slaughter us. He was debating what to do when a man in black jumped up from some bushes in front of me and ran into the vegetable patch. He was running as only a man afraid of dying can run. His bush hat and Ho Chi Minh sandals flew off from his efforts. I leaned against the tree and drew a bead on his back, then a new man ran in front of my rifle, yelling and pointing.

"There goes one! There goes one!" A split second later and I would have been squeezing the trigger. I still have the nightmare of that soldier in my rifle sights.

The VC stumbled and dropped his rifle as he entered the hedgerow, then turned and ran along behind it, parallel to the vegetable patch. His comrades had retreated in that direction. The row had gaps every twenty feet, and each time he reached a gap, rifles would bang away. When he reached the third gap, most of the rifles were already aimed there. He was lifted off the ground and knocked sideways by the bullets.

The platoon followed the man's path across the vegetable garden, running in small groups to offer fewer targets. Hobbs's men stepped over the discarded bolt-action Russian carbine and followed the hedgerow. I was with them when they reached the body. He was lying on his back in the grass, riddled with bullet holes, but was still trying to raise his head and say something. All that came out were pathetic gurgling sounds. Hobbs turned to me.

"We're going after his buddies. Kill the poor bastard and put him out of his misery."

I held my rifle at arm's length and pointed the barrel at the man's head. He smiled and closed his eyes, but I couldn't pull the trigger. I felt ashamed. The man opened his eyes and tried to speak again. I'm sure he was asking me to kill him. Gould saw my problem and strolled over.

"Don't worry, man. I can handle it. Give me your sixteen."

I walked away and watched the vegetable patch as a twenty-round burst sent the liberation fighter to his next life. I vaguely heard Gould ripping the Cav patch off his sleeve. Then he tapped me on the shoulder and handed back my rifle. Within five minutes, Gould had killed another Viet Cong as he rose up from a spider hole to shoot some Blues who had just walked past him. Then we captured a man who had been wounded earlier, in the firefight across the vegetable patch. It was almost totally dark now, so the slicks would pick us up from the vegetable patch, guiding on the squad leaders' flashlights. We walked down the rows of tomatoes and beans while door gunners traded fire with clacking bursts from AKs. Soon, only the door guns were firing. Two more guerrillas had died. The slicks took us back to Bong Son in total darkness.

An ARVN company searched the village the following morning. A Viet Cong from the local force company surrendered to them and told the American advisors a story. He said that his squad of nine men had entered the village the evening before, but that U.S. helicopters and infantry had appeared out of nowhere and killed or captured everyone but him. The news cheered most of us, except of course, John Martin.

* * *

On my first night back, Martin and I drew our beer rations and drank the cold cans of Pabst Blue Ribbon on top of a bunker, letting the cool breezes of the plains dry our sweat-soaked uniforms. I asked John what had happened while I was shivering in America, but he refused to answer. All he would say was that the platoon was "doing the same shit" as before. I wasn't wise enough to realize that he was trying to forget something.

"Come on, John. I hardly recognize anyone in the platoon. The only thing that's the same is the blue bandannas. Did they all go home?"

He shifted uneasily on the sandbags. "Not all of them. You want to know? I'll tell you. We walked into an NVA battalion in the Crescent on March sixth. Saito's squad killed some poor guy in a bunker, and then they came down on us, hard. A new man got hit, and Doc Hansen crawled out to help him. Then they shot Doc. Saito went out to pull back Doc, and they shot him in the head. Just like he would have done them. A head shot. I wish it had never happened."

"You didn't like Saito, anyway."

"I didn't want to see him killed. We lost seven men that day. We spent the night out there, and the only thing that saved us were Skyraiders and APCs. You ever smelled what napalm does to people, Matt?" I shook my head. "You should. It's just like smelling roast pork. Let's talk about something else." I had never seen Martin so bitter.

John told me that Sergeants Samuel, Hardy, and Jefferson had gone home. They were the first Blues I had seen make it through an entire tour of duty. Samuel's replacement was Sergeant, First Class, Kidder, a broad, crew-cut career man who took the Army life seriously. He had told Martin to get a haircut, and that put him at the top of John's shit list. He called Kidder a real lifer. Jefferson's replacement was a sergeant from Georgia named Hooten. He was a quiet draftee who had risen quickly through the ranks. The new leaders of Saito's and Hardy's squads were Blues with specialist ratings.

There was agreement in the platoon that the new ROTC lieutenant, Rosen, was a vast improvement over the former OCS asshole. Rosen treated the men with respect. They liked him for that but resented his habit of placing two squads ahead of him on patrol. It had been a Blue tradition that the officer walked behind the lead squad. To put it kindly, the soldiers thought that he was a nice, decent person but not a very brave one. When Lieutenant Rosen later moved his patrol position forward, his popularity soared.

Doc Hansen's replacement was a thin blond medic, Doc Claw, who had been wounded in the battle on December first. An AK bullet had severed one of the nerves in his left arm, and he couldn't completely close his hand. That's how he got his name. The name was used without malice; Doc liked being called Claw.

I told John that I had a lot of introductions to make, and he added, "You always will, around here."

The next morning at dawn, Blue was sent to search a bunker where a scout chopper had killed a single Viet Cong. The bunker was located on a hillside that had been hit so heavily by shells in the past that the trees were stark and dead, and the ground was littered with torn branches. We arrived at the usual red smoke and found the bunker, hidden by the big limbs that the artillery had blasted down.

The bubble chopper had chased the frightened man there and had hovered while the scout gunner dropped a grenade into the aperture. The strong smell of cordite mixed with the brutal odor of sudden death in the early morning air. It was the only bunker on the hill. We collected his carbine and walked for hours through that desolate stretch of mountains. It had become a daily routine.

The people in this seaside village were hostile and silent. We had killed three NVA in a village farther to the north and knew that the local fishermen smuggled enemy replacements and weapons down the coast each night in their sampans. The North Vietnamese would hide in family bunkers throughout the day, then continue the journey south at darkness. But these people were bothered by more than our search. Rosen grabbed Minh's sleeve and pointed him toward a silent crowd of villagers.

"Find out what's the matter with these people."

An old, leather-skinned couple finally gave us the answer. "They say mortars come two times in three weeks. They don't know who does it. Last night young girl dies. They say war is bad thing."

"Tell them we know nothing about that." Then Rosen turned to his radioman. "It was probably the damned Arvins."

We had searched huts and grenaded bunkers out of boredom, but now we came to a section where the villagers were even more sullen than the others. We became more cautious. Hooten grenaded a coconut log bunker and crawled inside with a flashlight. He came out smiling. He had just bagged two Communist tax collectors and had found belts, two Chinese pistols, and a thick roll of South Vietnamese banknotes. He flashed the money at me, then hid it in his shirt as Rosen walked up.

"We're almost done here. Frag all the bunkers from now on. There might be more where these two came from."

Hooten snapped a regulation "Yes, sir!" and moved off with his squad.

Now the game was serious. A soldier approached a bunker with a woman planted squarely in front of it. Rosen saw him trying to pull her away, and motioned for Minh.

"Ask her if there's anyone in the bunker."

The woman glared at Minh and refused to answer.

"Ask her again, Minh."

He got the same response.

"Alright. Get her out of the way and frag it."

The woman screamed as the charge went off. When the black cordite smoke had cleared, Doc Claw climbed into the bunker. A guardian angel had been watching us that day. The grenade had exploded beside an infant the mother had hidden in the bunker. The blast had partly collapsed the log roof and sprayed the walls with metal, but the child was untouched. Claw returned with the baby in his arms and handed it to the mother.

Both mother and child began crying loudly. Then the mother talked to us. The Viet Cong had told the villagers that we killed children.

The scouts spotted a man standing on the beach. When he saw the little chopper approaching, he ran to a place in the sand and started digging. As the chopper circled back for another look at this strange behavior, he tried to unwrap the oilcloth from around a rifle. He was dead before he could use it. Now Blue is on the beach. The man's papers say that he was released from a South Vietnamese detention center this morning as a reformed Viet Cong. He immediately headed for his buried rifle. The weapon is an old French MAS-36 bolt-action job, which couldn't be fired come hell or high water. The bolt has rusted shut in the damp sand.

We jumped into deep rice paddies in the Crescent where the gunships had killed a man with a rifle. The pilots were jittery because these paddies were near the place where Blue had lost seven men on March sixth. All we found was the body of an old man with the calloused hands of a farmer, not the smooth hands of a soldier. His rifle was a hoe. There was a young boy at a nearby hooch, grinding rice in the shade of a palm tree.

"Minh, ask him where his father is."

"He say he is over there working in the rice paddies." The boy pointed in the direction from which we had come. The lieutenant thanked him and moved us out of there in a hurry. We didn't want to be around when he found his father.

It happened again in May. Two men ran from a diving gunship and died in the watermelon patch behind their homes. Both had certificates from the South Vietnamese government proclaiming them to be "model citizens." They had been learning American farming techniques and trying to improve agricultural output for the other farmers in the region. The Blues, except perhaps Gould, were horrified by these mistakes.

* * *

April was another month in the mountains, those north and west of the An Lao Valley. It was a wild region, almost untouched by the battles raging farther to the east. Our days were spent walking down rugged mountain slopes through sparkling swift-flowing streams. I often thought during those days of a line from a song: "April, come she will, when streams are bright and filled with rain." The words strike a sharp contrast to a poem by T. S. Eliot, in which he speaks of April as the cruelest month. April may be cruel in London or in Boston, but it seldom is in the Annamite Mountains of Indochina. The next line, about April "breeding lilacs out of the dead land," could have been written about the other Vietnam, the land of dry rice fields and dead water buffalo and burning villages.

Blue often followed tiger tracks through the bamboo of the high mountains, and once, our point came face to face with a big cat. Both of them ran away. One day we were climbing a mountain and finally broke into the elephant grass above the trees. A female elephant and her calf ambled by barely thirty yards away. They were ripping out the tough grass, which cut our hands and faces, with leisurely movements of their trunks. Seeing an elephant in the wild is a stunning experience.

Whole sections of the mountains had been burned off by the hill tribesmen, planted in corn, rice, manioc, or melons, and enclosed with huge log fences. They offered perfect helicopter landing sites. Blue would land, cross the acres of fields to the single entrance of each corral, and bypass the deep elephant traps lined with pointed stakes. Elephants also liked corn, rice, manioc, or melons. The trail between the log walls and the elephant trap would be so narrow that we had to move along it sideways with our backs pressed against the logs. The last obstacle was always a baited tiger cage. Winding trails led past deserted Montagnard villages. These might be burned or spared, depending on the whim of the pilots circling far above us.

Once, we followed the trails for an entire day and found only a single giant wooden building under the canopy. It was filled with hundreds of pounds of drying tobacco leaves, hanging in bundles from the rafters. The fire made the hillside smell like a

83

smoker's paradise. When the NVA wanted a smoke, they would think of us.

On another day, we found rice storehouses high in the mountains. They were not protected by men, but by booby traps—Malayan gates, which were tree limbs bent back and studded with spikes; crossbows linked to vine trip-wires; ancient French bullets embedded in blocks of wood with nails for striking pins, buried upright in the mud of the trail; and punji pits, covered with twigs and dirt and lined with bamboo stakes. A crossbow arrow missed our point man by inches. We were saved from the bullet traps only because the recent rains had exposed them. Blue burned the rice, took the crossbows for souvenirs, and continued down the trail.

I flew as a door gunner on one of those April mornings. Below us was a line of elephants moving down a mountain trail. Each had a double pack of equipment slung across its spine on straps. Rockets and 40mm cannon killed some of the big animals and sent the others crashing through the trees. Many months later, my mother woke me from a troubled sleep. I was shouting, "Oh, no! They're killing the elephants! They're killing the elephants!"

My gunship flew over a jungle valley with hundreds of huts under the trees. Artillery covered the canopy with bursts, but when it ceased, there was only the black smoke floating in the treetops. The scout choppers hovered over the treetops, dropping phosphorous grenades on the huts hidden below. My pilot looked over his shoulder and said into the intercom, "Know what's going on down below, FO?"

"Looks like they're burning hooches."

"Right. We call it an urban renewal project." He grinned at his wit and gave a thumbs-up signal.

Two NVA ran from a hut beside a stream. All I could see were tracers from the little scout chopper and flames as phosphorus set the hooch on fire. Later, my gunship rocketed the streambed, and I fired the door gun into the jungle alongside it. As we climbed away from the attack, tiny men jumped from toy helicopters far below us. I wanted to be with Martin in the heat, not sitting in the cool seat of a gunship.

It was in those mountains that an occasional practice became a habit. The rebel yell became so popular among the 9th Cav Blues that today I can't picture a Blue landing without seeing soldiers standing on the landing skids of the slicks shouting things like "E-e-e-i-i, ha!" and "Ya-a hoo!" at the top of their lungs. The racket was supposed to scare the NVA, but it did more to boost our courage as the slicks dropped toward "landing zones" that might be boulder piles or fallen timber on a hillside or bomb craters in solid jungle. We usually jumped from moving slicks, but one landing in five involved hanging from the landing skids and dropping ten or more feet to the ground. Injuries were common, but the only man I ever saw evacuated before the end of a mission had broken his leg when he landed on a tree stump. We never saw him again. The Blues knew that among the smallest dangers awaiting us in those mountains were cobras, bamboo vipers, kraits, giant blue-black scorpions, yard-long day-glo orange centipedes, and three varieties of leeches. The rebel yells were a blanket over our fears.

An NVA had tried to shoot down the squadron commander's helicopter from a village, and as Kidder put it, "That's one man you don't fuck with." The huts were burning from an artillery shelling as we ran among them, ducking collapsing timbers. Then Martin stumbled over some cloth by a shell crater in a brick courtyard. But it wasn't cloth.

He grabbed my sleeve and pulled me over to the crater. "Matt, what will his family think?"

"Jesus! That was a man!"

We collected three smoke-blackened pieces of the old villager and covered him with a blanket from his home. Then we ran ahead to find the rest of the platoon on a hill behind the village. There were caves on the hill, but they hadn't been used for a while. Blue headed back toward the village.

Crack-crack-crack. Gould shot an NVA who was walking up the hill from the village. He slung the man's AK across his back, stooped, and sliced off one of his ears. I didn't know what had happened until I saw the small hole and glistening cartilage as I stepped over the body. Some of the NVA's bullets had been fired. This was the one who had shot at the squadron commander and caused the destruction of a village.

We arrived back at Bong Son just in time to grab our mess kits and run for the chow line. Gould and the cook were already squared off. "Hey, Sarge. Want some meat for your soup?" Gould was dangling the ear over a kettle full of thin soup.

The mess sergeant's expression was a mixture of fear and fury. "Get that out of here!"

Gould grinned. "Come on, Sarge. This soup never has enough meat in it."

The mess sergeant pointed his ladle at Gould's face. "Listen, you monster. If I ever catch you pulling a stunt like this again, I'll see that you're reported for war crimes."

Gould backed away. "Okay, Sarge. I was just having a little fun."

"Take your goddamned fun elsewhere."

Lieutenant Rosen called a meeting that night. We gathered in a filthy mob to hear what he had to say. He began with compliments. "I wanted to tell you that you men have been doing an outstanding job since I've been with you." His statement was greeted by silence. Fuck the lieutenant.

"The main reason for calling this meeting is that the colonel wants to thank you for getting the gook that shot at his helicopter. He says that Charlie Blues have come across again." This caused laughter and a chorus of grunts and coughs. The colonel flew around and played at war while the men under him got killed. Fuck the colonel.

Rosen was embarrassed and tried to laugh. "One more thing. There will be no more mutilation of dead gooks." He was trying to talk our language, but "gooks" sounded unnatural coming from him. "The next man who cuts off an ear will be court-martialed. Is that clear?" There was a bobbing of heads and a shuffling of feet that might be interpreted as a yes.

"All right. That's all I have. Let's keep up the good work."
More grunts. The lieutenant was glad the meeting was over.

Blue was in the An Lao once again. We had dug up the bodies
of three NVA killed by the gunships the night before and were
patrolling a mountain valley. Our point man was a fat specialist
named Arthur, who had just been transferred to us from the gunships. Arthur was notorious for making mistakes. There was
something about the valley. It was the feeling that I sometimes
got when I knew the enemy were close but still out of sight. I
had heard about Arthur's reputation, so I walked back down the
file to find Kidder.

"Sarge, I think there's Charlies in that banana grove down
there."

"What makes you think so?"

"I don't know. It's just a strong feeling. Besides, they like
campsites like that."

He was watching me with a curious expression. "Well, don't
worry. We'll find out soon enough."

"That's what I wanted to talk to you about. There's a new man
on point, and he might freeze if there's an ambush or something."

He shook his head. "Who's in charge here? Let's wait and
see, FO. I can't change the point because somebody thinks there
might be gooks around. That's what we're here for." And that's
a smart statement.

Arthur almost collided with a man in khakis eating rice on a
low boulder. The NVA grabbed his rifle and was long gone before Arthur remembered to shoot. He watched a whole flock of
North Vietnamese disappear down the trail. We passed the unfinished meal and found a big campsite with bananas on carrying
poles, baskets of rice, hammocks, and packs, all neatly hung in
trees to protect them from insects. I gave Kidder an "I told you
so" look, and he shot back a "How was I to know?" look in
return. Then he took Arthur off point.

Martin and I talked with Arthur that evening. The rest of the
platoon was avoiding him after the day's screw-up. The conver-

sation started with the weather. He didn't like the monsoons. "I'm glad the rains are almost over. Maybe in another month we can spend the days without getting drenched."

"Fat chance of that, Arthur. We'll just get soaked with sweat instead of rain. You should have stayed with those cool gunships."

"Gunships! I don't ever want to spend another day with that bunch. You know what they do in the gunships and scouts with the first man you kill? They make you go back to shoot him until there are only pieces left. Shoot until the pieces are smoking from the tracers. That way you're supposed to start liking it."

Martin gave me the strongest gesture he could. He spat in disgust. "This whole war is sick. Just like that poor farmer with the hoe who the gunships shot. It's all crazy. Somebody said they reported it as a new VC weapon. A rifle made like a hoe. Pretty soon we'll be finding farmers with automatic hoes. All those bastards did was guarantee that the farmer's son will be shooting at us in a few years. How'd you end up in this mess, Arthur?"

Arthur hung his head. "They drafted me. They drafted me and they put me in the infantry and they sent me to Nam, but they aren't going to make a killer out of me. All I want is to go home and forget this nightmare."

John jumped up and slapped Arthur on the back. "I'll second that motion!"

Two Blues restrained the prisoner as we flew over the An Lao Mountains. He couldn't take his eyes off the open door of the chopper. It was obvious that he preferred a quick death leap to life in a cage.

We found him in a village on the An Lao Valley floor that had been shelled all night. There wasn't enough left standing to burn. The place was littered with abandoned equipment, but the NVA had fled. Then a soldier looked inside a bunker and found our prize crouching in a pool of his own blood. He was a tough-looking fellow of about forty, with a crew cut and bulging muscles. Hobbs set him on a table to bandage his bloody legs, and the man tried to kick Doc Claw. Kidder put the muzzle of his rifle against the man's temple and clicked off the safety. He motioned Minh over.

"Ask him how big his unit was."

"He say there are two platoons in the village."

"How big was his entire unit?"

"He say again there are two platoons here."

"Ask him where they are."

"They go back into the mountains when the artillery comes. He knows Americans come after the artillery. He is wounded and tells them to go without him."

This Vietnamese was obviously not a recruit. He was stamped from the same mold that must be used for all professionals in all armies. I was fascinated by how closely he resembled Kidder. They looked at each other with expressions more akin to understanding than dislike.

"What is his job?"

"He say he is proud to be an aspirant and will soon be an officer. He fights the French for four years, and he is in the South four years fighting for the liberation." We had captured a senior NCO, an officer candidate. He had been a powerful man among his fellow soldiers.

The NVA began jabbering excitedly. "What's that he's saying?"

"He say he doesn't want to be a prisoner." The aspirant tensed his body and glared at Rosen as his words were translated.

Rosen's lips creased into a rare smile. "Tell him, sorry about that."

We left the smoking ruin and returned to Bong Son with our prisoner.

Blues crawled through the mud and grass along the trail. Gould had just walked into a patrol of NVA heading south. His rifle had jammed after one shot, but he still hit their point man in the chest. The wounded man's M-14, captured from the Marines to the north, was passed down the trail to Rosen. It would be easy to follow the trail of blood.

When we came to a spot where bright gobs of blood had spattered the leaves, Martin stomped his foot in anger. "There's only one thing you can say about Gould."

"What's that, John?"

"The sick bastard doesn't miss a shot."

CHAPTER 6

Arthur's Song

(May 1967)

Our commander had received a report that the Viet Cong had shot a woman the previous night for not giving them rice. If the report was true, it would be a good story for anti-Communist propaganda, so Blue was sent to investigate. We left Bong Son with two reporters and a photographer. The village was very clean, very prosperous. You could give the old headman a suit and he would go unnoticed at a Chamber of Commerce convention. Surely the war hadn't touched these people.

Rosen pulled the headman and Minh away from a silent crowd of staring villagers. "Minh, ask him if the story is true about the VC killing the woman."

"He say yes, it is true. They come last night with teacher and shoot her. The teacher tells the people about the VC and asks for rice. She say no. They are local squad. They live in those hills." Minh pointed to a line of low hills toward the sea. "They never see the teacher before."

"Where is the woman now?"

"He say they bury her this morning."

Rosen radioed the information to the gunships, and what he heard didn't please him. "Shit. We've got to dig her up. The press wants pictures of the atrocity."

A pair of Blues dug out her body. The mud wanted to keep the shovels and gave way only with a sigh. The old headman had tears in his eyes. He couldn't understand why we had to disturb her again. A soldier unwrapped her burial shroud and found the body of a woman that would have been the respected elder in any of the dozens of villages we had searched. She was about seventy years old, executed at close range by a single bullet through the temple. The camera clicked.

As we boarded the slicks, shots rang out from the low hills. It had to be a warning because the range was too far for the VC to hit us. The gunships swarmed in to attack them, rocketing the canopy and making long minigun runs. Martin thought he knew why the VC had fired on us. "I wonder if they felt guilty about our finding the woman?"

"I hope so, John. They're murderers!"

He sat in silence for a moment, then shouted over the roar of the chopper blades, "Yeah, Matt. But so are we!"

We were in the An Lao, walking from one red smoke to another as gunners marked the locations of NVA dead. It had been a turkey shoot for the door gunners. The NVA had been scrounging rice, and now their bodies were scattered over a wide area. Each smoke grenade marked the place where a man had been hunted and chased before dying. It was curious because none of these men, each with the smooth hands and pack burns of a soldier, had a weapon. Then Hobbs found a survivor hiding under a rock ledge on a barren little hill. The starving, trembling man told his story to Minh.

"He say his company is low on rice and they gamble to get it. His platoon comes to the valley to find any rice the people leave behind in the villages."

"Why weren't they carrying weapons?"

"He say they leave rifles behind because they add weight if rice is found. They think they can be back in the hills before the helicopters come."

We found the last body at dusk. It was a thin man of about twenty-five, lying on his back among the saplings by a peaceful stream. A door gunner had hit him in the stomach, and his intestines protruded from four small holes. I covered his face with a

92

poncho. Eighteen NVA had died for less than twenty pounds of rice.

We returned to the stream at dawn, but now there were only empty fields. Their comrades had come for them during the night. We followed a trail into the hills and found a jungle school for the children of the "An Lao Liberated Zone." There was a large hooch with blackboards, homemade desks, and elementary text-books; smaller huts for the teachers; and even a well-tended out-house located at a discreet distance from the other buildings. All of this we burned and headed merrily back to Bong Son.

The banana grove is hemmed in by high cliffs. The gunships have killed thirty NVA in a battle here, and we have been sent to collect their rifles and papers. Choppers hover over jumbled rocks above us, dropping phosphorous grenades. The NVA are shooting like crazy as they run from one pile of rocks to another, and ricochets from the door guns shred the banana trees around us. This is a strange place.

The commander won't let us go higher because there are too many Charlies in the rocks. So we form a line and search the banana grove. The smell of death is so strong you can almost reach out and touch it, but the bodies are gone. We comb the grove again and again, dodging the ricochets from the fight above us, but there is nothing left but battered trees. Where have they hidden the bodies so quickly? The stench clings to our clothes for hours.

We had spent the day walking through an old B-52 strike zone in the An Lao. The topsoil had been blasted away, and the rains and heat had turned the ground to stone. The NVA had stayed even here, retreating to the caves around that wasteland. My legs ached from pounding the hard soil, and all of us were soaked with sweat. The slicks pulled us out in the twilight, but the scouts saw seven NVA running into a part of what had once been An Lao Village. Surely they wouldn't put us in at this time of day!

Two bodies were sprawled over a paddy dike. We ran among the rotting hooches, spraying trees and hedgerows. Hobbs's squad gunned down two NVA who made the mistake of charging the line of Blues, then captured a man who threw away his rifle and fell to his knees, begging for mercy. The huts were burning as we pulled back to the rice paddies.

Kidder threw a smoke grenade to mark our location, then turned around to be sure that all the squads were in position. One of the "dead" NVA on the paddy dike was aiming his rifle at a Blue's back. The banging of Kidder's rifle sent us all jumping into the stinking paddy water, and then the man was really dead. Kidder ran over to the other "body" and emptied his rifle. He slid in another magazine and looked at our stunned faces, pausing to study each one.

"God dammit! You men better start checking those bodies more carefully! Walker! You were almost a dead man!"

What do you say to someone that has just saved your life? "Thanks, Sarge." Two Blues slapped Cav patches on the faces of the dead North Vietnamese, then we were running for seats on the slicks.

Blue is in Happy Valley for the first time in long weeks. An air strike has blasted a squad of NVA as they scrambled up a hillside. That's routine enough, but that's not why we're here. The Army is making a training film about the tactics of air cavalry troops because the Army wants more air cavalry troops, and we're the stars.

We landed in the middle of impressive fireworks and burned a new storehouse. There is a khaki-clad body leaning calmly against the trunk of a tree. Perhaps he is only sleeping. A soldier carefully searches his uniform pockets for papers, all under the watchful eye of a photographer, who is filming the scene from a bubble chopper hovering above us. It's such great fun. Some of the Blues turn and bow as our line reaches the top of the jungle hill.

Hobbs's squad had been scrambled for a mission at dawn, and they were back at the tents, bitching about lost sleep. Hobbs came over to my tent to tell me where they had gone.

"Scouts shot a gook messenger in VC Valley. We had to go

94

in and police him up. He was fucked up real bad. Don't think he'll make it. Gook had a carbine and a pouch full of documents. Want a souvenir?''

''Depends on what it is.'' He handed me the courier's gray canvas pouch, complete with a made-in-North Vietnam ball-point pen.

VC Valley was on the coast, just across the river from Bong Son. The platoon was on a ridge above the valley within an hour. We had a magnificent view of the town of Bong Son and our base camp. I could see the slicks parked in a field behind the Blue pup tents. There were hard packed trails in all directions on the ridge, but there was no way of estimating how recently they had been used.

Arthur was on point when he heard something rustling through the bushes. Kidder knocked down a couple of Blues as he rushed to the head of the file. He was still feeling the effects of Arthur's screw-up in the An Lao. He found our friend squatting behind a thornbush.

''What's going on up here?''

Arthur pointed to a bunker a few feet away. ''I've got a Charlie in that bunker, Sarge. What should I do?''

''What have you got between your ears? Frag the damned thing!''

Arthur wasn't carrying any grenades for some reason, so Kidder borrowed someone else's. Kidder stood behind him like an umpire to be sure he did everything right. One explosion, then another to be sure, and Arthur pulled a body from the camouflaged bunker. The man's face looked like hamburger, and Arthur turned white and vomited. Kidder took the VC's belt, hung with grenades and riddled with fragments, and hurled it far down the slope. He reached over and patted our killer on the shoulder.

''Nice job, Arthur. Let's see if we can find what he was guarding.'' Arthur just gaped at him and made a few grunting sounds.

The bunker was a lookout post for something on the hill, but we didn't have time to find it. Bravo Troop Blues were in a bad ambush in the An Lao. We trotted in a ragged line down a trail to the valley floor and were taken back to Bong Son to be ready if Bravo Blues needed our help.

As we waited in the shade of the slicks, Martin pointed to Arthur, sitting alone under a stunted tree by the barbed wire. "He's really down in the dumps about what happened this morning."

"Poor guy. The one thing he didn't want to do was kill somebody. You know? I hope we're through for today. I've already counted fourteen gunships going to help Bravo Troop."

John felt the same. "We've done enough killing for one day."

As gunships returned from the An Lao and others headed west, "Darling, Be Home Soon" blared from John's transistor radio. I listened to the words and wondered if our most recent "kill" had people waiting for him in a village somewhere. How many people were waiting for the men on both sides of Bravo Troop's battle?

Martin was listening, too. "That should be Arthur's song. He wants to go home even worse than me."

Bravo Blues were rescued without our help. They were withdrawn from the An Lao and given the greatest reward any group of Blues could receive. Those who had survived the ambush were given the rest of the day off duty. The Army called it a "stand down."

Blue landed in VC Valley at dawn the next morning. It was a thin valley with rice fields down the center and little clusters of hooches crowded against the hills. We soon learned how the valley had gotten its name. A soldier slipped and caught himself on the edge of a deep pit lined with stakes. The hole was covered by thin bamboo strips with leaves on top, and hidden by a layer of sand. We learned to spot the traps by the slightly darker color of the sand over them.

I was walking behind the point, against the artillery lieutenant's repeated orders not to do so. The point stepped through a gap in a hedgerow. Boom! We were both knocked down. I ran my hands over my body to find the inevitable holes, but there were none. There was a cluster bomb in the dirt at my feet. We had been lucky.

CBUs (cluster bomb units) were softball-sized yellow bombs,

full of explosive and ball bearings. The Air Force dropped them in clusters that broke apart in the air. The VC had wrapped the middle of this particular CBU with plastic explosive and linked it to a trip-wire. All we had gotten was the blast from the plastique. It was the only time I saw a plastic explosive belt fail to detonate a CBU. The point man was stone deaf and had to be evacuated. My head was roaring; I walked farther back for a few days.

There were punji pits and bundles of new punji stakes everywhere. We passed what must have been a punji stick factory and climbed a hill to a jungle campsite. We found a scene that had repeated itself many times by now—camouflaged hooch, belts on pegs, packs, a corpse in the mud. Everything was burning when we returned to the valley to eat C-rations. We set up a defense around a sturdy plastered building that had several large rooms and a tiled roof; it had probably once been the French administrator's home.

Rosen gave the usual order. "Burn this building after the break."

Hobbs nodded. "Right, sir."

Kidder didn't think it would burn and told Hobbs so. "You can't burn it, Sarge. It's plaster, not straw."

Hobbs wasn't convinced. "I bet you it will burn. Fire for hire can burn anything."

"How much you willing to lay on it?"

Hobbs rubbed his chin as if in deep thought. "How about a five-spot? Wouldn't want to break you." They shook hands on the bet in an empty room.

Hobbs enlisted his entire squad in the effort. They spent the break piling broken chairs, boards, baskets, and rags in the corners of the rooms. When the platoon moved away, they sprayed insect repellent on the piles and lit them. A gunship flew over the house, and AKs opened up from the hilltop above us. A door gunner fired as the chopper banked away, and Rosen grabbed his handset for a message.

"Gunships taking fire. There's an estimated platoon on that hill in bunkers. We're to pull back to the streambed"—he pointed to a stream behind the house—"and wait for an air strike." He listened to the handset again. "It's on the way! On the double! On the double!"

Jets screamed in from the south as we jumped into the streambed. A door gunner dropped a red smoke on the target, and a spotter plane putted over the stream, firing two phosphorous rockets where the smoke floated through the trees. The dense white smoke was barely through the treetops when the first jet released its bomb.

A tremendous brown column of earth kicked up from the hill-top. We hugged the bank and ducked while pieces of trees and huge clumps of earth crashed around us. A slowly tumbling tree trunk snapped off the top of a coconut tree above me and crashed into the paddies a few yards behind us. Three more bombs, each making the same rain of giant debris, and the jets were gone.

Echoes from the last bomb were bouncing across the valley when I saw two people on the blasted hillside. They were naked, running on all fours like a couple of animals. One was a woman with rather large breasts for a Vietnamese. They were swaying from side to side as she scuttled away. The concussion had blown off their clothes and probably driven them mad. I was too surprised to fire my rifle.

I grabbed Martin so hard his helmet fell off. "John, I just saw two people up there. I thought they were animals. They're naked."

He didn't believe me. "Aw, come on, Sarge."

Kidder had been listening. "Where'd you see those people?"

"There, below the crater. They were crawling on all fours."

"We'll take care of them."

Martin stared daggers at Kidder for a moment, then looked at me. "You should have kept your mouth shut, Sarge."

The place where the naked people had been was hit by a pair of gunships. As they rocketed the slope time after time, I regretted having told anyone. The gunships shifted their fire to a trail on the far side of the hill, and the platoon moved out of the streambed. I hoped the two survivors had gotten away.

Rosen put the platoon in a line and warned us to be careful. "Okay, everybody take it slow and easy. We've got the rest of

98

the afternoon to search that hill.'' He looked sheepishly at Hobbs. ''If that house weren't burning, we could use it for cover.''

Hobbs threw a grin at Kidder and rubbed his fingers together. ''You told us to burn it, sir.''

There had been bunkers on the hill until the first bomb scored a direct hit. Then there was an enormous crater. We found the shaft of one deep tunnel and pulled out odd items of equipment. The transistor radios, stamped with maps of North Vietnam, were especially nice. But that was all there was left. Everything else and everyone had been buried by the explosion. How many people were entombed at our feet? A German Mauser rifle was sticking muzzle-down in the lip of the crater, and pieces of khaki and black cloth were scattered in the mud. We left the place, feeling awed by the destruction one bomb had caused.

Blue was in the An Lao once again. The gunships had killed eight NVA along a mountain trail leading to a deep gorge. Hidden in the gorge was a sixty-foot hooch with long tables, dishes, ladles, and all sizes of pots and pans. The hooch was invisible from the air, and we had located it only because we knew something had to be drawing small groups of NVA down that trail. The North Vietnamese were hungry, and Blue had captured their mess hall.

One of the new replacements found the place where the trail climbed into the mountains. He was debating whether to follow it when a man in khakis silently walked up and stopped about ten feet away. The new dude realized he was staring at his first NVA, emptied his entire magazine at him, and missed. The NVA stood there for a moment longer, hungry and confused, and ran back up the trail.

The replacement's ego was shattered. ''I let him get away! Didn't even hit him! I don't know how I could have missed at that range.''

Hobbs was furious. ''I don't know how you could have missed, either. For God's sake, load that rifle. You won't get many more chances to pull a stunt like that.''

By the time he managed a weak "I'm sorry, Sergeant," the replacement was almost in tears.

We burned the long hooch and all its food and poked bayonet holes in the cooking utensils. As the platoon moved down the gorge, another chowhound was killed on the trail above us. Then Hooten saw a cave behind trees at the far end of the gorge. He yelled for whoever was there to come out, and when nothing stirred, he lobbed a grenade. Then he walked inside.

Hooten returned with a beautiful woman and her small son. She was wounded above the left breast by a sliver of fragmentation, and Claw had to remove her shirt to treat the wound. The result was electric. Her breasts were full and well shaped, and the brown nipples stood straight out. The men around her were young—very young and very lonely.

"Look at those tits!"

"Tits nothing, look at them nipples!"

"Shi-it, man! What a piece she gonna be!"

The woman tensed, trying to cover herself with her hands. But her hands weren't big enough. Now all eyes were on Rosen.

"Sir, no one would ever know if we called her in dead."

"Yeah, just say the grenade killed them. How about it, Lieutenant?"

Rosen shook his head. "Forget it. I've already called in the prisoners. Pop smoke! The choppers are on their way in for extraction." That took courage to say, considering our mood.

Gould had the last word. He stood with his hands on his hips, facing Rosen. "Shit. What a waste she'll be in a POW cage."

The Viet Cong patrol had just disappeared. Our scouts had chased them from the beach into a village, and then they had vanished. We jumped from the slicks as a last string of naval antiaircraft shells splintered a coconut grove about fifty yards up the beach.

The village seemed to be deserted. All that remained were empty hooches and a haze of blue smoke from the naval shelling. We couldn't find a trace of anything until a Blue leaned against a coconut palm stump and it gave way. Below it was a dark room connected to other rooms by tunnels. There were coconut stumps everywhere, and each one concealed another entrance. Rosen called the pilots.

"Okay. They're going to put delayed fuse artillery on this place to dig them out. Let's let someone else clean out these underground tombs."

The platoon had a rule that you never took the same route twice. There was too much danger of an ambush. But this silent village was eerie, and we were in a hurry to get away from it. The platoon followed the same trail back, but it was different. The first hedgerow we came to was booby-trapped with a CBU. The point had almost stepped on the wire. He found a booby-trapped Chinese hand grenade at the next hedgerow. Both traps had been placed there after we walked by the first time. We abandoned the trail and ran straight for the beach, parallel to the hedgerows and past more booby traps. The shelling began as our slicks lifted off the sand.

I hadn't taken a day off since my leave home in February, and May thirty-first seemed like a good day to do just that. There were no special missions planned. I had saved six beers from the daily ration of two beers and had a book to read. All that was left was to check with Martin one last time.

"I'm going to take the day off I've been threatening you with. That means you'll have to bring in the artillery if there's any trouble. Think you can handle it?"

"Yeah, Sarge. I'll handle it if I have to. I handled it when you were gone for thirty days. I've got the maps and all the call signs. I hope we have a quiet day." "Sarge" meant that John wasn't happy. He always reverted to that little formality when he was uneasy or pissed off.

I was reading Michener in the shade of a tree when the platoon saddled up. I stopped John as he ran by the tree. "Where're you going?"

"It's no big thing, Sarge. We're going after a chopper that's down with engine trouble. Go back and read your book." He ran ahead to the slicks.

Blue was always taken to secure downed choppers. On a good day they were down from mechanical troubles; on a bad day they had been shot down. But even choppers that had been hit tried to get away from the place where it had happened. There was always the chance of finding injured crews or an NVA ambush, but those landings usually resulted in a morning of loafing. It was a good way to rest after a night on the bunkers.

When the empty slicks returned to camp, I questioned one of the pilots. "Where'd that chopper go down?"

"No sweat. It's down in the secure area east of Bong Son. Nothing out there but smiling farmers." I took my book back to the tree.

I was on my third beer and feeling light-headed in the 110-degree heat when the rotor blades began turning. Gunship pilots boiled out of the operations tent and ran for their choppers. One of them shouted to a cluster of door gunners who were grabbing their machine guns and throwing on flak vests, "Blue's in contact! Receiving fire from a pagoda! One KIA!"

One man was already dead on the "routine" mission. So much for the beer and the book. I jumped aboard one of the slicks as it taxied for takeoff. I plugged in an extra set of headphones and listened to the action. The ARVNs wouldn't let Martin shell the pagoda, and the Blues were fighting back with rifles and machine guns. Then the ARVNs changed their minds, and howitzers pounded the building. Gunships were being shot at along the entire length of the village. An infantry company was landed at one end, and the scouts saw NVA running away through the village. The slick I was on would take a squad of Blues to seal off their escape route.

We landed in a rice paddy next to the wrecked helicopter. Blues were laying facedown in the water, tensing for the fire they knew would come. Eight of them ran toward us in a crouch. A replacement saw that I had one of the seats, hesitated for a second, then ran back to the cover of a paddy dike. "Thanks, Sarge. I didn't want to go anyway." The slick banked away from the village and circled back to a place where a hovering gunship was firing its cannon.

We jumped from the slick and ran toward a grass embankment. Two bodies in the grass were the work of a 40mm cannon. One had its left eyeball hanging on its cheek, still connected to the optic nerve. The other body's legs were attached only by thin strips of muscle. There wasn't time to think about how grotesque they looked. Pop. A carbine round whistled by my head. Hobbs saw the man who shot at me and fired a burst down a trench. Pop-pop. Now he was firing at Hobbs. Another long burst from Hobbs, and he was dragging a body from the trench.

A Blue started shooting beside me. He was the one who had missed the NVA at the mess hall a few days before. He set the haystacks behind me on fire with tracer bullets, and something started cracking. Under each haystack was a body. The bullets in their rifles and the ammo in their pouches were cooking off from the intense heat. The stench of burned meat was suffocating.

The Blue smiled at me. "I saw one of those haystacks move when the Charlie in the trench fired." He wagged his finger. "Better keep your eyes open, Sarge."

Hobbs listened to a message from the pilots and shouted to us, "This is it! This is as far as the gooks got! Platoon's going to sweep toward the grunts. We wait until they bring in the other three squads. Burn the hooches!"

I walked over to the hooch where the first two NVA had died, pulled my Zippo lighter from my pocket, and lit the thatch. A young woman with a baby in her arms ran out and beat the flames out with her shirt. She was naked from the waist up. I tried again, and she knocked the lighter out of my hand. I tried a third time. She slapped me.

"What the hell, lady. If it means that much to you, keep the fuckin' place!" She shouted what could only be a curse. "Same to you, bitch!"

Three slicks landed with the rest of the platoon. Rosen formed us in a line and we walked deeper into the village, passing a bunker that looked too old to be used. No one bothered to look inside.

"Choi hoi! Choi hoi!"

We looked around. A teenage NVA soldier was standing in the

bunker with his hands raised above his head. He was waving one of the "safe conduct passes" that our psychological warfare teams dropped by the millions over Communist territory. *"Choi hoi! Choi hoi!"* He was shouting it in desperation. Minh ran back to the bunker and made the NVA lie on the ground. They talked rapidly until Rosen got there.

"What's his unit, Minh?"

"He say he is with NVA company that moved here last night. He is private and doesn't want to fight the helicopters anymore."

"What are they doing here?"

"He say tonight they attack the American base at Bong Son."

"Where's his rifle?"

"He say he throws rifle in the river so we take him prisoner."

A slick took the prisoner away while Rosen got us back in line. There was a river on our left and rice paddies on the right, so our line could cover the width of the narrow village. An old man in black pajamas stepped in front of the line. As we moved forward, he walked backward. Minh shouted for him to stop, but he turned to run, and rifles started banging. He disappeared into the village. The platoon was already out of sight when Martin looked in a hooch and saw the old man lying on the floor. Blood was streaming from a bullet hole through his wrist. He groaned when I placed a field dressing over the gore.

I started to leave him there, but Martin grabbed my shoulder and spun me around. "You can't do this. He'll bleed to death."

"The platoon left him behind. We've got orders to sweep."

"He's a human being, Matt!"

I found Lieutenant Rosen farther along in the village, and his face told me that he knew why I was there. "Sir, we have a wounded man back there. He needs a doctor."

He hesitated. "The man shouldn't have run. We've got to link up with the infantry."

I had to reach him somehow, for Martin's sake, if nothing else. "Sir. You don't want an old man's death on your conscience."

That was the right approach. Rosen reverted to his usual compassionate self. "All right. Get Claw back there and have him look at the wound. I'll contact the gunships and have them pick him up.''

Claw gave the farmer a shot of morphine and led him to a gunship for evacuation. The next day we learned that the old man was the leader of the local Viet Cong company. It had been his idea for the NVA to use his village to stage the attack on Bong Son. The plan had failed because a chopper had developed engine trouble on that fateful morning. The Blue landing, covered by the troop's gunships, had convinced the NVA that they had been discovered. If we had not stopped the NVA in that village, they would have been coming through Bong Son's barbed wire defenses fifteen hours later.

The platoon was beside the river now. NVA squatted like frogs in the tall reeds along its bank. When they saw us approaching, they jumped in the water and stayed under as long as possible. Heads appeared, gasping for air, and the rifles and machine guns fired. Bodies bobbed to the surface of the river and floated downstream until they lodged against an earth dam.

Beside the dam was a long trench where the gunships had received fire. For fifteen minutes, the gunships had pumped rockets along the trench, while a single defender fired back. A door gunner had finally killed him. A young boy in black was sprawled there with a Model '98 Mauser, longer than he was, clutched to his chest. The battle was over. The Blues, the infantry, and the gunships had killed ninety-six NVA and Viet Cong.

There was something else behind the long trench. A hooch had been burned by helicopter rockets, and beside it was an animal pen. A mother water buffalo and her calf had been chained in the pen, and all that was left were two peacefully kneeling carcasses. The calf had raised its head, as if to call for help over the charred timbers. The mother's head was turned toward the young animal. The pen smelled like a cookout in a neighbor's backyard. If the brutality and sadness of war could be described in a single photograph, a picture of that scene might do it best.

When we were safely back at Bong Son, I asked Martin who was killed. There wasn't time to ask before.

''It was Arthur. He was lying next to a hole in a paddy dike when they started shooting. It was carbine rounds from the pagoda, not very accurate. Some hit the water in front of him and he caught a ricochet. Just one lousy bullet.''

"I should have known. He was so upset over being here that he didn't even bother to take proper cover.''

Martin nodded. "He was a good man, Matt. Everyone was always riding him, but he didn't give a damn what they thought. All he wanted to do was go back home. Then he had to lie in front of that hole.''

We sat in silence for a long time. Arthur was going home. We would miss him.

CHAPTER 7

Games in the An Lao

(June 1967)

June was another month spent in the An Lao Valley. Bravo Troop had done its stretch in May, and now it was Charlie Troop's turn. The valley was quieter than before. Large enemy units were still there, hiding in the rugged hills around the valley, but they had broken up into groups of between ten and fifty men. Larger groups would attract the 9th Cav helicopters and, with them, the tremendous firepower of the 1st Cavalry Division. Our task was to hound the smaller units until they left the valley completely.

Blue returned from the first June day in the An Lao with dozens of pairs of Ho Chi Minh sandals, packs, and seven NVA bamboo helmets. A platoon of NVA had run away from us like scared rabbits and had thrown most of their equipment away so they could run faster. We made a great show of parading the captured material in front of a small cluster of Vietnamese children by the barbed wire and bragging about the "beaucoup VC" we were killing in the An Lao. A group of gunship pilots saw the show and came over.

"Would you guys mind giving us a few of those souvenirs?" said one.

"Yeah. We fly cover for you but never get a chance to collect any gook equipment," said another.

The gunship pilots had saved our asses many times in the past, so we gave them everything we had collected. "Sure. Take the stuff. There's more where that came from." And there was.

The platoon was in a deep ravine on the eastern edge of the An Lao Valley floor. Two bodies were facedown in a shallow stream, killed in mid-stride by a door gunner. Hooten saw a cave above them and stepped inside, and the occupants opened fire. Hooten jumped back, firing his rifle on semiautomatic, and gunned down five NVA. One of them was wounded and still shooting. Hooten's grenade blew away his face. When he returned from the cave, he was toting an armful of carbines and belts.

"I've got five belts here. They've all got stars. Anybody need one?" A couple of replacements lined up to get their belts. Hooten's bravery would have won him a high medal in 1969 and beyond, but on this day, no one even thanked him.

Hobbs's squad killed two more people in the bushes on the far side of the stream. When Hobbs stooped to collect their rifles, he saw they were women. A Blue stripped them of their leather belts and packs. We gathered all the weapons and a thick stack of papers and jogged back to the paddy fields to wait for an air strike on the ravine. Minh shuffled through the papers and made an announcement.

"This is the message center of the Third NVA Division. These are the division dispatches." The discovery would please intelligence. Soon, they would know the locations, communications, and day-to-day problems of the entire enemy division facing us.

First napalm, then 250-pound bombs, exploded in the ravine. I turned away after the napalm strike and watched those beautiful mountains on the western wall of the An Lao that bombs could never destroy. Then I was lucky. A muddy bootlace was undone, and I bent down to tie it. Whoosh! Something hot passed the skin on my neck and a gush of water drenched me. The man beside me was staring with wide eyes.

"What the hell was that?"

He formed a circle with his hands. "Sarge, you should've seen what just went by your head. A chunk of metal as big as a hubcap." The skin on the back of my neck was really tingling now.

As the last jet streaked down the valley, we climbed into the ravine, past the sticky black resin of napalm. The bombs had been wasted. There were nine NVA packs, no more, and the trail ended a few feet from where we had been before. The message center had been wiped out. Nine Blues ripped Cav patches from their sleeves, and we pulled back to the paddies to wait for the slicks.

One of the platoon's jobs was to detonate unexploded bombs and shells, so that the NVA couldn't use them for mines and booby traps. We had found a real beauty. On a low hill in a ruined village was a fat 500-pound bomb. Hooten placed a thick band of plastic explosive around its middle and set a fifteen-minute fuse. We pulled back to a streambed and waited for the charge to go off. Fifteen minutes passed, and twenty, then twenty-five. Rosen began giving doubtful looks to Hooten.

"How long did you set that fuse for, Sergeant?"

"Fifteen minutes, sir. It should have gone off by now."

"We're going to have to check it. Wait five more minutes and then take a team to have a look."

Hooten wasn't happy about the risk involved but managed a low "Yes, sir." When the time was up, he reluctantly left for the bomb. Hobbs was sitting with his back to the earth bank, with a radio handset pressed to his ear. He was interested in what Hooten was telling the lieutenant.

"You ain't gonna believe this. Hooten's squad found Ho Chi Minh prints leading up to the bomb. Some gook stole the C-4."

Why not? "I'll believe anything that happens in this valley."

Hooten set a short fuse this time, and his men scrambled down the bank only seconds before the bomb exploded with a great roar. After the rain of debris was over, we went back to the hill. There was no trace of the man who had stolen our plastique.

The scout choppers had been fired on from a narrow wood. It was only a few yards wide and was nothing but old trees and clumps of bamboo. Open rice paddies surrounded it. This mission would be easy. We walked through the woods in a couple of minutes, and Rosen told the pilots that nothing was there. Clack-clack-clack. He dropped the handset like a hot coal.

"All right. He's in there. Let's get him this time."

We searched the thicket more carefully this time. Then we arrived at the other side. Clack-clack-clack.

Kidder screamed at us. "I want that little bastard! We're not leaving this place until we get him!"

Blue stayed in the woods for another hour, kicking tree limbs, probing the earth with sticks, and walking back and forth, again and again. Finally it was time to leave. The man didn't fire when we walked into the paddies. Perhaps he was gone, after all. As the slicks pulled away, a long clacking burst chased us out. Somewhere in that wood, an NVA was having a good laugh at our expense.

The artillery lieutenant is going home in a few days, and he wants me to practice directing the guns from the air. The Blues need an FO on the ground, so on the next mission, he wants me to find a high mountain and pretend it's a chopper. We have already talked about it a couple of times. It doesn't matter to me right now. I'm stoned out of my mind.

I don't like the stuff, but Martin has been bugging me for weeks to smoke some grass with him. He's my friend, so I'm doing it. The smoke hurt my lungs, but now I can only feel the taste in my throat. A platoon is surrounded near a bridge to the west. I never realized how pretty flashing helicopter lights are at night. The miniguns make such fantastic streaks through the air. What a light show!

The lieutenant wants to brief us on shooting artillery from the air. He would have to pick this night. Martin and I walk to his tent. I think that I am airborne already, floating about a foot off the ground. He's sure to notice that I'm acting strange. Got to be careful.

The light in his tent is too bright. He's saying something, but it's hard to hear because of the light. "Now, Sergeant Brennan, when you have a target, it is either clear or not clear . . ."

"Not clear!"

He has a curious look on his face. "Ah. Sergeant Brennan, the target has to be either clear or not clear, and . . ."

"Not clear!" I want to say something intelligent, but it doesn't sound that way, even to me. He has a strange look. He's strange-looking. I never really saw him before. He's too thin, and his short haircut makes him look like a scarecrow. His nose sticks out like a beak. He ought to get some sun. His pale skin is . . .

"Ah. That's all for now, Sergeant Brennan."

I want to show him that I've been listening. "Not clear!" Martin laughs all the way back to our pup tent.

We jumped into the elephant grass at dawn. Thousands of new punji stakes had been planted there. Walker, the man who was almost killed by the "dead" NVA in the An Lao, punctured his leg. I caught one, too. I pulled back the pant leg and made mud with my spit to stop the bleeding. A platoon from the 12th Cav landed behind us, and two of their men were evacuated with punji wounds. The two platoons separated to search the mountain.

Blue reached a large clearing under the canopy and found the remains of a feast in months gone by. The bones of dozens of pigs were lying in a jumble, where men had tossed them after gnawing away the meat. A big NVA unit had dined in this box seat above the valley. Perhaps they were watching us that day.

I picked one of the few intact parts of An Lao Village, in the war zone below, and called down 155mm white phosphorous shells on the straw huts. Orange tree bursts and other deadly blossoms set the whole area on fire. The flames were already spreading to the coconut groves around the village as we added our C-ration cans to the bone pile. The 12th Cav platoon was burning a big village under the canopy. Smoke drifted through the treetops above us, and I caught occasional glimpses of flames through the jungle growth. Fire above and fire below.

After the break was over, Rosen sent Hobbs's squad down an overgrown stream. I tagged along. We made our way from boulder to boulder, clinging to the overhanging vines to keep balance. We had to cut a path through a maze of "wait-a-minute" vines and thickets of bushes with inch-long thorns. Then Hobbs received a message.

"Blues are at a small NVA camp. Had a hooch and a guy in

111

a coffin. They're waiting for us there. Rosen says go down another fifty meters, and if we don't find anything, join up with them.''

A single shot. Silence for a moment, then another shot. Then many rifles began firing. Ricochets chewed into the treetops high above us. Hobbs grabbed his radio headset and listened. "Rosen wants us back there on the double. Platoon from the 12th Cav is pinned down. Two men hit!''

"On the double" became ten minutes of agonizing climbing. We found the rest of the Blues at the bottom of a clearing. Above us were the soldiers of the 12th Cav, crouching behind boulders and firing at the trees higher up. Bullets were hitting around us as Rosen ran over to Hobbs.

"They were crossing that clearing. The first shot killed the lieutenant. The second one got a machine gunner through the eye. We're going up to those rocks." He turned to the rest of us. "Everybody keeps his head down and runs till we get there.''

We covered the distance in one ragged rush. I rolled behind a boulder and called the artillery lieutenant. "Warbler Three-One, this is Three-One Mike, over.''

"This is Warbler Three-One. The only thing in range is one-five-five. How does it look down there? Over.''

"This is Three-One Mike. Negative on the one-five-five. I say again, negative on the one-five-five. We're in too close for anything but Willy Peterous. Over.''

"Warbler Three-One. Roger that. Will adjust from here. Out.''

White phosphorous shells exploded in the trees above. That might scare the NVA, but the chemical rounds wouldn't hurt anybody in those thick woods. Jets were already circling over us, but we were too close to the target for bombs. The Phantoms used the phosphorous smoke to mark the target and roared over the clearing with 20mm miniguns firing. The trees lit up like a string of exploding firecrackers.

After a few more shots from the snipers, the clearing became silent. The slicks clattered in to extract the 12th Cav platoon. The loss of their officer and a machine gunner had so unnerved the grunts that they fought each other for seats on the choppers. The

112

slicks returned for us a few minutes later, and we watched the first 500-pound bomb hit the trees as our flight cleared the mountainside. The 12th Cav soldiers' fear had infected us as well. The Blue platoon that returned to Bong Son was silent and shaken.

That fight had been the last straw for Walker. He was sure he would be killed if he stayed with the Blues, and he asked to be a door gunner. There was a gunner with the gunships, Bates, who was positive that the Blues were the only safe place to be. They went to see our commander the next day, and soon Walker was a door gunner and Bates was a Blue. The day after the switch, Blue was scrambled to secure a downed chopper in the Fish Hook area north of the An Lao. Walker's gunship had been shot down.

We landed in a grassy valley next to the machine and pulled four bloody crewmen out of the wreckage. We weren't sure which of the two door gunners was Walker. The chopper was a total loss, so a new sergeant from Illinois, Paxton, placed a demolition charge along its belly. Jets were bombing the antiaircraft position on a ridge above us. As the slicks lifted us out of the valley, the chopper disintegrated in a cloud of black smoke. Bates shook his head with relief. He had been right about the Blues after all.

The sun was brutally hot. Blue had been following a hard trail through barren foothills when Paxton took two prisoners. They were standing together now, a boy and a girl, in the mouth of a cave. Paxton reported to Rosen.

"I was walking up the trail and saw the cave. Next thing I know, the kids are handing me these grenades." He reached in his leg pocket and showed Rosen an American and a Chinese grenade. "I almost shot them."

Minh questioned the children and turned back to Rosen. "They say they are brother and sister. Both are sixteen. They are medics for NVA, but have not seen their unit for weeks. All they leave them to fight with are grenades. They say killing is bad."

Rosen accepted their story. We all felt sorry for them. "Okay. Let's get them back to the valley so a chopper can pick them up."

Hobbs's squad had the prisoners now, and they brought up the rear as we headed for the valley. Down the trail from the cave, Hobbs found a wide, bloody leaf and some string. He timidly lifted the leaf by its edge and looked at the teenage girl. She blushed and hung her head.

Hobbs dropped the leaf and wiped his fingers on his trousers. "Ha! I wondered how they handled that!"

Blue had walked since dawn under a burning sun. There was one last hillside to search, then we could go home. Rosen sent Hooten's exhausted squad to make the patrol up a rocky slope. They were back within five minutes, staggering under the weight of a wounded North Vietnamese on a stretcher. Hooten was the last man in the file.

"Where'd he come from, Hooten?"

"He was in a cave, sir, on this stretcher. He's hurt bad. I think he's been hit by artillery."

"Okay. Have Claw patch him up. Then we can get out of here."

Clack-clack-clack. The bullets careened off the rocks in front of us. The platoon was in an open field without cover, but there was a hedgerow behind us. We had thought we were too tired to walk back to the hedgerow before. Paxton's men rushed for it while bullets dug up the grass around their feet. The rest of us followed, one small group at a time. Somehow we all made it to the hedgerow, but the wounded NVA was still at the base of the hill, caught in a cross fire. What followed was like a scene from a grade-B Western. The bad guys were in the rocks, the good guys were down below, everyone was shooting like crazy, and nobody was getting hurt.

Games can't last forever. It was almost dark, and something had to be done before we spent the night as sitting ducks. The gunships made a series of minigun runs on the hill, roaring in a couple of feet over the hedgerow. The hot minigun shell casings burned several Blues. The NVA tried to shoot down the gunships, which got their attention away from us.

Rosen shouted to Hobbs, "We need a prisoner! Can you get that Charlie up there?"

Hobbs stared back through bloodshot eyes. "Why should we risk it? He's the one who got us into this mess!"

Rosen's temper was also short. "Sergeant, I said we need a prisoner! Make an attempt to get him!"

Hobbs didn't look at Rosen when he answered. "Okay, sir. Let's go, Gould!" We covered them as they ran forward, firing long bursts at the hillside. Then they came running back, jumped the hedgerow, and landed squarely on the backs of two Blues. Groans and curses. Hobbs and Gould were panting like dogs in August.

Gould winked at me and carefully avoided eye contact with Rosen. "Gook's dead, sir. Sorry about that."

The slicks picked us up behind the hedgerow, one load at a time, while the gunships rocketed the slope. A spotter plane floated down in the twilight, waiting to bring in his Phantoms. The long day was over.

I cleaned my rifle and loaded more bullets that night. Martin was meanwhile sketching a scene in chalk by candlelight. John was determined to contribute as little as possible to the destruction of Vietnam, so I knew there was some reason why he wasn't cleaning his rifle like the rest of us. I had to ask him tactfully.

"I fired seventeen magazines this afternoon, John. How about you?"

"One round, Sarge." He had wanted to be sure his rifle wouldn't jam.

"One round? You've got to be joking. Why didn't you shoot more?"

"My foot hurt, Sarge!" You can't argue with logic like that.

Gould left for his small town in the Midwest the next morning. Other Blues had become old men almost overnight in Vietnam, but Gould had thrived on the war. He looked younger and more innocent the day he left than he did when I first saw him. He's probably a local sheriff now, being a combat veteran and all. And friend, don't cross him.

My leave replacement arrived two days later. Now I could go home for sure. He was Walmsly, a chubby sergeant whom I had once known at the command post. Walmsly was excited as he walked toward my tent, smiling from ear to ear. He'd lose the fat soon enough.

A big wave. "Hi, Brennan. I can't wait to get started. What's the Blues like? I've heard so much about them."

He was fresh blood. In a month he would be changed forever. "It's hard to explain. We'll be going on a mission later. Why don't you come with us"—you silly bastard—"and see for yourself."

"That sounds great! I've been trying to get a slot as an FO for four months now. Had to extend to get a chance."

So the fools were waiting in line. "The grass is always greener. You might wish you'd gone home."

He shook his head and laughed. "Not a chance. Don't be so selfish. FO experience looks good on promotion boards back in the States." Martin took a long look at Walmsly. They were going to love each other. Blue scrambled on a mission a few minutes later.

I was on point, passing baskets of rice drying on the rocks. Walmsly was limping badly now. He had sprained his ankle on the jump. I silently prayed, "Please, God. Keep him going until tomorrow." I walked to the far side of the NVA camp, just in time to see a man's leg disappear through the ceiling of a cave. I squatted down, motioned for the soldiers behind me to do the same, and slowly stood up.

I was face to face with an NVA in a green uniform, standing on the roof of the cave. The barrel of his AK was flashing. I fired at the same instant, and he was flung back against the rocks. His bullets had wounded the man behind me. His nickname was Tennessee, and he had painted a big rebel flag on the front of his helmet. A bullet had hit the flag dead center, parting Tennessee's hair above the forehead. He wiped away a trickle of blood and grinned.

I found the NVA among the boulders in a pool of blood. He was only a teenager and carried a shiny, new Russian AK. There were two chest wounds and a broken arm, but the Blues were just staring down at him. I wanted to know why.

"Why don't you give the kid a hand? He's hurt pretty bad."

"Hell, no. He wounded Tennessee," said one.

"Let the motherfucker die. He wouldn't patch us up if we was hit," said another.

I wanted to change the mood. "Look. You call that a wound? Tennessee has cut himself worse shaving." They still wouldn't move.

Now John was beside me. "Come on, Matt. We can handle it." We started to bandage the wounds and Claw joined us. He had been hanging on the edge of the group, waiting to see if anyone would help the boy and get him off the hook. Claw gave the boy a shot of morphine. There had been a lot of men in this camp, but they had left a boy as the rear guard. It didn't seem fair to me.

The big pile of captured equipment made a nice bonfire. The boy was fascinated by the leaping flames and raised himself on his good elbow to get a better view. The artillery lieutenant wanted to fire some shells above us, where the other NVA had fled, and checked his range with a smoke marking round. Whoosh. The smoke canisters crashed through the treetops above our heads. Blues scattered in all directions as the steel canisters ricocheted around the boulders. The camp was full of red smoke. The wounded boy laughed, shaking all over with drug-induced happiness. He thought the burning equipment, the red smoke, and the ducking soldiers were hilarious. His glazed eyes were dancing.

The boy needed quick medical help, and the gunships found a clearing to evacuate him. Paxton's squad, every man a new arrival, carried him away on a stretcher. They returned after only a few minutes, and Rosen was suspicious.

"Did you evacuate him already, Sergeant?"

"Sorry, sir. He died on the way to the LZ." I had wanted the boy to live. Part of that feeling was the guilt I felt for having shot him.

When we arrived back at Bong Son, I began packing a travel kit for the trip home. Martin was beside me when Walmsly limped over to the tent. "Hey, Brennan. Know the gook you patched up this morning?"

Of course I knew him. "Yeah."

"Well, those guys in Paxton's squad held his head downhill until he choked on his blood. They say it's because he wounded Tennessee."

I wanted to scream. Those replacements hadn't been in Vietnam long enough to hate that boy in the hills, and most of them didn't know who Tennessee was. He was just their excuse. It wasn't the experience of war that had made them cruel, but rather, something in their training.

"Now you know what you got yourself into, Walmsly."

He didn't know. "Well, that's what we're here for."

John exploded. "Aw, shit! Do you have to leave, Matt?" Walmsly jumped. He didn't even know why Martin was upset. Tomorrow night those two lovebirds would be crowded together in a six-by-seven-foot tent.

It's such a good feeling to walk through the gates of Sin City again. It has been so many months. This walled compound is the brothel complex that the 1st Air Cav built for its soldiers. It has caused a lot of protest in America, but we are grateful. The girls are clean. Army doctors examine them and give them shots every week. The bars have good beer and American music. The madames treat even smelly infantrymen with respect. Hell, the French took their whores with them in trucks when they were here.

There is an all-white bar that caters mainly to Southerners and an all-black bar for the other group. Most of the bars are integrated and have such charming names as the An Khe Star Bar and the Lido. The girls represent all the stocks of Indochina. There is one woman who might be the girl next door. Her father was French, and the Vietnamese of her mother doesn't show. Another girl could be from the ghetto. Her father was a Senegalese soldier in the French Colonial Army. She has an Afro and the blacks are very protective of her. My girl is a mixture of Cambodian and Vietnamese. These peoples hate each other, but they got together at least once. Her name is My.

We spent some days together during my summer in An Khe, and there was never any talk of money. If I had known her under other circumstances, I would be madly in love with her. She has been my closest friend since the summer I spent in the bunker of many sandbags. She tried to talk me out of going to the 9th Cav. Even she knew about their reputation. I know that a big shot in An Khe proposed to her, but maybe she's changed her mind. She was having second thoughts the last time I saw her. Just to see her smile one last time.

But there was no smile in the doorway that day. As I turned to leave, the madame grabbed my arm. "Sergeant Matt. It's good to see you again."

"Mamasan, where's My? The girls won't tell me."

"They don't know you. They're new girls from Qui Nhon. My married the major. She lives in a big house in An Khe." A look of compassion crossed her tough old face. "Go and see her. She would want to see you, Sergeant Matt."

"No, Mamasan. It's not the same anymore." The soldiers who paid her never mattered, but now she had promised her life to a man, and that was different. I couldn't sit in the same room with her and just talk.

My lust was gone. I walked down the line of bars and did a stupid thing. Another Blue had given me a big artillery simulator firecracker. Might as well have some fun. I tossed it into the An Khe Star Bar, and it went off with a shriek and a loud bang. I didn't think it would make so much noise. A Korean soldier threw his "Boom Boom" girl off his lap and tried to hide under a chair. Then he saw me standing in the doorway like a fool and realized what had happened. He pulled a trench knife from his boot, and I lunged for the nearest chair just as someone tackled me. His buddies were holding both of us down.

I apologized and he accepted, all through the good graces of an English-speaking Korean. He and I sat in the Star Bar for the afternoon, drinking and smiling uneasily, trying to act like comrades in arms. They wanted me to choose a girl and join in their fun, but all I could think about was My. Once, he turned to me and said something through an evil smile.

119

"What'd he say?"

"He said you American infantrymen are all crazy."

"Please tell him thanks for the compliment." It was so stupid, our sitting there as friends by a twist of fate, while other men were our enemies by the same twist.

Two days later I was changing planes in Seattle for the last leg of the journey home.

CHAPTER 8

Indiana

I had a good time on leave. The summer's warmth was far better than the chilling days of February. I reached home just in time to be the best man at my sister's wedding—wore my uniform, of course. I had six ribbons and a Combat Infantry Badge, and I wanted people to know from where, and from what, I had come. Vietnam veterans were still treated with respect in my hometown in those days. A young man in greens stares back from the wedding pictures.

I did all I could to forget the war. I swam, danced, drank beer and little else, and dated five girls, changing them as if they were pairs of socks. After all, I was a grown man of twenty. There had never been a My, either. On my many walks through the fields and woods of Daviess County, I tried to again experience nature without danger. It was no use. Everywhere I looked there were possible ambush sites or ominous noises. A campsite could be located in that draw. The woodpeckers could be the muffled sound of machine guns. Those wheat fields on that hillside—how many slicks could land there? There wasn't time to forget, but by the end of those full weeks, Indochina seemed to be only a distant reality.

I was drinking beer in the shade of a tree in our town's little park one day when a battered '57 Chevy pulled up on the road below. It was Charlie, a recent high school graduate and one of the town's small elite of roughnecks. He had thrown a party for me the night I returned, using beer he had stolen from a liquor store. Charlie wanted to talk about the Army.

"What's Vietnam like? Do you think I could make it as an infantryman in the Cav?"

"It's not a question of making it. Anybody can make it. It's like nothing you can ever imagine. The newspapers don't tell it the way it really is. Nam is mostly just being bored and sweaty and dirty."

"Come on. Do you think I could make it?"

To put it mildly, Charlie was not the military type. I couldn't imagine him conforming to a world of hierarchies and regulations. "Charlie, when I first met you, you said they couldn't pay you enough to get shot at. Why're you so fired up about the Army all of a sudden?"

He leaned over, as if to confide some great secret. "Some friends and me robbed a couple of liquor stores on the West End a few weeks ago. We were broke and wanted some beer. Just took eight cases. That's the beer we drank the night you got back. The cops are getting wise, and I want to go somewhere for a while."

"Go somewhere else. The Army doesn't take people with police records, anyway."

Charlie didn't have a police record, yet. We argued back and forth for a while longer, and he finally convinced me to ride with him to the local recruiting station in Vincennes. I went along mainly to be sure that the recruiting sergeant didn't tell Charlie a pack of lies to fill his quota. We drove the twenty miles to Vincennes in record time. The recruiting sergeant was about ready to retire and was telling it straight. I was more interested in his secretary. She was tall and blond and smiling at me. The last was of great importance.

How should I begin? "Hi."

"Hi." God, what a nice smile.

"Ah, do you work here?" She must think that's a dumb question.

"Yeah. I come in on Tuesdays and Thursdays to do the typing. Are you thinking of enlisting?"

"No. I'm already in." Maybe I can impress her. *"I'm a staff sergeant."*

"Did you ever go over to Vietnam?"

"Yeah. I just got back from eighteen months over there."

"I wondered where you got that deep tan. I figured you might be working out on the railroad." She likes me. I can tell.

"No. It's the tropical sun." That's milking it for all it's worth. *"Ah, would you like to do something sometime?"*

She's smiling again. *"Sure, I'd love to."*

I fell head over heels in love. I had only a week of leave left, but that passed and then two more. I was now officially AWOL, but the Cav was lenient with people coming back to Vietnam from leave home. I think they were just happy we came back at all. One day I told Cathy that I was returning to the war and gave her a tiny diamond engagement ring. Two days later, she rode with my family the fifty miles to the Evansville Airport. It wasn't the same as leaving on a cold morning in March. I was crying by the time the plane left the runway. I didn't want to go back to the killing.

CHAPTER 9

Dusty Delta

I reported to the artillery headquarters in An Khe and learned that I had a new assignment. They were sending me to Delta Troop of the 9th Cav. I had now survived longer than any other artillery sergeant in the 9th Cav, and the battery commander wanted me in a safer unit for a rest. I couldn't change his mind. Delta Troop was the squadron's "rat patrol" unit. They traveled in jeeps instead of choppers and didn't fight well when they had to move on foot. If I had an obligation to be in Vietnam, I wanted to spend the time with Martin and the Blues, not in a unit that the Blue platoons ridiculed.

When I arrived at Bong Son, I left my travel bag at the Delta Troop artillery tent and crossed the camp to my old friends in the Blues. Martin was reading, sitting on the sandbags around his tent. I sneaked up behind him.

"John, my man, how's life been treating you?" He jumped to his feet and we hugged each other. "What's been happening around these parts the last month?"

"Month? It's been more like seven weeks. They were wondering if you'd come back. Nothing much happened. It's always the same shit."

"That's what you said the last time. The clerk at Divarty said Walmsly got hit."

"That was a long time ago. We were chasing some VC in the An Lao about a week after you left. Walmsly was so clumsy he was tripping all over himself just trying to stay on his feet. He shot one of them, I still don't know how, and the guy's buddy threw a grenade. Walmsly was the only one hurt. Let's sit in the shade and catch up.'' Martin limped as we walked toward a tree.

"What's wrong with your foot? Hurt it again?''

"I wish. You always have to know, don't you? About a week ago I was riding with Hobbs's squad when they pulled us out of the An Lao. They shot us down, Matt. I jumped right before the chopper crashed and chipped some teeth and hurt my back a little. Hobbs rode it down and got messed up pretty bad. He's in the hospital in Japan right now. Let's talk about people, not things.''

Martin told me that the platoon had remained in the An Lao throughout the summer. A few Blues had gone home, and more had been injured on the landings or hit in the constant skirmishes. Walmsly had been replaced by another sergeant from the command post. The new artillery lieutenant was named Romero. He hadn't said a word to Martin about getting a haircut, and that rated a gold star in John's book. They had spent a few nights talking on the bunkers, and Martin thought of Lieutenant Romero as a personal friend and a man who understood his philosophy of life. It had taken a long time for me to feel comfortable around John. I was sad that powers beyond my control had taken me away from him and Brave Fighter Blues.

I returned to Delta Troop in time to watch a convoy of dusty jeeps grind by. A soldier pointed out the artillery lieutenant. He was riding in a jeep with a back seat piled high with AKs, carbines, and Chinese burp guns. I walked over and introduced myself.

"Sir, I'm Sergeant Brennan from Divarty.''

"Hi. Lieutenant Fortin. We just made believers out of some dinks in the Tiger Mountains. Haven't seen burp guns since Korea. Why don't we go over to my tent and have a beer?''

Now we could discuss my future over cans of beer. "Sounds good.''

He reached into an aluminum cooler and handed me a cold can of Pabst Blue Ribbon. Everyone in Delta Troop had a cooler full of beer on ice. If the Blues had known about it, the 9th Cav would have had a riot on its hands.

Fortin began, "I'm glad to have an experienced recon sergeant again. The other man went home several weeks ago." He beamed proudly. "I was a recon sergeant, like you, in Korea."

I said, "Glad to be here," and wanted to add, "It's better than being in Siberia."

"Here's the set-up, Sarge. We have three identical platoons, code-named Red, White, and Blue. There are three artillerymen with the Troop—me, you, and the driver. Each of us takes a platoon and acts as the FO."

"Is the driver good at shooting artillery?"

"Yes. Ted's damned good at it. You'll meet him when he gets off the road. The way we work it is that you go out on the road for two days and spend the third day on standby in case the air cavalry troops need our help. The standby doesn't go out much, so it's really a free day to write letters, catch up on sleep, or go into town." He winked to emphasize what you could do in town. "You'll be on standby tomorrow so you can get your gear squared away. Any questions?"

"No. It sounds pretty clear-cut. Thanks for the beer."

Ted returned at dusk. He seemed professional and independent. He was only a private now, but I had no doubt that he would be retiring from the "green machine" in twenty or thirty years. It was written all over him. Ted was a tough city kid from Cleveland who loved danger. He was so different from John Martin that I hoped we could work together without friction. Ted wanted to get some rest, so that he would be ready for tomorrow's convoy. John would have been finding ways not to go.

Delta Troop had three platoons, each with four machine gun jeeps, a radio jeep, two 106mm recoilless rifle jeeps, a light truck with a mortar, and another light truck with an infantry squad. They had patrolled jungle roads in 1965 and 1966, but now their lives were less dangerous—guarding convoys and shooting back at snipers. The platoons would sometimes be used as infantry to help the Blue platoons, but life here was many times safer. The major problems facing these jeep soldiers were keeping the road dust from caking their bodies and weapons and guessing where each day's crop of VC land mines were planted.

I spent as little time as possible with Dusty Delta. I'd ride with the convoys for two days out of three and use the days on standby to make landings with the Blues. They were happy to have the extra rifle. Charlie Troop was now operating in a place called the Song Re Valley. It was a high, nearly treeless river valley that the NVA were using as a highway into the An Lao. The fighting there was like the early days of 1966, before the Cav turned the Crow's Foot into a wasteland. Back then we were near the coast; now the same things were happening far up in the mountains. The Cav had extended its reach.

On the first days in the Song Re, we sat on a barren plain below a Special Forces camp and waited as gunships and jets attacked NVA and tent camps on the open plain. Things got deadlier for us as the choppers hunted for enemy camps in the surrounding mountains. The hills around the valley were ringed with heavy machine guns, and scouts and gunships started to go down. The Blues' main job was to cut through the brush and rescue the crews. One of those killed in the crashes was Romero. It was a great personal blow to John, who had become his friend.

One evening I stepped into my tent at Delta Troop well after dark. Blue had spent the day in scrub-covered hills pitted with new spider holes, and I was exhausted. Ted was waiting for me.

"Lieutenant Fortin says no more landings with Charlie Blues."

"Why not?"

"We'll be going out every day now. One of the platoons is going to start guarding convoys to the An Lao. Engineers are going to level some villages there with bulldozers."

I rarely had the time to see Martin after those days in the Song Re Valley.

The helicopters were burning and one of our bunkers had collapsed from a direct hit. The mortars were hitting behind us now,

127

but they had already killed four men along the wire. Ted was behind a machine gun, rapping out rounds at flashes in the trees. The NVA had attacked right through Bong Son Village. The flares and artillery shells made the night look like a painting of hell. Crash! A new soldier had stood up behind a bunker for a better view, and was blown apart by a Russian antitank rocket. It was a long night.

Ted shook me awake at dawn. "Let's go, Sarge. We've got to sweep the village."

"It'll be a waste of time. They're long gone by now." Then I remembered the last rocket. "Who was the man killed by the bunker?"

"I don't know. Some guy just in from the World. The cook got his, though. They put the dude's body in the back of the mess tent. This lifer mess sergeant went back to take a look and puked all over himself. One of the KPs saw it. Serves him right. He's always hassling us when we come in off the road."

I remembered the mess sergeant as a friendly and good-natured person. "He never bothers me."

Ted was scornful. "Hell, no! You're a sergeant, remember?"

A tree in front of Ted's machine gun was painted in blood. There were drag trails along the wire, and the ground was littered with packs and bloodstained clothing. The attack had cost the NVA dearly. Some of the huts in the village had been destroyed by the flares, and we finished the search to the wails of parents crying for their lost children.

Ted had another comment. "Poor damn people. This shit didn't even have to happen."

"Yeah. It's a shame, but the gooks attacked through the village."

He shook his head. "No, that's not what I mean. The Arvin police caught two NVA scouts selling Cokes to GIs a couple of days ago. They were sitting by the main gate. Guess they didn't make them talk in time."

I remembered seeing the scouts when we returned from a jeep patrol a few days before. They were muscular men in their late twenties, dressed in tattered black and khaki rags and crouching by a wooden ice chest. I had thought it odd that such healthy men

128

of military age should be peddling soft drinks for a living. I had blamed the war for their poverty.

I was an FO again. A Delta patrol would move down a road behind mine-sweeping teams and set up near areas where the VC had base camps. The platoon would blast away with its single mortar and two recoilless rifles, and I would bring in the artillery. On some days, I would fire 400 to 500 shells, leaving mountains smoking by the time it was over. The eight-inch shells were especially nice. They broke huge holes in the canopy and sent rocks and tree stumps twisting through the air on their shock waves. These barrages struck the An Lao Valley and the Tiger Mountains. From past experience, I knew that the targets in those jungles were Communists, not civilians.

On convoys to the north, we would park the trucks and jeeps on bluffs overlooking the South China Sea and swim naked with laughing Vietnamese children. The Army didn't issue bathing suits and underwear rotted in the tropical heat. But there was danger near those beautiful beaches. The engineers would build a bridge of wood and complete it every third day. On the fourth morning, it would always be burning. The engineers would curse their bad luck and start over. We never parked the vehicles twice in the same place. A platoon started to do that one day, and a sharp sergeant grabbed a metal detector on a hunch. Yesterday's picnic site was infested with land mines and booby traps.

There was a rocky hill that overlooked the beaches. No one had the desire to climb it in the shimmering heat, and besides, an American platoon had lived there for some weeks after Delta Troop arrived. One evening after we returned to Bong Son, Alpha Troop scouts saw men running for cover among the boulders. Their Blues killed four NVA in a twilight battle among the outcroppings. It had been an observation post.

Even Bong Son wasn't safe. One day in September, the ARVN police and Cav MPs made a routine search for ARVN deserters in the village. An unsuspecting Delta Troop soldier walked over to the wire to take a leak. He looked down to see a VC hiding in the grass underneath the barbed wire. Our man brought him in, guarded by the AK-47 he had been lying on. The VC had been visiting relatives in the village. That incident reminded me of the day Blue had killed two Viet Cong in the foothills of the eastern An Lao. They had carried French MAT-49 submachine guns. The interesting discovery was a packet of photographs showing those two posing on Bong Son's main street with their French submachine guns hung around their necks.

There was only one Dusty Delta casualty during this quiet period. An overweight ROTC lieutenant had joined one of the platoons. We had been guarding bulldozers as they crushed hooches and destroyed old coconut groves, and it had been time for chow. The officer had his first C-ration meal brought over by one of his soldiers, but he saw that there was an extra meal in the ration box. He ran to get it, straight through a field of punji stakes in the inch-high grass. A stake went completely through both sides of his boot, just above the ankle. I never saw such a dumb way to get a Purple Heart. He was groaning but still eating when the slick arrived to evacuate him. I wonder what he tells people when they ask him how he was wounded in the war.

I finally took a day off duty. The convoys had been peaceful, and I wanted to write Cathy a long letter. A new sergeant took my place in the artillery jeep. A blackened and twisted hulk of steel was towed by my tent in the late afternoon. I was shocked when I realized it was my artillery jeep. The shock was greater when I saw a battered Ted walking toward the tent.

"What happened, Ted?"

"We ran over a mine in that pass south of Duc Pho. The sergeant lost his leg. I think it was hand-detonated. The gook saw the antennas and thought we were the command jeep for the convoy."

Ted's face was cut up badly, and his arm was starting to turn black. "Are you hurt bad?"

"Nothing to lose sleep over. Only a couple of scratches. But you know something? If you had been in that jeep, you'd be missing a leg right now."

"You ain't telling me anything new."

Ted was back on the road the next morning.

* * *

The convoys to the An Lao are over, and the standby platoon goes out more often now. I'm frightened by the clumsy way these jeep soldiers move through brush. We have landed on a hill within sight of our camp. It doesn't make sense for the NVA to be so far inside a heavily defended area in daylight. There are two bodies beside a rocket crater and a bunker under the only tree on the hill.

A machine gunner, a small and sad-looking teenager named Bolten, lobs a grenade. His tattered uniform makes him look like a refugee from a poorhouse. When the black smoke is gone, Bolten drags a body from the bunker. The corpse has a Chinese pistol on its belt and a pack strapped to its back.

Now we know why they were here. Pistols always indicate officers or administrators. These were tax collectors. The one with the pistol was the official; the others were "enforcers." Bolten finds a thick roll of bills inside the pack and tries to hide it in his shirt. The lieutenant grabs his hand and knocks the bills to the ground. Bolten smooths his crumpled uniform and glares.

"Come on, Lieutenant. That money can go for a good cause."

"What cause, Bolten?"

"Booze and broads. Have a heart, sir. It was my kill." The other soldiers look at the lieutenant and stir expectantly.

"Sorry, boys. You get paid. The piasters are going to the squadron orphanage." The platoon was picked up, still bitching, minutes later.

The southern part of the An Lao War Zone had become so tame that the few remaining NVA had reverted to a classic guerrilla war of booby traps and sniping. This didn't help the tank crew that was killed by a mined Air Force 500-pound bomb, but it did keep losses at an "acceptable" level. The 9th Cav was largely responsible for creating this quiet region, and the squadron was keeping it pacified by frequent daylight helicopter patrols and a series of night ambushes. The Viet Cong had sworn never to stop fighting for their An Lao Liberated Zone. The summer and fall of 1967 was the only time when part of the valley was safe

131

enough to allow small units to operate there and have a reasonable chance of surviving.

I went along with a Delta Troop ambush squad on one moonlit night. Our little group was landed near woods and walked west until we found a narrow trail. It was a quiet night. I awoke at dawn and stretched, and then my heart almost stopped beating. We had ambushed the mouth of the horseshoe valley, where Blue had been ambushed months before. The raw edges of the B-52 craters had been rounded by the rains, and grass was sprouting from their bottoms and sides. Around them were gigantic new craters from the 2000-pound shells of the battleship *New Jersey*. A mountainside behind the valley had collapsed in an avalanche created by the huge shells. I was glad when the helicopter picked us up.

A few nights later, another ambush squad heard sounds coming from the riverbank by a bulldozed village. They directed gunships and artillery shelling in the darkness. When it was over, twenty NVA were dead. The North Vietnamese threw the bodies in the river to hide their losses, but they were found wedged against a dam farther downstream. The tank's crew had been avenged.

We were playing hearts in the shade of bunkers when the White platoon sergeant took off at a run toward the slicks. "Let's go, White! Let's go! Alpha Troop's got a downed bird! Everybody to the helipad in five minutes! On the double!"

The Alpha Troop slicks took us to a burning village northeast of Bong Son, less than a mile from where Arthur had died. Gunships made a series of ripping minigun runs at the place, and then we were on the ground, running past blazing huts. Three NVA ran around the corner of a hooch in front of us. Two of them were shot down. The third man dropped his rifle and raised his hands. We grenaded the bunkers that dotted the open courtyards.

The platoon spread out in a line. We started to cross a hedge-row with a square, open pit twenty yards in front of it. A machine gun hammered through the bushes, and for the first time since June, I remembered just how good dirt felt next to my face. It would keep me from harm. We fired blindly at the hut behind the pit until somebody noticed that the bullets were cutting branches two feet above the ground. The machine gun was firing at an angle. It had to be in the pit.

Minton took a grenade and ran for the pit. A burst ripped by him, and he threw the grenade too soon. It exploded behind the pit. He unclipped a white phosphorous grenade from his belt and crawled closer, bullets clacking over his head. A muffled whump from the pit. Bullets cooked off from a hot weapon. Minton gave us a thumbs-up signal and jumped up. More bullets from the pit, this time fired from a rifle. Minton was trapped in the open. He looked around at us, face contorted with fear, and knew that he couldn't make it back to the hedgerow. He sprayed the lip of the pit and heaved another white phosphorous grenade with his free hand. Another whump and it was over.

Inside the pit were the bodies of four NVA. They had carried an RPD machine gun and two rifles. The fourth man had drums of ammunition for the machine gun in carrying pouches slung across his shoulders. They had been horribly burned by the phosphorus, and one smoldering corpse grinned up at us through a charred face. The jeep soldiers held their noses and fished for the hot weapons with poles torn from the walls of a hooch.

Minton got a Silver Star for his bravery. My reward was some verse that haunted me as I stared into the pit.

> Death in a pit from phosphorus,
> A big grin
> For those who must go on.

A gunner from the downed chopper ran to us from somewhere behind the pit. He was still wearing his flight helmet and flak jacket and cradling a machine gun in his arms. The platoon sergeant pulled him to cover and questioned him.

"Where's the rest of your crew?"

"A gunship pulled them out as far as I know. Gooks had me pinned and I couldn't make it."

"Can you tell us what the hell's going on here?"

"All I know is they shot us down with a twelve-seven. This

village is supposed to be government controlled, but there's beaucoup VC around here. Man, you guys look beautiful.''

It was almost dark, so we ran to the closest rice paddy for extraction. I stumbled over more NVA bodies on the way out. I had a complacent feeling about the battle. There were already a lot of dead NVA here. There couldn't be many more of them in the village. As the slicks lifted us over the edge of the inferno, a 12.7mm machine gun rattled, sending big tracers arcing across the nose of my chopper. The rounds seemed to come straight at us like red fireballs, then veer at the last instant and streak away into the black sky. The complacent feeling was gone. I watched as two gunships rocketed the antiaircraft position.

I was sitting in the shade of a bunker the next day when Ted walked over with some news. "Hey, Sarge. You know that Alpha Troop chopper you guys went after yesterday?"

"Don't forget that easy."

"I just saw the interrogation report on that prisoner you picked up. There was a battalion of the 2d VC Regiment in that village. Came down from the Marine area two days ago to attack Bong Son. The APCs and infantry are up there now, kicking their asses back north. Their big mistake was shooting at the chopper.''

Prisoners and documents were important sources of information. It was during this time that we read the translation of a document captured in the Crescent. It instructed the NVA to throw away their khaki uniforms and to start wearing black pajamas if the newly issued green uniforms had not yet arrived. The NVA copied our jungle boots and the color of our uniforms. We copied their packs and many of their tactics.

There was also a strange series of actions in the Cav area. The gunships from Alpha and Charlie Troops began catching groups of NVA replacements, all armed with new Russian and Eastern European weapons, making their way to the battered regiments in the area. It was a turkey shoot; the raw troops were surprised in the open or got lost in caves. Hundreds of North Vietnamese were killed before they could reach their units. No one suspected that they were on their way to beef up the regiments for the Tet attacks of early 1968.

The presence of the 1st Air Cavalry made Binh Dinh Province one of the quietest places in Vietnam during the Tet Offensive. While provincial capitals and American bases were being buried under rocket and mortar barrages, Bong Son was attacked by a couple of long-range shots from a recoilless rifle. No one was hurt. When an entire NVA regiment moved into position for the decisive attack on Bong Son, a 9th Cav scout ship spotted the camouflaged antennas of their command post. The regiment was surrounded and destroyed. Other Viet Cong battalions tried to capture the coastal city of Qui Nhon. They attacked a day before the Tet Offensive was scheduled to start and apparently didn't take the nature of the Korean reaction force into account. An eyewitness told me that the Viet Cong survivors were lined up on the beach and shot.

I was reading by candlelight when someone knocked on the flaps of my tent. It was Red, formerly the Red platoon leader of Dusty Delta. Red had been my only living friend in the troop. The four-man mortar team that I had traveled with on convoys and spent long nights with on guard had been killed by a single 82mm mortar round during the NVA attack on Bong Son. Their loss hurt me so deeply that I erased them from my mind for many years.

I had fired artillery into the mountains with a special hatred after the death of the mortar crew, and Red enjoyed the fireworks. Our first conversations had been about the lethal possibilities of various sorts of artillery shells. Red was as unhappy in Dusty Delta as I was, but that was about all we had in common. He had griped for months about not being allowed to lead a Blue platoon, and one hot day in August he was told to pack his bags and leave immediately for Bravo Blues. Red was packed and gone within fifteen minutes. I had not expected to see him again.

"Don't just stand there; come in."

He was all smiles tonight. "Don't mind if I do."

"Well, how are things with your new Blue platoon?"

More smiles. "They're great! Just great! I've never been happier. I've got a tough bunch of boys, and do they ever love to fight. How's it going with you?"

"Same old thing. Driving down the road and getting dirty."

He clenched his teeth. "I know how you feel. I hated even coming back here, but I had to pick up my mail. The only thing Delta Troop ever gave me was hemorrhoids."

"I've escaped that so far."

Red was a war-lover, and he was excited by Bravo Troop's latest toy. "Some of the gunships have got police sirens, see. The pilots turn them on when they make a rocket run, and it drives the gooks crazy. They run around like chickens with their heads cut off. Then"—he drew his finger across his throat—"Blamo, baby!"

"Sounds like the Stukas the Germans used."

He nodded. "Yeah. The same principle, and boy, are they effective. The gooks never know what hit them." He left after a while, saying that he had to get away from the place that had disappointed him so.

It was early October. I sat in a jeep on a hill above Colonial Route 1, showing a new artillery sergeant the ropes. Pete had spent a year in the command post, living a secondhand war and watching the 9th Cav Blues swagger by with their stupid NVA belts. Now he had extended his tour to see the war firsthand. The fact that I had survived for so long had encouraged him to volunteer. I wanted to tell Pete to read about the war and be content but knew that I wouldn't have listened to the same advice ten months before. Now all I could do was teach him how not to make mistakes. Our target was a giant boulder, bulging from a jungle hill about a thousand yards away.

"What corrections would you give if you wanted to hit that brown boulder?"

"Drop five hundred, repeat platoon two."

"You sure about five hundred? That would put you in those paddies next to the road. The farmers wouldn't like it."

"Oh. Five zero. That's what I meant to say."

"Okay. Just remember that one wrong correction and you're

likely to grease your own people. Give it to the 'guns.'' We watched as black explosions bracketed the boulder and set the dry jungle on fire.

Pete was supposed to be Ted's replacement, but things quickly changed. Ted was waiting for the jeep when we returned from the second day of training. "I've got news for you, Sarge."

"What news?"

"Red's dead. Bravo Blue got hit in the An Lao again. Machine gun got Red." It was always the stinking An Lao.

"What a waste. He couldn't wait to go over to Bravo Blues."

"That's not all the news." He grinned maliciously. "You're going to Bravo Blues, too. Sergeant May went home a couple of days ago."

I didn't know whether to be happy or scared. I wanted to go to Charlie Troop, not Bravo Troop, and life in Dusty Delta was pretty easy duty. I asked Ted a question that I thought I could answer myself. "Is Bravo Troop still in the An Lao?" Of course they would still be in that goddamned valley.

"No. They just moved up to Chu Lai to replace the Marines. Lieutenant wants you to pack your gear and catch a chopper back to An Khe first thing tomorrow. Peterson's taking your place. I'm here with Delta again."

He waited for a reaction, but I wouldn't give him the pleasure. "All right. Thanks for the news, Ted." Pete looked at me with pity in his eyes. "Hell, Pete, Bravo Troop's not that bad."

Martin was in An Khe the day I arrived there. He was going home the next morning, so we stayed awake all night, talking about the events of the past year.

"Patterson's on his way to Long Binh Jail, Matt. He was playing cards with a new sergeant, and the sergeant accused him of cheating."

"He always did cheat at cards."

"Yeah. But this was a new dude. It wasn't his place to say. Pat pulled out his forty-five and shot him."

"He's come a long way from the day he tried to play John Wayne in the Suoi Ca. This place is just like the Old West."

John nodded solemnly. "Yeah. Just like the Old West. If somebody crosses you, you shoot him."

"Remember January fourth? I was there a few weeks ago."

"I remember it. I don't ever want to see that horseshoe valley again, not even in my dreams. Remember that big green leech that kept hassling you in the middle of the firefight?"

"That damned leech!" We had a good laugh. "And the Suoi Ca. You know, it was such a beautiful place. The mountains were like living poetry."

John had an idea. "Let's propose one last toast to them, Matt."

We raised our cans of beer and pretended they were champagne glasses. "To the Eighteenth NVA Regiment: may they sleep on firm straw pallets tonight, and may their rice rolls be full."

We grew more serious toward dawn. We talked about Cathy and the pink panties she had mailed from 12,000 miles away. Martin had found a hair trapped in one of the seams, and the whole Blue platoon had come over to see it. I carried the panties with me on missions for good luck. We were all obsessed with whether our luck would be good or bad. John talked about how the past year had changed him. He had wanted a master's degree before, but now he would be content to work in a factory and take the time to forget the horrors we had experienced. He removed from his wrist a copper Montagnard bracelet, which he had once souvenired in the An Lao Valley and handed it to me.

"It's the only thing I ever took from a VC. I want you to keep it as a token of friendship."

"Thanks. I'll wear it. I promise that."

We walked together to the rocky helipad behind the 9th Cav buildings. From here a chopper would take him to Pleiku on the first part of his long journey home. I missed him already. I knew I would never be closer to another human being. He finally broke the silence.

"Matt, you were always the first one on the slicks and the first one off. What's the hurry? Slow down, don't play hero, keep your head down, and all that bullshit. Please come by and eat some of my mother's good cooking when you get back."

"That's a tall order. I'll remember the invitation."

The pilots started the engine and the blades began to whine. Martin was smiling as he stepped aboard. I only felt empty inside. He shouted something.

"What?"

"I said, 'I love you, Matt!'"

I couldn't reply, waving instead. As the slick lifted off in a cloud of dust, I felt that my manhood was no longer compromised and said, "I love you too, my friend." I still have his bracelet.

CHAPTER 10

Flashing Saber Blues

I reached Bravo Troop's tent encampment at the huge air and Marine base of Chu Lai later that afternoon. What a contrast Chu Lai was to the crude bunkers and barbed wire of Bong Son. Here were jet runways, wooden barracks, asphalt roads, flagpoles, mowed lawns, and every form of service the military could provide. Bravo Troop had occupied a grassy field with its tents and choppers. Around that field, rear echelon Marines lived a life from another world.

The troop operated from an armored base far to the west in the Que Son Valley. They were already gaining notoriety from a photograph of one of their many landings in the An Lao. The picture of Blues jumping from a slick onto a rocky outcrop would become probably the most published photograph of the Vietnam War. But this was a unit with another reputation to maintain. They had killed 471 NVA in three months at Duc Pho, north of Bong Son, and were grimly determined to top that score at Chu Lai. And we did. A total of 915 dead enemy soldiers in three bloody months earned the troop its second Presidential Unit Citation. The count was boosted by an unofficial policy that prisoners were to be taken only if there were orders to do so. Our new commander was aware of the troop's hatred of the NVA and would often insist that prisoners were to be taken on a particular operation. His interventions saved the lives of 305 VC and NVA. You have to think about those

"Charge of the Third Brigade," Chu Lai, October 1967 (AP/WIDE WORLD PHOTOS, INC.)

Early Delta Troop patrol. Scout chopper flies cover, January 1966 (U.S. ARMY)

Alpha Blues in the foothills of the Suoi Ca Mountains, December 1966 (U.S. ARMY)

Charlie Blues jump from slick, 1966 (U.S. ARMY)

Bravo Blues ride the skids into a landing, Bong Son, March 1967 (U.S. ARMY)

Charlie Blues wait to board slicks as gunship escorts lift off. Special Forces Camp at Bong Son, January 1967 (1ST AIR CAVALRY DIVISION)

Charlie Blues scramble for a mission at Bong Son Camp, 1967 (U.S. ARMY)

Bravo Blues in village, Bong Son, March 1967
(U.S. ARMY)

**Wounded Blue is evacuated by medevac, Bong
Son, March 1967** (U.S. ARMY)

Bravo Blues prepare to sweep through a village, Bong Son, March 1967 (U.S. ARMY)

Blues search a fighting hole, Bong Son, 1967 (U.S. ARMY)

Bravo Blues await orders to advance into a Viet Cong hospital complex, An Lao Valley, April 1967 (U.S. ARMY)

Minh questions captured NVA near Bong Son, May 31, 1967 (AUTHOR)

Bravo Blues prepare to move out on a patrol through the An Lao Valley, July 1967 (1ST AIR CAVALRY DIVISION)

Bravo Blues in the An Lao, August 1967 (U.S. ARMY)

Blue fires grenade launcher at enemy positions inside village, Duc Pho, June 1967 (U.S. ARMY)

Blues search the body of NVA soldier for documents, Duc Pho, June 1967 (U.S. ARMY)

Bravo Blues land in the An Lao Valley, August 1967 (1ST AIR CAVALRY DIVISION)

Captured sapper demonstrates his technique,
1969 (1ST AIR CAVALRY DIVISION)

Author and friend, Charles Roberts, Fertile
Crescent, March 1967

Author with marine cover and souvenir AK-47, An Khe, March 1968

Vietnamese woman cries as helicopter carries her husband off for interrogation, Chu Lai, December 1967 (CATHERINE LEROY. TIME/LIFE, INC.)

Skull with a Viet Cong bush hat, Chu Lai. Sign read "Merry Christmas, Charlie," December 1967 (AUTHOR)

Blue searches NVA killed by a LOH, 1969 (AUTHOR)

Author as an officer near Zuan Loc, 1969

107mm rocket damage at Quan Loi Base Camp, 1969 (AUTHOR)

Dead NVA near Saigon, March 1969 (AUTHOR)

Bravo Blues at Quan Loi, 1969 (1ST AIR CAVALRY DIVISION)

Both sides of standard surrender pamphlet, "Safe Conduct Pass" (AUTHOR)

"Hunter-Killer" team from Cavalry aerial artillery units, 1969 (1ST AIR CAVALRY DIVISION)

numbers to understand why the Communists hated the 9th Cav so much. In three months, a unit with a combat strength of about a hundred men eliminated over twelve hundred enemy soldiers from the Chu Lai area.

The Blues were at Chu Lai that day, so I got the chance to get acquainted. There were some interesting fellows in the platoon. Charlie Troop had its Gould, but this was a unit of Goulds. Four of them had recently been sentenced to twenty years in Leavenworth Prison for the rape-murder of a woman in a village. A night ambush patrol had abducted her from her home. The radioman who had turned them in had been hustled out of the platoon before the others could kill him. Some of the Blues had already obtained his address in the United States and had sworn that any survivors of the platoon would hunt him down in America. I agreed with what the radioman had done, but I wasn't foolish enough to tell anyone.

There was a squad leader named James. He had been a scout gunner and a door gunner before coming to the Blues. When he went home for discharge, he had been decorated and wounded a number of times and had killed 173 men. He would sometimes look at me with sad eyes and say, "Matt, you know why I extended?"

I always knew what his answer would be. "Why is that, Skip?"

"Because I like to kill." His obsession really did bother him.

"Hippie Doc" was an ex-member of the Hell's Angels and looked the part. He was a powerfully built man about six foot four. He had a huge handlebar mustache and a completely shaven head, except for the barbarian topknot. The story went that Hippie Doc had once bandaged a wounded NVA and then stabbed him to death as he thanked Doc for saving his life. He was a good person and a damned fine medic—that is, if you were fighting on his side.

And there was Hill, a huge black machine gunner who wore size thirteen boots and carried an enormous Bowie knife that was always razor sharp. Hill had once stomped an NVA to death with those boots. Once when the former commander wanted trophies, he had cut off the heads of three NVA whom they had killed in the An Lao. The story didn't shock me by then. In August, I had met a 4th Infantry Division grunt wearing fourteen left ears around his neck on a green nylon cord. He had just returned from Duc Pho.

Billy, the black platoon sergeant, was idolized by his men, just as Sam had once been in Charlie Troop. Billy struck a sharp contrast to Red's replacement, a diminutive blond-haired, blue-eyed lieutenant. The soldiers called him Little Boy Blue. Thanh, our interpreter, was a wiry ex–Viet Cong who was usually into the fighting before the Americans could catch up with him. He was the complete opposite of Minh, Charlie Troop's college-educated interpreter. My radioman, Ray, was different from the rest. He was a draftee, a Nebraska Indian, a gentle person and a frightened one. He had no friends, perhaps because everybody else was black or white. I could never break through the shell that he, or our society, had placed around himself.

My only friend in the first days was a squad leader from Louisville, Barnett. He was tough like the others, but he was a draftee and wanted most of all to go home. He fought because he wanted to keep his soldiers and himself alive, not because he liked it. I usually rode with Barnett's squad, just as I had once ridden with Hobbs. So this was the platoon that Red had loved so much.

The scouts and gunships were different in Bravo Troop. In Charlie Troop, the little scout helicopters had worked in pairs called "white teams." The pairs of gunships were called "red teams." The common arrangement in Bravo Troop was a scout chopper below with a gunship covering it from higher up. These were the "pink teams." Because of this arrangement, scout pilots and gunners had a short life expectancy. It was often only weeks. Some did go home, usually wounded, and most had killed fifty or more NVA before their luck ran out. But scouts can't have all the fun. There was a group of Bravo Troop door gunners called the Mag-7. To become a member, you had to kill one hundred Communists. It was called the Mag-7 because there were seven founding members. Membership doubled at Chu Lai.

Marines had been in the region west of Chu Lai for years. They didn't have our helicopters and had been forced to fight an old-fashioned infantry war with the NVA choosing the ground. No one doubted the bravery of the Marines, but in Vietnam, courage was no substitute for innovation. Our first helicopter recons surprised NVA platoons in the open, day after day, in "liberated zones" that had gone unchallenged for years. They had never fought attacking helicopters like those of the 9th Cav, and their toll was enormous before they learned a few basic lessons. When the enemy started using camouflage again, and when the heavy machine guns atop the ridges became more practiced, our choppers began to crash. One of our troop commanders was shot down thirteen times at Chu Lai. Rescuing the commander became almost a joke after a while.

Something else was different at Chu Lai. We were fighting the 2d NVA Division, and they were not the frightened, hunted men of the 3d NVA Division to the south. The 2d NVA was far better armed, had the support of an intact Viet Cong organization, and had not been bludgeoned by the 1st Air Cav for two straight years. They were just as ruthless as us. At Chu Lai, I didn't learn to fear the NVA, but they taught us all respect.

Blue boarded the slicks on my second day and was flown over the flat, rocky countryside west of Chu Lai. I missed the coconut palms of the Bong Son Plains. Here was an ugly region of stunted trees, looking more like dwarf cedars than anything else. When we landed at the armored base, a slick pilot brought over a chessboard, and we sat down to a game in the shade of his machine. We didn't finish it.

Billy grabbed his harness and shouted to the platoon. "Let's go Blue! Got a mission!"

The village below us was neat, and the rice paddies were ready to harvest. The gunships led us in, rocketing a hedgerow and the trees behind it. Then we jumped. Five NVA in green uniforms were already dead beside the hedgerow. Three more broke from

143

its cover and rushed at us, firing their AKs from waist level. They were shot down in one deafening volley from twenty rifles. Bullets clacked by from deeper in the village, and we belly-crawled among the bodies, using them for cover. A scout chopper hovered over our heads as the gunner fired into the first hooches. At least a dozen AKs shot back. Billy hesitated, listening to a message from the pilots.

"Pull back to the paddies! Pull back! They don't want us in deeper! Pull back to the paddies!"

The scout chopper drew the NVA fire as we ran along the hedgerow. Abandoned weapons were everywhere. The hedgerow concealed a long trench. Barnett looked to one side as we rounded the corner and saw two more NVA below the bushes. He killed them with one long burst, then lobbed a grenade for effect. We hid behind the paddy dikes as slicks clattered in at rice paddy level to extract us. That was my introduction to Chu Lai. The NVA there were living in prosperous villages, untouched by years of war.

The scouts and gunships continued killing NVA in the village all day. I silently prayed that none of the helicopters would be shot down. The vacation with Dusty Delta was really over.

I was with James's squad on a one-ship raid. The scouts had cornered a wounded VC somewhere in a streambed. The troop commander needed more information about this area, and we were going to capture the man. Hill stepped forward and fired his machine gun in an arc across the stream. When the hammering stopped, a man in black pajamas with a bullet hole in his shoulder stood up behind a boulder in the middle of the stream. He was about ten feet from where I stood. He raised his hands to surrender, and three rifles and a machine gun banged away. The VC didn't seem surprised at what was happening to him. His expression didn't change as he dropped back into the water with a loud splash. I was too stunned to speak.

When we arrived back at the armored base, a scout gunner walked over to the place where James's men were lounging in the shade. "Why didn't you guys take that gook prisoner? We could have greased him."

Hill laughed harshly. "Man, you know better'n to ask questions like that."

The gunner backed away. He was afraid of Hill. "What the hell? But we do need prisoners once in a while."

Thanh brought us a middle-aged Vietnamese woman. She had escaped from a village with an NVA garrison, and Blue was being sent to rescue her family. Our pink teams had already scouted the area and reported that it looked deserted. Send in Blue.

The troop had a gung ho commander who loved phosphorous rockets. This was one of his last missions before going home, and he wanted to do it right. It had been a picture postcard village before the gunships made run after run with high explosive and phosphorous rockets, blowing hooches apart and setting fire to everything. The troop made war more violently, but with the same weapons I had seen so many times before.

Now we were in the furnace. Billy was on one of his last missions, too. He was nervous as he formed the platoon into a line. I was walking past a burning haystack when something moved in a bunker in front of me. I hesitated a split second before firing, and an old farmer ran out. The Blue beside me had seen the whole thing.

"Why didn't you shoot him, man?"

"He's a farmer!"

He spat at the farmer in disgust and clicked his rifle off safety. "Hell, that's no excuse."

As if to emphasize the farmer's right to live, the woman ran up to him and grabbed his hands. They embraced, then went back into the bunker and led out three terrified little boys. Thanh questioned the farmer about the NVA company we had been expecting. Then he turned to Billy.

"He says the company is away at another village. They left behind two clerks in this village. They live in a hooch ahead of us."

145

Billy looked at the pinched faces around him and said softly, "Let's go, Blue. Nobody takes chances."

The fires were behind us when we reached the clerks' hooch. It looked empty, but there was a big rock bunker underneath the entire floor. Blues covered both entrances to the bunker, while Hill shouted the usual brutal words.

"*Lai day! Lai day!*"

A green-clad NVA emerged from the front entrance, his arms raised in surrender. Hill shoved him out of the way. "Dude's buddy must still be in there. *Lai day! Lai day!*"

A soldier emptied his rifle into the rear entrance. The man inside scrambled to a far corner and shot his pistol. Another long burst into the front entrance. Another pistol shot.

"Come out, motherfucker! *Lai day! Lai day!*"

A Blue shrugged, ever so coldly, and lobbed a grenade into the bunker. The crash reverberated off the rock walls, then he was dragging out a corpse in a green uniform. He returned a second time and found two pistols, a stack of typed papers and carbons, and a portable typewriter in a green cardboard case. The farmer wasn't joking when he told us they were clerks. I could imagine the horror of two American clerks trapped by the NVA infantry.

The prisoner's eyes were shifting from his comrade's body to an open rice paddy, then back to the body. I knew he wanted to run and hoped that he wasn't stupid enough to try it. Suddenly, a Blue pushed him in the direction of the paddy. The prisoner stumbled and fell. The Blue yanked him to his feet, pointed him in the direction of the paddy, and yelled in his ear, "*Di di,* motherfucker! *Di di!*" He gave the NVA a hard shove, and the man ran for his life. The Blue let him fight his way through the water to the middle of the first paddy field before he killed him with one short burst. He turned back to the other impassive faces and laughed, "Got some." We had to step over the body as we filed into the rice paddy for pickup.

Billy was relieved that the mission was over. As the slicks lifted us out of the paddies, many AKs opened up from the next village. They had been close enough to see the clerk die. Perhaps they were the clerks' company. The place we had been was a pleasant region, an Asian farmer's paradise. It was as prosperous and secure under NVA control as the area around Bong Son was under ARVN control. I wondered if the form of government really mattered to those Asian farmers.

Billy made one last landing with Blue to collect the remains of a scout pilot and gunner. They had been killed from a bunker on a jungle hill at the western edge of the Que Son Valley. The chopper had exploded and burned. It was just long enough to see again the mist creeping through the jungle trees. Just long enough to smell again the reek of burned flesh and stinking paddy mud. Just long enough to be a pallbearer once again. Then Billy was gone. Only a face in a long line of faces.

Tomorrow night we'd make the ABC "Six O'Clock News." A red-haired Australian and another man, perhaps a Japanese, were traveling with Little Boy Blue. The Asian cameraman was dressed in the same fatigues we wore, while the Australian fellow wore Chino trousers and a neatly pressed safari shirt. I hoped the NVA didn't find the target too tempting to pass up. As the platoon moved out of a rice paddy, a gunship roared overhead, firing rockets at a treeline. I pointed my arm, telling the news team to get down or be hit by fragments, and the Australian snapped a picture.

We ran into the village, making a great show of throwing grenades into wells and empty bunkers. The blast had to be just right, or they'd turn off the camera and hunt for special effects elsewhere. They filmed three wells being grenaded before they had the effect they were after. Some of the Blues "captured" a couple of scared farmers hiding in a hooch. The newsmen filmed away. Soon the folks back home would see our smiling faces on the tube. The Blues were going to be stars.

I picked up a copy of the *Stars and Stripes* two days later and saw myself in a blow-up on page one. A mustached soldier with grenades and a belt of machine gun ammunition across his chest was shouting and pointing. The caption read, "The Charge of the Third Brigade. A squad leader of the Third Brigade of the First

Cavalry Division leads a charge across a rice paddy near Tam Ky. Four Viet Cong were killed in the assault.'' That was me telling the news team to take cover. My parents sent the picture from the hometown newspaper, along with others showing us ''fighting in a Viet Cong village'' as we lobbed grenades into empty bunkers and ''capturing Viet Cong'' as farmers were led through the doorway of a hooch. Other Blues were receiving the same pictures from their families.

We had also made the evening news. We had been in the village for a reason. The door gunners had shot four NVA in a trench behind an old woman's home. The platoon had collected their rifles and equipment and burned the hooch. People in America had seen a wailing little woman standing outside her burning home, but no bodies or weapons. I still wonder today who edited out the footage of the dead NVA and biased the whole report. The Army was flooded with letters of protest. We were being called villains. About a week after the village incident, Little Boy Blue called a platoon meeting.

''We've got orders from higher up that there will be no more burning of hooches in populated areas. Is that understood?'' His answer was a chorus of hoots and laughs. ''What this really means is watch what you do when there's newsmen around. Our CO got his ass chewed because we burned that gook's hut.''

More calls and grunts. Someone in the back of the group said softly; ''Little Boy Blue, come blow my horn.''

The lieutenant quickly developed hearing problems. ''What?'' A long moment of embarrassed silence, then ''That's all I have. Dismissed.''

We were in another of the prosperous villages in the enemy zone. Several NVA had already been killed by the scouts. One of them had been shooting from an underwater platform in a well. He would pop up to fire, then duck underneath the water when the choppers hovered over. A scout gunner had killed him by dropping a grenade into the well. Village wells at Chu Lai were often concealed entrances to underground tunnel systems. We always tried to collapse them with grenades or plastic explosives.

As we walked in a line through a grove of trees, a Vietnamese ran at us, waving a pistol in the air and shouting. He fired a shot, then ran into a hooch. Hill emptied two entire belts of machine gun ammo into the hooch. The man had been shot through both legs and crawled into the courtyard, leaving a glistening trail of blood. Thanh kneeled beside him. A brief exchange in Vietnamese.

"Are you a Viet Cong?"

"Yes, traitor!"

Thanh drew his pistol and shot the man through the head. Another squad had found a wounded NVA lying in the grass a few yards from the courtyard. They switched their rifles to automatic as the man begged for mercy. Five rifles sent his body jumping along the grass. The bullets tore him to pieces. A Midwestern rifleman, Dubois, wanted a momento.

"Has anybody got any color film left? I just shot my last picture."

Always the same answer. "Sorry, man. I'm all out, too."

As we returned through the village, soldiers set fire to the hooch where Thanh had killed the Viet Cong. I stayed behind when they were gone, watching an old woman wailing beside the body and the flames. Green rice shoots waved in the breeze behind her. This one time, I wanted to stay there with her and not return to the armored base with those human scorpions. I gathered a handful of rice and took it to her, holding it out in the palm of my hand. She stared through me and started to cry again. Her arms were raised to heaven, calling down the wrath of something in the clouds. I let the rice fall to the ground and ran to find the platoon. The slicks soon took us back to the armored base.

Paul from the Division Press Office was visiting. He was an old friend of this Blue platoon and spent most of his time flying as a door gunner or making landings. At night, he'd tape-record messages to our family and friends and send them to hometown radio stations. That was supposed to be why he was with the troop. Everyone liked Paul. He was a quiet, polite, scholarly young man with glasses, whose main ambition in life was to be a professional newsman. He looked like everyone's idea of the nice, clean-cut boy next door. Here the resemblance ended.

Paul had won the troop's respect by making the most dangerous landings at Duc Pho. One day there, he was with a gunship when they slaughtered an enemy squad in a mountain valley. He volunteered to gather the weapons, jumped, and almost got his head blown off by a Viet Cong in the bushes. Paul ran him down, shot him, and captured the British Webley revolver he now wore on his belt. Paul was never without his prized pistol. It had a big lanyard ring on the butt and broke open at the top for loading, and he was always eager to demonstrate the loading technique and tell the story of how he acquired it. Everyone in the Blues marveled that such a nice person could be so brave.

Paul and I were talking about the An Lao one evening. "That's one bad valley, Matt. Bravo Blues were always getting in contact there. You knew Red. In some ways, it was worse than Duc Pho. Duc Pho is what made these guys so vicious. I saw them change. The gooks down there were some bad dudes."

"All they talk about is Duc Pho and the An Lao. Charlie Troop lost a lot of good people in the An Lao, too. I hear the Cav was fighting there even in 1966."

He nodded. "They've always been fighting there, even the French. No one knows how many men have died for that one place. There ought to be a song about it when the war is over."

"We had one in Charlie Troop. It rhymes with the airborne running cadence.

"Bo-diddy, bo-diddy, really got to go,
Gonna air assault in the old An Lao.

NVA guerrillas a runnin' all around,
Firing thirty cal machine guns a close to the ground.

> Four choppers in to the old LZ,
> One goes down, but not the other three.''

"That kind of tells the story. You know? Nobody in America will ever hear about the An Lao. It would just be a place with a funny name."

"They all have funny names."

Paul was with us for the battle of November tenth. The armored squadron from our base was moving toward the western edge of the Hiep Duc Valley. Troop gunships were scouting villages through a pass, a few miles farther to the west. The villages were supposed to be the armor's objective, but they would never reach them. APCs were already being destroyed by 75mm recoilless rifles, and tanks were trying to knock them out. Our gunships were being fired on from at least a battalion of NVA in the villages, and a Cav infantry company was landed nearby. Then two of our gunships were shot out of the air, and we were sent to rescue the crews.

The slicks flew over the green wreckage of old Marine Corps choppers. Once they had come this far. Soon, the brown wreckage of Army choppers would litter the same paddies. We passed a staggered line of blasted Marine APCs, destroyed in some forgotten battle. A thousand yards beyond them were five burning Army APCs. The tanks looked like brown beetles as they crawled around a hedgerow, firing cannon into what looked like clumps of bushes. This had been "Indian country" for longer than the Americans had been in Vietnam, and the Cav was finally overstepping itself by trying to retake it.

The villages had been bombed by B-52s in the past, but were now rebuilt and prosperous. Among the hooches were incredibly tall coconut palms, looking like a forest of giant telephone poles. To the north of the second village was a grassy hill littered with the wreckage of Marine and Army helicopters. Someone long before had named it Million Dollar Hill, because of the expensive machines that had crashed there. The two brown choppers were ours.

The crew we were after had run for the safety of the infantry

151

company. One shipload of Blues banked away from our flight and was landed near the hill. The Blues and the crew were pinned down for long minutes and were finally rescued by a brave slick pilot. As the rest of us waited above the battle, all that reached our ears was a continuous crackle of rifle and machine gun fire. The commander decided that he wouldn't risk twenty men so far outside of artillery range, so our flight headed back to the armored base.

As we passed over the tank-recoilless rifle battle, bullets rattled past the slicks from a tiny hamlet of three hooches. Two rocket ships dived at the target. When the first rockets hit around the hooches, a huge black explosion and a shock wave rose from the hamlet. The blast almost knocked the rocket ships out of the air and slammed the slicks sideways. When the smoke was gone, only denuded palm trees and raw earth remained. The hooches had disappeared. The NVA had been guarding an ammunition dump. This region was pure death.

Back at the armored base, the Blues from the rescue ship looked pale and nervous. Paul had been with them, and he was obviously shaken by the experience. I was curious, as usual.

"What happened down there, Paul?"

He sucked in a deep breath before answering. "The gunship crew was hiding in some bushes and ran to us as soon as we landed. They had been caught in a cross fire between the grunts and the gooks."

"That fire sounded pretty bad down there."

"God, I never heard so many AKs in my life. You wouldn't have wanted to be there. The grunts were scared to death. They said the rice paddies in their LZ had deep pits with stakes and steel animal traps in the bottom. They couldn't get out their wounded. They were all digging and shooting at the same time. It was a mistake to put them in. We wouldn't have got out of there at all, if some lift pilots didn't have a lot of balls."

We talked with one of the rescued door gunners later in the afternoon. He was still trembling from his experience.

"We started making a rocket run on this village, and the whole place opened up on us. The chopper in front took hits and went down, then we started taking hits. We circled back to draw their fire. Our rocket tubes were so full of holes they couldn't be used, so we went in with door guns and the last of the minigun ammo. The whole ship was shaking from hits, and I knew I'd never live to see the end of that run. I just kept shooting at flashes and hoping I was taking a bunch of gooks with me. Then we auto-rotated into that clearing and saw the grunts waving at us. Poor bastards. They're still out there, and a lot of them ain't coming back.''

This was a more even war than the one being waged at Bong Son. The 9th Cav wasn't fighting squads and platoons now. Paul left for greener pastures later the same evening.

CHAPTER 11

One Keg of Beer

(November–December 1967)

We were on one-ship raids called Hawk Flights. Single slicks swooped down throughout the western Que Son Valley, taking prisoners. Finding them was easy because the North Vietnamese were harvesting the rice fields alongside the farmers. I was riding with Barnett's squad when our door gunner started shouting.

"James's boys just killed three gooks with carbines. Blues will sweep the area." He paused for a moment, then shouted with more urgency. "Six is down! We'll rendezvous with the other birds and go in to secure him! They have a prisoner!"

We laughed at the thought of the new major getting himself shot down again. The other slicks arrived, and we were flown to the northwest. Below us was the gunship, sitting in water up to its belly in a rocky rice paddy between two long villages. The slicks dropped toward the gunship, the door gunners opened fire, and the world below me lit up. Dozens of flashes from both villages.

A man in green ran along the edge of the village I was facing, fired a volley from his AK at my slick, reloaded, and fired again. I shot in his direction until he stumbled, either hit or diving for cover. We were ducks in a shooting gallery. A tracer came through the door beside me and disappeared into the roof of the chopper. Our slick shuddered with hits.

The slicks came in at high speed beside the downed gunship, and we had to jump ten feet into the paddies from the speeding

154

machines. The pilots wanted to get out of there in a hurry. The fall knocked a canteen and a grenade loose from my harness. My helmet was lost somewhere in the muddy water. The slicks crossed part of the long village to the south, followed by the deep stuttering of heavy machine guns firing above the continuous clatter of AKs. Barnett's eyes were a study in terror as he told me that two of our four slicks had been shot down.

One Blue was already dead with a bullet through the neck. We formed a circle defense around the gunship crew and its prisoner. This young NVA had been standing in the center of the rice paddies as the major flew over. It looked like an easy way to capture a prisoner, but he was a decoy to draw us into a trap. He was drugged completely out of his mind. He had probably been given morphine to ease the pain if he was shot.

Two NVA broke from the rocks to our east and ran for the village to our north. Two Blues killed them. Two more NVA ran from the rocks to our west. Hill toppled them with long bursts from his machine gun. Now bullets came at us from every direction, ploughing into the paddy dikes, careening off rocks, kicking up water spouts. We swam in the stinking water and tried to keep our weapons dry.

I heard the major telling Little Boy Blue to attack a low ridge to our south. Our grenadiers fired about thirty grenades into the brush along the ridge. They exploded out of sight. Four machine gunners stood up in a line and sprayed the ridge. The major turned to Little Boy Blue.

"Okay. Let's move to the high ground."

The Blues started backing away from the ridge. It had to be well defended. Our lieutenant was thinking. "Sir, I'd like to have a squad check the ridge before committing the entire platoon."

The major saw how afraid we were. "Okay. Get them moving."

James's squad ran into the bushes and was pinned down by a hail of bullets. Then they were scrambling back. James ran up to the major. "Sir, there's a trench up there! They were firing at us from all along it, but we couldn't see the flashes!"

155

The major grabbed a radio handset. "We'll have the gunships hit it."

Two gunships roared in parallel to us, sending rockets crashing down the length of the trench. A scout chopper popped over the top of the ridge and crossed the trench at an angle. The major listened to the scout's report. There was a heavy machine gun at each end of the trench. Behind it were rock bunkers about every fifteen yards. One of the bunkers had been cracked open by a rocket, killing two NVA. Assaulting the hill with eighteen Blues and four gunship crewmen would be suicide.

A scout chopper hovered over a pile of boulders to our north. A single shot, then another. The scouts told the major that they had a "gook with a pistol" hiding in the rocks. The gunner fired his machine gun as the chopper made a tight circle and headed back to the boulders. It hovered there for an instant before a long burst of submachine gun fire tore pieces of plastic and metal from its body. The scouts weaved about a hundred yards down the paddy and crashed. A gunship roared over to pick up the crew. It was chased all the way in and out of the paddy by machine guns from the villages. Barnett jabbed his thumb in the direction where the scouts had crashed.

"Gook was squeezing off rounds from a grease gun to lure in the scout bird. Then he zapped him. These boys know what they're doing."

The afternoon became a nightmare for us as one chopper after another was shot down. Other ships flew through the incredible racket to rescue the crews. Some of them made it. At one point in the battle, the NVA blew up one of our downed slicks. Gunships killed the demolition squad as they ran toward another one. Pairs of gunships circled over the villages, one drawing heavy machine gun fire while the other dived on the weapons. It started getting dark.

Another twelve-seven was firing from a ruined building to the west. Something had to mark it for the gunships. Two of us stood thirty yards apart and slowly fired tracers at the building. The target was where the tracers crossed. The whole thing took less than a minute, but it was one of the longest minutes in my life.

We dropped back to cover just as the AKs cut the air where we had been standing. Two gunships rocketed the ruined building. No more fire from there. It was totally dark now and artillery support was my responsibility, but Ray had the radio. He had refused to jump with the rest of us and had been fortunate enough to be aboard the only slick that wasn't shot down. He was now back at the armored base with a bunch of shipless crews. Ray had done this to us twice before.

A whoosh from the ridge. Something erupted in the water beside the major's gunship. The next round slammed into its side, breaking it apart like a toy. We pressed ourselves farther into the mud and water as the gas tank exploded and thousands of rounds of ammunition cooked off. The flames were turning the rice paddy around us into daylight as the major radioed an orbiting chopper.

"Saber relay, this is Saber Six. I just had my bird totaled by a recoilless rifle. Over." A pause. "Roger that. Out." He motioned for Little Boy Blue. "We've got an infantry company that's going to try to break through to us."

Grunts from the 4th Infantry Division had landed on the other side of the ridge. We huddled behind the bushes on our side of the ridge as the gunship burned and bullets from the infantry battle whizzed over our heads. The far side of the ridge was a drumbeat of grenade explosions and crashes. Sergeant Cruz, Billy's replacement, lowered his handset. His expression told us that he didn't have any good news.

"Hell. The infantry didn't make it. They got to the ridge and then had three killed and five wounded trying to take some bunkers." More crashes. "Now they're being hit with mortars." The NVA were using us as bait in a bigger trap.

The flames from the gunship fizzled, the firefight was dying, and there was almost complete silence for a few minutes. The major told us that reinforcements were on the way to our paddy. Six slicks brought in another grunt platoon, guiding on the squad leaders' flashlights. They came in low over the ridge, and we scrambled away from spinning tail rotors and jumping men. The slicks took off due north over the other village. Someone should have warned them. Strings of big tracers crossed over the village, and one of the slicks disintegrated in a ball of flame.

Cruz was listening again. He spoke with a tired voice. "They lost two choppers to twelve-sevens." As if to finish the thought, a mortar round whistled in and covered me with stinking rice paddy mud.

Dawn finally came. The grunts had spent the night facing north and digging. We had stayed below the ridge, expecting the NVA to come through the bushes at any moment. The illumination flares had kept them away. The word was passed that Blue would be extracted by the troop's one remaining slick, covered by the one remaining scout chopper. That was all that was left of twenty-six helicopters.

The scout pilot flew bravely along the village to the north while the gunner poured tracers into the trees and hooches. The slick followed the rice paddies between the two long villages, flying only a few inches above the paddy dikes. The major's crew, the prisoner, and a few Blues jumped aboard and it was gone. A command helicopter, carrying the battalion commander of the grunts with us, flew over at about fifteen hundred feet. A machine gun stuttered, and the chopper began spinning like a top. I watched through exhausted eyes as a door gunner was flung from his seat and fell to his death in the paddies. The helicopter followed seconds later, spinning around in circles until it crashed and exploded. Scratch one colonel.

I wanted no more fighting that day. If only Martin were there. I wanted to see that reassuring face one last time. I turned to Barnett. "You think they'll use us to sweep those villages?"

We saw each other's fear. "Naw. They'll use the grunts. We've got only two choppers left. It's too big for us to handle."

"I don't know if it matters. Tomorrow we'll be in another hassle and might all be dead."

He frowned at me. Those were forbidden words. "That could happen, but you just don't think about it. Cool it. You've been shot at before."

We were the last slick-load out of that paddy. The slick flew over the south village, climbing as quickly as possible. A machine gun started firing from the village, and we responded like crazy men, firing every rifle, machine gun, and grenade launcher we had at the flashes. Then the NVA machine gun was behind us. We were later told that one of the units facing us was an antiaircraft battalion. They had shot down twenty-seven Cav helicopters.

I found Ray sitting on top of a bunker at the edge of the armored base. He saw me coming and tried to avoid my eyes. "Why didn't you jump?"

He looked away. "The choppers were too high. I was afraid of breaking a leg. I'm sorry. It was too high to jump."

"God dammit! Everybody else jumped. That's the third time it's happened. I'm not going to make any more excuses for you. Catch the next chopper back to An Khe and tell them I said you could come back. I won't make an official report. Get a job driving a jeep or something and lay off the booze. Got it?"

He slid down from the bunker. "Yes, Sergeant. Thanks."

I had to make sure that Ray stayed away from the Troop, or the Blues would settle his bravery problems for him. "Ray?"

"Huh?"

"Don't come back around Bravo Troop. Don't ever show your face around here again." He nodded and quickly walked away. I never saw him again. I don't even know how he managed to get out of the armored base.

The platoon was taken back to Chu Lai one load at a time. The day's troubles weren't over yet. As Barnett's squad got off the slick, a Marine MP spotted us. He walked over with his hands on his belt. "You guys need a shave." He saw that I didn't have a helmet. "Where's your cover, soldier?"

Barnett interrupted his lecture. "Look, our tents are right over there. We'll clean up when we get there."

"That still doesn't tell me why you look like a bunch of tramps. I'll have to report this to your commanding officer." Goddamned fucking jarhead!

We started laughing and he turned deep red. "Go ahead. His tent's right over there. The major looks like a tramp right now,

159

too. Man, we haven't slept in a couple of days, and we spent the night in a fuckin' rice paddy. Get off our case, will you?''

His voice was subdued when he asked, "You guys burps?"

"No. We carry around all these guns 'cause we like how they look."

He shuffled his feet like he wanted to run away and forget that he ever saw us. "Sorry. I was in the burps myself for a while. We just don't see many this far back." I wondered if he was baiting us again.

Barnett explained. "We're an air rifle platoon. Sort of a special unit."

Sheepishly he said, "Oh. I didn't know that. Please have a nice day."

The respite from war only lasted a few days. Soon we were waiting at the armored base as our new helicopters scoured the countryside for signs of the enemy. They weren't hard to find at Chu Lai. An area of "good hunting" was the coast along the South China Sea, about halfway between Chu Lai and Da Nang. On one of the first recons along this stretch of coast, a scout chopper surprised and killed a column of thirteen NVA. The major wanted to send the Blues to collect the weapons and papers, but first he sent another pink team to look the place over. The pink teams passed each other in the air, one coming back to the armored base to refuel, the other heading toward the coast. There was a period of about five minutes when the sky above the bodies was empty. When the second team arrived, there were only dark bloodstains in the sand and drag paths leading into the hedgerows and palm trees. The commander didn't send the Blues to investigate.

There was a place on the shore where a river emptied into the sea. Coastal fishing sampans brought NVA replacements down the river each night and landed them along the south bank in an area that we called the "one-man bunkers." Men sat in those tiny bunkers in the sand all day long, waiting for a helicopter to fly over. The bunkers were almost impossible to locate and destroy, and their only purpose seemed to be to shoot at aircraft. The pilots dreaded pulling reconnaissance flights over the one-man bunkers. No matter how many NVA they found and killed, more would always be waiting the next day.

One rainy day in November, Blue was landed on a narrow island in the river north of the one-man bunkers. Five NVA had been killed by the scouts before we arrived, and James's squad killed three more who were hiding in the tall grass. The whole affair reminded me of a rabbit hunt. Blues sank the sampans along the beach with grenades and then walked in a line toward a large earth bunker. Cruz motioned for us to approach the bunker with caution.

"Gunbirds took fire from here. Let's see what we've got."

Dubois looked inside one end of the bunker, and a burst from

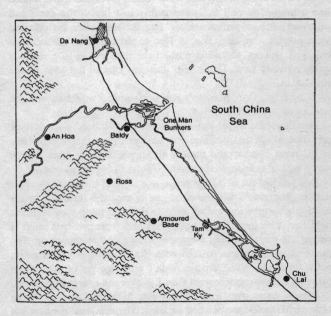

161

an AK missed him by inches. He hopped out of the way while two other Blues rolled grenades into both entrances. The cordite smoke lingered in the humid air of the bunker, so James pulled on a gas mask and crawled inside. He dragged out the inevitable bodies—a man and two women in green uniforms. The Vietnamese had carried medical bags, grenades, and two rifles, including a captured Marine Corps M-14. The bunker was a protective storehouse for crates of medical supplies, and the island had been some sort of medical facility. That explained why eleven NVA had put up no real resistance to our attack. They had probably never been in a battle before.

James found a badly wounded little girl of about seven hidden under a pile of baskets and rags. She was dressed in a pint-sized green NVA uniform and had waist-length black hair. She looked like a limp little doll as James gently laid her in the grass and pillowed her head with a medical bag. Dubois raised his rifle and took careful aim, and Hippie Doc exploded. Doc grabbed the collar of Dubois' shirt and pushed the rifle to one side. Dubois wrestled away from Doc's grip, but was careful not to raise the rifle again.

"Come on, Doc. She ain't gonna make it. I might as well put her out of her misery."

Doc thrust his finger to within an inch of Dubois' nose. "Back off! You touch that girl and you answer to me, baby!" No one in his right mind would mess with Hippie Doc. Dubois walked away with a hangdog expression. He didn't say another word.

Doc patched the child's grenade wounds and called for an evacuation chopper. When it arrived, he carried the little girl to the waiting crewmen and asked them to do everything they could to help her. The loving way he treated and protected that child is one of the most touching memories I have of that crazy war. The medevac chopper was painted with big red crosses on its sides, belly, and nose. The crosses didn't stop dozens of AKs from firing as it flew south toward Chu Lai over the one-man bunkers.

Barnett came over to talk later that night at Chu Lai. "The little girl Hippie Doc patched up died. The one-man bunkers got her."

162

"What a shame. Does Doc know about it yet?"

"He knows. I just saw him crying out on the flight line. He doesn't want anyone to see him. He's taking it real hard." Doc was going home in a few weeks. He had experienced enough brutality.

We were in the area of the one-man bunkers. A gunship had been shot down and we were sent to guard it. One squad was still there while the rest of us walked ahead of a company from the 4th Infantry Division. They had been in a battle earlier in the day and weren't anxious for another. About a dozen young NVA prisoners carried many of their packs. The Vietnamese were all strong, well-fed new troops from the one-man bunkers. Each stared silently ahead as he stumbled under the weight of two or three heavy infantry packs.

We entered a sandy hedgerow area. AKs clacked from the hooches to the east, and the Blue squads ran forward, spraying the huts. I had a grenade launcher and fired it like a mortar, trying to put some grenades behind the NVA. I had seen an NVA killed that way in Charlie Troop. A new grenadier had fired his elephant gun at rifle flashes on our side of a hill, but he was aiming too high. We found a dead NVA in a clearing on the other side of the hill, surrounded by little 40mm grenade craters. He had been running away from us, but his luck had been bad that day.

We were almost to the hooches when we looked around and realized that we were alone. The infantry had changed direction to the south. A big Chinook helicopter with our gunship slung beneath it flew over our heads to the south. At least twenty AKs opened up and a Chinook crewman dropped a red smoke grenade to mark the target. Our gunships rocketed the area and told us to watch for more one-man bunkers dug into sandy embankments beneath coconut palms.

The Blue platoon headed south, firing as we walked. Again we were alone. The infantry company commander had decided to stop and eat lunch. The Blues were openly cursing them, and moods were getting ugly, when our commander called us back

163

for pickup. No matter where they walked, those soldiers would eventually have to fight.

There was another side to Chu Lai. The evenings there were quite pleasant. The defenses of the base were manned by Marines and ARVNs, so we spent the nights cleaning weapons or sipping drinks at a beachside club. The base was occasionally rocketed, but the NVA were after the big planes at the airfield, not our puny helicopters.

The other diversion was pestering the Marines and Sea Bees. Blue had never forgiven the Marine MPs for their harassment on several occasions and returned the compliment at every opportunity. The Sea Bees were our enemies only because we vaguely knew that they had something to do with the Marines. In all our dealings with the Sea Bees, they treated us with respect. They even let us eat in their mess hall, overlooking the fact that we often smelled like walking garbage dumps and wore Army insignia. We repaid their kindness by stealing two of their big generators.

The Blues made it clear to passing rear echelon types that our tents were off limits to them. Someone placed a skull with a Viet Cong bush hat at the entrance to our tent street. That seemed to frighten them a bit. The Marine MPs complained that the skull wasn't sanitary, but it stayed in place. But that was only the evenings.

December fifth had been a quiet day. Blue hadn't even left the armored base, and I was in the middle of my fourth game of chess with a slick pilot. The pink teams were making one last circuit over the Hiep Duc—Que Son Valley, and then we could go back to Chu Lai.

Cruz dropped the handset he was monitoring and shouted, "Let's go Blue! On the double!"

As the slicks lifted over the barbed wire of the armored base, the door gunner beside me explained the mission. "Somebody shot at the major's gunship in the Que Son Valley. Broke the gunner's arm. Major's mad as hell and wants the gook that did it.''

The slicks dropped toward a ridge north of an artillery base called Ross. The gunships were rocketing a grassy knoll on the ridge while a scout ship hovered over a twin knoll, pumping tracers into a jumble of boulders. We jumped onto the grassy knoll as the last gunship was climbing away from its rocket run. Cruz pointed to the red smoke floating above the short trees and boulders on the other knoll.

''They've got bunkers up there. James's squad move toward the hill. Second squad cover them with your machine gun.''

James's boys ran into a depression between the knolls while the machine gun chipped and scarred the boulders above them. As the first line reached the boulders, we ran to join them. There were four bodies in American camouflaged uniforms beside the first boulders. I thought for a brief second that we were attacking an ARVN reconnaissance unit, then two men in green NVA uniforms raised themselves up from a pit dug underneath the same boulders. Two Blues shot them from a distance of about one foot. Dubois had fired point-blank into a man's head. Now he wiped brains from his helmet and face and cursed. The other one had been wearing glasses. I lifted them off the ground and noticed that they were bifocals. He was the first NVA I had ever seen with glasses.

A body in a khaki uniform was lying facedown in a trench behind the boulders. I looked down at him, and he was suddenly pointing an SKS rifle at my stomach. Two Blues shot him as they walked by me and kept right on walking. James sprayed a bush above the trench, and a body in black pajamas rolled away. He stopped long enough to remove a leather belt hung with a Chinese compass, a map case, and a Russian pistol. He tossed the equipment to me.

''Here, Matt. I got an outfit like this a minute ago. Dude moved when they shot his buddy in the trench. This is great!'' He meant the killing.

There were more bodies in camouflaged uniforms scattered across the knoll. The scouts had been busy. Most of the dead

NVA wore golden rings engraved with Vietnamese characters. I thought at the time that they were wedding bands, although I had never before seen the enemy wearing them. They were probably the command rings of high officers.

The platoon reached the crest of the knoll and headed downhill, blasting the trees below us with rifles, machine guns, and grenade launchers. Two NVA ran out of the trees and charged our line, firing short bursts from their AKs. Bullets knocked them back down the slope until they collapsed in two khaki heaps. More AKs flashed from hooches hidden under the trees. A gunship hovered over our heads like a guardian angel and blew the hooches apart with rockets and cannon shells. A thatched roof rose about ten feet into the air and then burst into flames. Now Cruz was ordered to pull us back to the grassy knoll for extraction.

Souvenirs were everywhere on the knoll. We grabbed pistols, compasses, Chinese binoculars, map cases, pouches of documents, and rifles. One of the maps had the crossed sabers of the 9th Cav still visible under the plastic. It had American positions marked in red and Communist positions marked in blue. It was the same system we used—good guys in blue and bad guys in red. I looked down at Ross through a pair of Chinese binoculars and could see every tent, bunker, and artillery piece in the base. These had to be NVA forward observers planning a rocket and mortar attack.

We hid the trophies under our shirts to keep the officers from seeing them. Half the platoon looked pregnant by the time the slicks came in. The Blues stayed awake until early the next morning, counting booty from the "gook FOs." We had an American .45 automatic, six Tokarev pistols, two Makarev automatics with red stars on their handles, nine wide leather officer's belts, and three wide canvas belts with big stars on their buckles.

The major had heard about the trophies by the next evening, and all the pistols were collected. These Blues had previously had some bad experiences with officers taking their souvenirs for "intelligence purposes" and then keeping them. To be as fair as possible, we had given all the compasses and binoculars to the pilots who had protected us on that knoll. A group of us went to ask the major to return our pistols, and he told us what we had found that day.

"First of all, don't worry about the pistols. We needed them to confirm some things. The pistols will be returned. You men did a good job out there two days ago. But if you had turned those pistols in sooner, we might have known what we had bagged and could have inserted an infantry company or something.

"We wiped out what we believe was the command post of the Third Regiment, Second NVA Division. The documents and other evidence show that nine of the seventeen kills were officers. Some of them were division staff, including the division's commissar and its intelligence officer. There was a full colonel, a regimental commander, three majors, and four senior captains. Some of the equipment they had was taken from the troop's helicopters on November thirteenth. You men might be interested to know that the highest ranking NVA officer killed until now was a captain." We were interested.

I didn't know it at the time, but that raid marked the high point of morale among the Blues. In many ways it was one of the last triumphs of an era and a style of war that the Army in Vietnam would never again experience. That night the Blues went to the beachside club and celebrated, singing their favorite song for hours.

> Glorious, glorious,
> One keg of beer for the four of us.
> We're happy as can be,
> My comrades and me,
> For we are members of the in-fan-try!

We landed on the knoll a few days later. The trench and the pit underneath the boulders had been used as graves. One bloated purple corpse had been left unburied, staring at the sky from the mud of a trail. Perhaps he was the one who had shot at the major's helicopter. As I stepped over the body, a large black roach crawled from a bullet hole in its forehead. It would have shocked me once.

167

The gunships finished the destruction of the 3d NVA Regiment's command post about a month later. This time it was the common soldiers, the sergeants, and the privates. They were found wandering through rice paddies north of the armored base. A company of the 4th Infantry Division swept through the area as our choppers hunted down each cluster of enemy soldiers. I listened on my artillery radio as a skeptical battalion commander issued orders to his troops. He told the company commander to "see how many dinks are down there and how many are really dead." A group of us crowded around the radio and listened, cursing the 4th Division colonel for his smart-assed remarks.

The company commander's reply came about thirty minutes later. "They're all dead. We've got bodies everywhere." The colonel ended the afternoon with praise for our gunners and an apology to our major. Ninety-nine NVA were dead. Many of them had been carrying two or three rifles from those who had died in other battles. The Blues were still angry. We didn't want other soldiers doing our work.

We are south of the Marine base called Baldy. The gunships have been in contact here. It's an old B-52 strike zone, and the Blues run from crater to crater, shooting it out with the people hiding there. It's a strange group. There's an old man, two women, younger men of various ages. They have an even odder assortment of weapons. Old American rifles, carbines, two bolt-action French rifles, two German Mausers, grenades. This is the first bunch of pure Viet Cong we've seen at Chu Lai.

The four Vietnamese killed by the gunships have enormous bags of rice strapped to their backs. The rice bags are stamped with the Hands Across the Sea emblem of the American aid agency. The Blues have killed four of these people as they popped out of craters to shoot at us. After the NVA we've fought in recent months, they fight like a bunch of amateurs out for a Sunday picnic. It's too easy. Soldiers check a few more craters and slit the rice bags, stomping and scattering the grains in the mud.

A figure in black pajamas jumps from a nearby crater and runs

168

for a distant hedgerow. Barnett knocks it down with a burst from his rifle, walks across, and rolls over the body with his foot.

"Oh, my God! It's a little girl!"

He's almost in tears when another Blue stops and digs a Chinese grenade from the mud under her tiny hand. He holds the grenade out to Barnett.

"See? Look, man, she would have used it on you if she had the chance!"

The time for my Christmas leave had arrived. I boarded a Caribou transport for the trip back to An Khe. The Caribou's first stop was Baldy. As the plane circled thousands of feet above the one-man bunkers, there was a loud pop. The bullet smashed a knob from the instrument panel and knocked the crew chief down. He was wearing a flak vest and wasn't hurt. A Red Cross girl fainted and rolled off her seat into the aisle. I started laughing. Those damned NVA in the one-man bunkers were at it again.

The rest in Hong Kong was a wonderful time. I spent a thousand dollars in seven days and enjoyed every penny of it. At least there I could enjoy Christmas carols and a soft bed and other soft things. My only regret was that the leave was over almost before it had begun. While I waited at An Khe for a chopper back to Chu Lai, I met a certain Private Page. Page had been drafted after flunking out of college, and he wanted no part of Vietnam. He thought I needed a lecture.

"It's not the same in the States now, Sarge. You've been out of touch. The conscience of the masses is being stirred. People are turning against our meddling in the affairs of Vietnam. Experience has shown that peoples' war cannot be defeated."

I had never been confronted like this by a fellow soldier. What he was saying sounded to me a lot like the ideology we were fighting. "What's all that got to do with you, Page? You're here now, and you'll fight to live, just like the rest of us. It's not a philosophical question anymore. It's a question of survival."

"Hah! Nobody makes me do what I don't think is right. I'm not going to be a baby-killer. I respect what the NLF is doing." That's sure to piss off the sergeant.

"I respect the NLF, too. You'd be surprised how few babies we have to kill. Listen, what's your job with the troop going to be?"

"A scout gunner, whatever that means."

Private Page was in for a rude awakening. "A scout gunner? Mark my words, Page. They start killing to live, and then one day they start liking it. It gets like a drug you're hooked on. Tell me how you feel in a month."

He shook his head violently and pointed an accusing finger. "That's not me you're describing. You can't categorize people like that. Our ideals are what make us unique."

"Page, those fancy words you learned in college are mostly just words." I felt pity for the changes to come in Page. "Let's wait and see."

We arrived back at Chu Lai the next morning. Barnett told me that it had been a "quiet" time for the platoon. They had rescued a couple of helicopter crews and killed two armed NVA women in the foothills north of the Que Son Valley. The women had been wearing American camouflaged jungle fatigues. The Army couldn't supply us with the coveted fatigues, but apparently the NVA had already received theirs. Hippie Doc had gone home to Los Angeles. I would miss him. He may have been a hard character; I don't know, but what I had seen was his compassion for the poor little girl on the island.

We celebrated New Year's Eve that night. The Blues sat on their cots in our big squad tent, telling war stories and getting drunk. The bunkers around Chu Lai opened up at midnight, sending flares and tracers arcing over the base. Then an AK ripped the air behind our tent. Blues grabbed grenades and rifles or crawled under the cots. Another clacking burst. Dubois and Hill took their M-16s and ran toward the sound of the firing. They were back within minutes, holding out an AK and a bottle of whiskey. Dubois flung the rifle into the dirt and kicked it under a cot. Cruz rushed through the doorway.

"Who was firing that thing?"

Dubois spat in the dirt. "Some fuckin' jarhead who bought it from an Army truck driver. Hill hit him a couple of times and took his whiskey.'' He examined the bottle in the light. "Real Southern Comfort.''

Hill laughed his evil laugh. "Serves da jarhead right!'' The Blues cut the whiskey with hot sauce in a fifty-fifty mix. Some of them used the souvenir skulls for drinking cups.

A year ago yesterday I was hiding behind a paddy dike in the horseshoe valley. Parts of the 2d and 3d NVA divisions had attacked bases throughout the Que Son Valley on the anniversary. Our old friends from the Suoi Ca and An Lao had marched a hundred miles north to participate, but the Americans were waiting. Blue had captured the plans for this attack when we wiped out the regimental command post. Now our scouts and gunships were hunting down stragglers across the valley.

The slicks circled over the ridge where we had found the regimental CP, then dropped toward Ross, crossing over a staggered line of teenage bodies in green uniforms. Machine guns had killed them while they assembled for the attack. The defenders of Ross didn't even know for certain that anything was there. A two-wheeled cart pulled by a water buffalo was piled high with more corpses. The farmer was taking them to Ross for burial. The scene would have been different if a man hadn't gotten nervous in December and fired at our commander's gunship.

Our days in the twin valleys were almost over. A new American division, the Americal, was relieving us. The Cav, the 101st Airborne, and the 4th Infantry Division were leaving behind shattered enemy regiments and several thousand dead North Vietnamese regulars. Let the Americal mop them up.

The last landing at Chu Lai. Blue is on a grassy hilltop near Baldy, at what was once an ARVN artillery base. Below us are railroad tracks running through a pass. They have been cut in several places by big mine craters. There is a concrete post in the grass. The inscription reads, "Dan Drachea. 90 days to go. January, 1963.'' What kind of man stood on this barren hilltop five years ago and thought about going home? Did he live or die? This war has been going on a long time, even for us Americans.

171

CHAPTER 12

Tet

(January–March 1968)

The troop was preparing to move north of Hue, and I was aboard one of a pair of gunships flying north to contact the Marines at our new base. My gunship left the perpetually mist-shrouded pass above Da Nang and arrived over the city of Hue. Below us were pleasant streets and peaceful suburbs. We flew at low level over the Perfume River, the massive citadel, tennis courts, and modern apartment complexes. This was a beautiful city, a side of Vietnam that I had never seen. Everything below us was so relaxed and natural. I wondered whether the people of Hue knew about the war raging in the mountains and rice paddies around it.

A coastal road guided us to Camp Evans. We landed in a field outside the barbed wire and walked through the gate to a Marine aviation bunker. The Marine and Army pilots eyed each other and exchanged overly polite greetings. One of our captains began the briefing.

"What's the general situation around the camp?"

A Marine captain walked over to a wall map. "It's pretty quiet right now. We haven't been mortared in six months. The major problem our infantry is facing is in this valley to the southwest." He poked a finger at the map. "They're running into a lot of booby traps there."

The map was blotched with red circles. "What do those circles indicate?"

The Marine captain explained. "When we receive antiaircraft

172

fire, we draw a fifteen hundred meter circle around the point and avoid the area.'' He looked guiltily at our captain. ''We don't have the helicopters you have. We can't afford to lose them.'' Our pilots grinned at each other.

Our captain pointed to a long red mark along the coast. ''How about that long village by the coast?''

''We've had a lot of trouble from there. We consider that stretch of coast VC territory. They've got twelve-sevens in there, so we fly around it.''

Now the major made his jab. ''We don't hide from machine guns. The Cav will take care of that village.'' And it would. Nine months later it was flatter than a newly plowed field. The village was leveled by artillery and bulldozers.

I knew Evans would be a safe place to spend my last forty days. Bravo Troop's helicopters swooped in a few days later. We parked the choppers in the same field outside the gate, and the Blues dug foxholes to guard them. That night I sat in a hole and dreamed of Cathy and home. I looked across the flat, open country stretching north to the DMZ and felt the same misery I had experienced twenty-five months before, during my first night in the field at An Khe. I wondered why I had stayed so long and what good I had done by being there.

A Marine patrol left the camp at dawn and walked down a dirt road past our foxholes. Each Marine had a heavy M-14 rifle, a flak vest, and not much ammunition. Each of us carried at least twenty magazines of rifle ammo, two smoke grenades, four hand grenades, and a belt of machine gun ammo. We were walking arsenals compared to them. We stared at each other in silence for a moment, then a Blue said in a loud voice, ''I wouldn't give two cents for the whole bunch.''

Another Blue said, ''Cool it. They probably think the same thing about us.'' The Marines walked quietly past us, never saying a word.

The troop moved inside the wire that day and began the tedium of building bunkers. The Marine defenses along our section of the barbed wire had been little more than reinforced foxholes. Army engineers occupied our foxholes outside the gate. Delta

Troop's rat patrol jeeps and trucks arrived in the afternoon and parked in the grassy field behind the engineers. Evans was mortared that night. Two of our choppers were hit. Delta Troop had two men killed and the engineers lost eight. If Bravo Blues had still occupied the first night's foxholes, the mortar shells would have destroyed some of the coldest killers in Vietnam, merely by chance. I walked over to Delta Troop the next morning and found Pete standing beside his wrecked jeep.

"Say, Pete. How're things with Dusty Delta these days?"

He frowned at the question. Pete didn't like the name Dusty Delta. "They were better before last night. I'd rather be at Bong Son. They've been mortaring us ever since we started north."

"We'd all rather be at Bong Son. We just came up from Chu Lai. The Charlies up here are different from anything they've got down south. Where's Ted?"

Pete laughed. "You won't see him again. We spent the night before last at a Marine base west of Hue. Charlie hit us with about forty rounds of eighty-two mike mike. One landed next to Ted's tent and put holes in all his gear. He was going to come up here for a couple of days, but after that he caught the first chopper out of there. Didn't even say good-bye."

"So something finally got under his thick skin. I was beginning to think he wasn't human. He hit a mine one day at Bong Son and was back on the road the next day. God, how I wish we were back at Bong Son."

He shrugged and looked away, thinking about something. "Maybe and maybe not. Things were getting hot down there, too. We got into some really deep shit on December sixth. That was the worst day. Alpha Troop's Blues got pinned down, and I went in with the standby platoon. It was in those secure rice villages northeast of Bong Son. We had to break through to the Blues, and there was a machine gun between us and them. The first squad that charged up the bank lost every man except Bolten, and he killed the gook machine gun crew. Just kept shooting with his machine gun until they were all dead. That dude saved our lives. They put him in for a Silver Star."

I remembered the day Bolten had killed the VC tax collector

and tried to keep the money. "I can't picture Bolten as a hero. He always looks so sad and lost. What unit was it? The NVA."

"The Twenty-Second NVA Regiment. They wiped it out before it was over."

"You mean a battalion of the Twenty-Second Regiment."

"No, man. Believe me. I mean the whole damned regiment."

I didn't believe Pete until I saw the place from the air in early March. Whole villages had been flattened by the shells, and the paddies were plowed up by the treads of tanks and APCs. It was in the same area where Arthur had died and where Minton had won his Silver Star. It looked like a large force had been surrounded by armor and had then contracted in upon itself. A regiment had been destroyed there. The 22d NVA Regiment had been repaid for violating the Christmas truce at Bird one year before, but the defeat had served the Communist cause. By always attacking through the prosperous government areas, they forced us to destroy that prosperity and the illusion of security.

The evening after the mortar attack, I listened to a radio broadcast on the Armed Forces Radio channel. A female voice said that the People's Army of Vietnam welcomed the 1st Air Cavalry to Camp Evans, "with a special hello to the boys of B Troop of the Ninth Cavalry." She said she hoped that we had written goodbye letters to our families and girlfriends back home. I hoped that the People's Army didn't know just how much damage the boys in B Troop had caused.

The departing Marines shook their heads at the swarms of helicopters suddenly filling the sky over Evans. The Cav infantry was landing at the base of the mountains west of Hue, and our pink teams were finding NVA everywhere. On one of the first days out, the pink teams smashed an intended ambush along the road north to the DMZ, killing more than fifty NVA. I saw Private Page one afternoon with an armload of East German and Czech AKs. Last month's ideologue was laughing. It was beginning to look like another Chu Lai.

One afternoon, a gunship was shot at by a lone NVA in the middle of a rice field. The man was surprised when the helicopter dived at him, instead of flying away. A door gunner told me that he just stood there, gaping and waiting to die. The Mag-7 was welcoming new members. The scout gunners couldn't believe their "luck" at finding so many NVA so easily. None of us questioned why large bodies of enemy troops should be moving around a formerly quiet Marine camp. We drew the wrong conclusion. We thought the Marines had been screwing up, just like they had done at Chu Lai. The truth was far more ominous.

The Battle of Hue began with a confused report that the local Viet Cong had captured a bridge inside the city. The troop was asked to investigate. As the flight of gunships left, we stood by the lift ships, arguing about whether the bridge was really inside Hue. We were sure a new radioman had messed up. "Everyone knows there aren't any VC in Hue."

Within two hours, several squadron helicopters had been hit and other gunships were receiving heavy automatic weapons fire at all altitudes above the city. One of Bravo Troop's gunships had been shot down, and two of the crewmen captured. They were

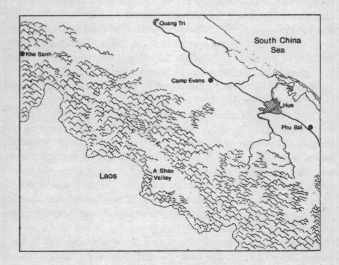

rescued by a brave slick pilot, Wonder Warthog. Wonder was a gutsy fellow. He buzzed a field full of NVA and landed his ship almost on top of the soldiers guarding our crewmen. Wonder's pump shotgun and the door gunners killed ten NVA. Two troop pilots died that day. One of them, Hanna, a quiet boy from Indianapolis, was on his second mission in Vietnam.

That evening, General Westmoreland announced widespread attacks throughout Vietnam. The bridge had been inside Hue, after all.

Hue was burning. The slicks orbited away from the city as Skyraiders dived again and again into the inferno, releasing black bombs. Whole blocks of apartment buildings collapsed from the explosions. The air above the center of the city was filled with dust and black smoke. We touched down in a rice paddy on the edge of the city, and two frightened American advisors ran to us. Behind them, our gunships rocketed a suburb from which AKs were clacking. Then the slicks were off. We watched as more bombs exploded along the pleasant streets of Hue.

That was Blue's last experience with the Battle for Hue. Our services as a recon platoon were not needed when the scouts could fly in any direction from Evans and find NVA units. The scouts and gunships did participate in the Cav attack into the northern part of the city and earned a reputation for destroying strongpoints and catching NVA as they ran from one position to another. Bravo Troop's choppers killed 156 enemy soldiers at Hue.

The platoon watched helplessly as an infantry company fought NVA digging bunkers on a hill in front of our bunkers. Then we patrolled past the half-finished holes. They looked like raw sores in the grass. We heard a man running away and passed an NVA pack and a fishing pole stuck in the bank of a tiny stream. He wasn't catching anything. On another hill was a neat pile of mortar rounds. A square pit was already waiting for the mortar tube. That was warning enough. Weeks of mortar shelling started that night.

That wasn't how I had planned to spend my last days in Vietnam. Intelligence had reported that the NVA tanks in Laos had poison gas shells, so we were ordered to carry gas masks. I sat each night on a bunker, carrying only a gas mask, an artillery radio, and seven hand grenades. If the NVA attacked, I would do nothing but be an FO and blast the hills and woods to our front. I hoped they would try to use the bunkers they had been digging. I had an artillery concentration planned on top of them. If they breached the wire, seven grenades said that they would go no farther. Seven is supposed to be a very lucky number.

The helicopters burned behind us at night, but I was safe. The NVA listened to Armed Forces Radio. When "Holiday" by the Bee Gees played, they mortared us. It was my favorite song, and they must have liked it, too. Whenever the song began, I grabbed my transistor radio, ran to a tiny bunker I had dug into a bank, and listened for the whistle of the first mortars. Then I enjoyed the rest of "Holiday." They were singing, "Don't believe that it's all the same." It happened every night for two weeks. When I hear "Holiday" today I hear the whistle of those rounds.

Evans was surrounded by an NVA regiment. Air Force cargo planes flew over faithfully every day, parachuting rations and ammunition. Mortar shells exploded around us at all hours of the day and night. I listened for "Holiday" and feared the crashing of the rounds. They made me feel so helpless. You can fight an enemy rifleman, but a mortar round is a blind thing. It seeks you out in your miserable hiding place and crushes you before you know it's there.

Our pink teams continued recon flights around Evans, although mortars and bullets were destroying them faster than they could be replaced. One day a scout pilot was wounded so painfully that he couldn't hold the controls. The gunner took over and somehow flew the chopper back to the camp. It crash-landed on a grassy slope, and medics ran to help the pilot. Out of the gunner's seat stepped Private Page. He was still dazed by the flight.

"I can't believe it. He just told me what to do, and I flew the damned thing back. Am I glad that's over!"

"You'll probably get a medal. You saved his life." I had to

know something. "Say, Page, what do you think of the scouts now?"

"Saved my life, too." His eyes came back into focus. "Know something, Sarge? I've got seventy-nine kills already. Just up here."

"I thought you were the one who wasn't going to compromise."

He smiled the whole issue away. "People change, Sarge. I like the scouts."

"That's good." His convictions were just as shallow as the next man's.

Dusty Delta often tried to break through to the 1st Air Cav units fighting their way into Hue. A rat patrol convoy would grind through the camp gate and turn south along Route 1. Always the muffled sounds of mortar, rocket, and rifle fire, and the jeeps and trucks would come bouncing back to Evans. One day I asked Pete what was going on.

"We go down the road to Hue, and every time the NVA try to ambush us at the same place. We start getting AK fire, sometimes mortars, and our mortar and recoilless rifles shoot back. Then the gunships come over and shoot up the trees. They kill thirty or so NVA, and we come back to camp and try again the next day. It's always the same treeline."

"That means they're losing at least a platoon a day just keeping the road closed. And to think we used to have to hunt for them. What's the rest of Dusty Delta doing?"

"Road patrols north to Quang Tri. It's generally quiet in that direction. Some Arvin APCs wiped out the NVA battalion blocking the road." I had seen the APCs, piled high with captured equipment, rumble by Evans one night at dusk. The ARVNs were shouting and waving captured AKs and North Vietnamese flags. They stopped long enough to offer us "bargain basement" prices on AKs. They would barter a captured AK-47 for one case of C-rations. Unfortunately, none of us needed an AK-47.

Pete wasn't quite finished. "There's something that's bugging me."

"What?"

"It's Combat Bolten. I can't get him out of my mind. Ever since December sixth he's been a crazy man. He rides gunner on a jeep. Always the first one to start shooting back. He lives for it. A couple of times, guys actually had to stop him from running into the treeline south of here. I think he's about ready for a rubber room at the funny farm."

"Too bad. He just doesn't seem like the type." In the distance, a sad sack figure walked toward the latrine, cradling his freshly oiled machine gun in his arms. "There goes our hero now."

One morning in late February, the slicks took us north to Quang Tri. We had to wait there in case Delta Troop's convoy got into trouble. The sky was heavily overcast, so the slicks made the journey at low level. The paddy fields around the city were cratered from thousands of artillery shells, and we crossed over a wide zone of death. Muddy craters everywhere, the sprawled bodies of NVA and farmers, the carcasses of hundreds of water buffalo, everything swollen and rotting. It was so silent and still there below us. Parts of the city still smoldered from recent battles. Block after block of ruined houses and deserted streets. The rain only made it seem more pathetic and disgusting. Near nightfall, the slicks returned to Evans over the same areas of rot and chaos.

I was a "short-timer," living through my last days at Evans. Our lives had degenerated into a combination of crushing boredom and fear of the sporadic mortaring. A group of men who had thrived on constant action and danger now looked for unfamiliar ways to keep their collective sanity. One recreation was something I called the C-4 Dance. We used the plastic explosive to heat our C-rations, and the only time that it was chemically unstable was when it was burning. I remember nights in a dirty squad tent, watching soldiers lighting wads of C-4, and then leaping through the air and stomping on them. Fortunately, the stuff never exploded, or the "dancers" would have lost at least a foot. We were manufacturing our own dangers.

Another diversion was the "gross-out session." Blues would dump the contents of their C-ration meals into the dirt and grind the food under their boots. Then they would scoop up the slop with dirty hands and stuff it into their mouths. A variation involved eating the meal directly off the ground with a plastic spoon. We grew fond of unique drinking vessels on the rare occasions when we received a beer ration. We removed our boots, which never left our feet for longer than a few minutes, and filled them with beer. I have a vision of Blues gulping stinking, muddy liquid out of worn boots as watery red mud ran down their chins and necks.

It was Friday. I had been on the bunkers all night and Barnett wouldn't wake me for the trip north to the Marine base at Dong Ha. I might get hurt with only four days left at Evans. When the choppers landed at the Marine base, the mortars came. The four men sitting on my usual side of the slick were wounded before the pilots could lift away. I didn't have the chance to say good-bye to them.

It was Saturday. A Blue was telling us how he had watched a 122mm rocket collapse a section of concrete aircraft hangar at Da Nang. It had buried a group of screaming Marine replacements who had just arrived from America. Cruz stopped the brutal talk by asking if anyone had a reason for going back to An Khe.

One Blue was going home and another had leave. Dubois had a doctor's slip that said he had a skin infection that couldn't be treated at Evans. Dubois had schemed for a month to get Dubois out of Evans, ever since a mortar fragment had hit his flak jacket and knocked him into a garbage ditch. Now he had found a soft doctor. The lucky ones boarded the slick and waved good-bye. I watched it climb over the wire and disappear and wished I was on it.

It crashed in the cloudy pass above Da Nang. Our gunships searched for the wreckage for days but finally gave up until things quieted down around Hue. Many months later, a soldier asked me if I had known any of the men who had been shot down in a chopper above Da Nang during Tet. I thought of the cowardly Dubois and the other, less memorable men.

"Yes. I knew three of them and the pilots. Did any of them make it?"

"No. One of the gunships found the wreckage in August. They all died in the crash."

On Sunday morning, the Catholic chaplain said mass and offered prayers for those who had died in the last month. He was impressed that every man in the Blues had attended his service. He must have thought the whole platoon was Catholic. After the blessing, the Blues lined up and the chaplain's assistant handed out black plastic rosaries. The word was out about the rosaries, and everyone had agreed that they would bring us good luck. By the next morning, most of the soldiers were wearing the rosaries around their necks for ornament. The platoon had finally got religion. My last memory of the Blues of Bong Son and Chu Lai is of a group of black and white soldiers, smiling and waving, with the black plastic beads gleaming around their necks. My war was almost over.

The mortar shells that hit An Khe landed far away and I wasn't afraid. I had seen war firsthand and survived, and the memories were overwhelming any other thoughts I might have had. I was suffering a personal crisis. Soon I would return to Washington, Indiana, where the people remembered me as a bookworm and an unpromising athlete. But I had been with the 9th Cav since nearly everyone there had arrived, and with the division even longer. Men liked to hear stories about the now distant days of Pleiku and "Crazy Horse," or hear about people like Sergeants Samuel and Hardy. I never had to buy a beer when a 9th Cav Blue was in a club, and now I was returning to the obscurity of life in a small Indiana town. When Barnett returned to An Khe for leave, we walked into a clump of young trees behind the 9th Cav buildings, and I told him what was on my mind.

"Vic, I'm afraid to go home. I don't like the war, but the only friends I have now are in the Ninth Cav. I don't know what to expect back home."

Barnett understood. "You'll make new friends, FO. You haven't been out in life much. It happens every time you start something new. There's not a man in the Ninth Cav who wants you to stay another day. You're an example of one who made it. The Blues would lynch you if you stayed any longer."

"But look what's coming. We aren't going to be sitting in the bull's-eye at Evans much longer. The Cav's getting ready to break through to Khe Sanh and save the Marines. You might need some artillery."

He shook his head. "It's all over for you, FO. If you stayed much longer, we'd all be gone and leave you behind. Just write a letter and tell us about all the pussy you're getting. Go home and start living like a human being again."

I spent my last night in An Khe at the NCO club. Paul the newsman was there, along with a new friend. Paul was going home, too. "Matt, this is Jerry. He's my replacement. I've got two days left."

I nodded at the boy with Paul. He was still chubby from American food and beer. "Hi, Jerry. Welcome to the Cav. I'm leaving for home tomorrow."

Paul jerked his thumb in my direction. "Matt here has just completed twenty-seven months with the Cav. That must be some kind of record." Then he asked in a low voice, as if afraid of what the answer might be, "What did the Blues do during Tet?"

"Nothing. We sat inside the wire at Evans and got mortared. I dug a little bunker and marked the days off on a calendar. How about you?"

"Nothing much."

Jerry was restless. He wanted to say something, and he fluttered his hand to get my attention. "Nothing much? This guy's too modest. He shot fourteen gooks in Hue. They gave him a Silver Star the next day. Come on, Paul, tell him about it."

Paul blushed. He seemed like such a gentle fellow. "Did you really do that, Paul?"

He blushed again. "Yeah. You know how they build things up after they happen. I was hiding in a shop in the center of Hue. The odds were about even. They came by in pairs. All I was trying to do was save my neck. The best part is that the newsmen I was supposed to be baby-sitting heard about it and offered me a job when I get back. It's what I've always wanted to do. I can't tell you how excited I am about it.''

''Paul, that's great! I hope it all falls in place for you.'' And for me.

Three days later, I was a civilian, boarding a jet in Seattle for the long flight home.

CHAPTER 13

The Long Summer

Returning home was far more complicated than I would ever have imagined. I was unable to communicate with anyone, so Cathy and I parted as friends. She had wanted to stay engaged, but my adjustment to civilian life was too enormous for anyone to understand or share. I had to do it alone. I was unable to sleep at night, so I read and exercised myself into a state of exhaustion, hoping that sleep would follow. The greatest psychological obstacle was realizing that there were no mortars firing in Indiana. I was always listening for the thunk of a mortar shell leaving the tube. When everything else failed, I drank myself to sleep.

By early April, I was desperately in need of someone to talk to about the hell I was going through. I finally decided to drive to Dallas and visit James from Bravo Blues. One cold spring morning I threw a sleeping bag in the backseat of my new Plymouth and headed south. The Tennessee and Arkansas Mountains reminded me of the Suoi Ca Mountains. While driving on the super-highway between Dallas and Fort Worth, I saw a huge billboard poster of me leading the "Charge of the Third Brigade." It was an advertisement for a local television station. I couldn't believe what I was seeing. There I was, frozen in action beside a Texas highway, thousands of miles from that rice paddy at Chu Lai.

I arrived at James's home, expecting some understanding and

185

support, but he couldn't help me. I told him about the billboard, and he replied that he wouldn't drive near it. It reminded him of the Blues. His medals were on his dresser in a tiny cardboard box, and at night he would line them up at the foot of his bed and proceed to drink himself to sleep. He was trying to forget 173 dead men. James's parents gave me a cold, detached welcome. They did not want anyone around their son to revive his memories of the war. We talked about our common experience, of gunships, AKs, and NVA, and then we were silent. The visit had been superficial and damaging for both of us. I returned home to Indiana and never heard from James again.

I enrolled at a junior college and lasted one week. After Vietnam, the boredom of the classroom was insufferable. I became infatuated with a local girl, but her father didn't want her dating an ex-soldier. I thought it was poetic justice when they drafted her brother. The spring and summer became one long brawl of drinking, dancing, and generally raising hell. The lowest point of the summer was the night I spent in the county jail.

I had managed to locate three other veterans, and we celebrated the Fourth of July at a dance in a neighboring town. We finally left for home at about 2:00 A.M. A local policeman whom we had all known in high school, but who didn't recognize us now, watched me drive into the parking lot of an all-night diner on the edge of town. He stopped us at the door and asked to see our IDs. My friends complied, but I got cute. I took my driver's license out of my wallet and ate it. He arrested all four of us for public intoxication, disturbing the peace, and disrespect to an officer of the law. It didn't matter that I had been driving safely, and he never gave us the chance to disturb anybody's peace. He was just on the prowl and probably bored, so he arrested a bunch of strangers who had driven into his town at an odd hour. I paid the twenty dollars and costs the following morning and continued on my wild spree.

Eventually my savings ran low, and I found a job driving spikes on a railroad track gang. It was a good job. If I worked hard for eight hot hours a day, there wasn't time to be bored and I was exhausted enough to sleep. Boredom was always the problem. Every day was the same as the one before. If a person was lucky, he could look forward to living like that for fifty more painfully long years. I had become addicted to constant danger in Vietnam, and the constant security of life in Indiana was unbelievably melancholy. I knew I had to find some way to cope with my unrest.

I enrolled at Indiana State University in September with the usual menu of freshman courses. ISU was an alien place to me, and the student life seemed trite and incredibly petty. Students dressed to impress their classmates and attended lectures to find dates for the weekend. The pursuit of learning was far down the list of reasons for attending college. The Greeks controlled most of the campus social activities, and if you didn't belong to a fraternity, your recreational options were limited. There was a fraternity on campus with a majority of veterans, but they had been typists and truck drivers. They urged me to join, but we had nothing in common. It made me angry when I overheard them telling the sorority girls elaborate, false war stories.

Another thing that struck me as ridiculous was the racial tension at ISU. Blacks and whites were not on speaking terms. It was confusing after experiencing the integration and sharing among blacks and whites while fighting with the Blues. Julian Bond arrived on campus and gave a fiery speech that ended with, "God told Noah, here's a sign. No more water, fire next time." That speech did nothing to bring people closer together. It only made the racial divisions deeper.

The students carried umbrellas even in the lightest rains. Having spent months in heavy rains with no dry clothing at all, I found those umbrellas the most difficult part of student life to accept. With all my heart, I hated the umbrellas as a symbol of just how superficial my new life had become. When other students told me, "You ought to buy an umbrella at the campus bookstore," I silently cursed the umbrellas. My only escape from these strange customs and experiences was to study extremely hard. But ISU was so easy that in four weeks I had read most of the semester's assignments. There was too much free time to contemplate the America I had returned to.

My country had changed in the past three years, and I had not changed along with it. Not only were fashions and hairstyles different, but so was the prevailing morality. My morals were trapped in the previous generation. To me, "free love" was a threatening concept. Americans were searching for answers to many questions, and one of the major ones was why we had gotten ourselves involved in the quagmire in Indochina. I couldn't understand what the debate was about. I had never questioned the reasons for the war. I was an idealist who felt that Vietnam required our sacrifices because it was a just cause. There had been so much Chinese equipment that I believed the NVA were pawns of Communist Chinese expansion into a region that had been a tributary state prior to the arrival of the French. That was my simple philosophy.

Veterans were a curiosity in Indiana in 1968. We were not yet ignored, not yet called dope fiends and sociopaths, but no one cared about what we had been through, except other Vietnam veterans. The only questions I ever received were from young men who might be drafted. They wanted to know what to expect. They would be disenfranchised veterans themselves in a few years, and it isn't over, even now. Put your war record down on paper and try to get a teaching position at a good university, regardless of your brilliance as a student. Let an employer find out that you were a grunt in Vietnam and try to find a job where you can wear a tie instead of dirty work clothes. Watch an "objective—the way it really happened" documentary on the war and see how fair the producers are to everyone else, usually at the cost of the Vietnam veteran's self-image and pride.

My view of Americans was of a people who competed in petty ways for money, power, and status symbols. I missed the sharing, the genuine comradeship, and the simple life-and-death choices of Vietnam. I had returned to a nation of mixed-up values and political assassinations, and the changes were too complex for me to understand. Millions of veterans had readjusted to a different America after their wars, but Vietnam veterans had to do it alone. I stopped trying at ISU. I wasn't strong enough, and there was no one to help me.

I withdrew from all classes on a rainy October morning. It went well until I reached the office of my history professor. He asked me why I was leaving ISU, and when I told him, he gave me a lecture on the immorality of the Vietnam War. I didn't know what the hell he was talking about, and I certainly didn't want to hear it. I left the withdrawal slips at the administration office and walked two blocks down the street to an Army recruiting station. I made a deal with the recruiting sergeant. I would re-enlist if I could go directly back to the 1st Air Cav. He made arrangements over the telephone while confiding that he was in the recruiting service to avoid going back to Vietnam. He could stay in America as long as he met his monthly quota of volunteers. He wanted to stay and I wanted to go.

The most painful part of returning to Vietnam was saying goodbye to my family once again. My father had always been strongly opposed to the war, and he was terribly confused by my decision to go back. He called me a quitter, and he was right. I only knew that I was disillusioned and unable to understand my surroundings. I needed a life that I could emotionally handle. I told my family that I would apply for the officer's commission that the Army had offered me twice before. The first time it was offered was at the command post when I was still nineteen years old. I thought this excuse would appease my father's anger, but it didn't change his conviction that I would die if I returned another time to the war.

Throughout this strange period in America, I had wanted to see John Martin and talk to him about his adjustment. I wanted his perspective on everything that had happened to me. But he was gone, traveling around the world on his Vietnam savings. The last postcard I had received from him was from Afghanistan. So, John had been right about me when he said that I would end up being a lifer. At least I understood the rules in

Vietnam, and at that point in my life, I had to be involved in a game I could understand. I was relieved that there would be no more unimportant mind games with a bunch of half-assed students.

Whatever crazy reasons I used to justify my return to the war, going back was the greatest mistake of my life.

CHAPTER 14

Return to the Cav

One week later, I arrived at Oakland, California, the replacement center for the United States Army, Pacific. The tiers of bunks were filled with silent draftees, waiting as if for their own funerals. The boasting paratroopers of 1965 were only a memory. There was a Special Forces sergeant in my barracks, a quiet man who set himself apart from the herd of long-faced draftees. He had fought for two years in Laos and North Vietnam, had gone home for eight months, and then returned for the same reasons I had. He had been lonely and bored. The sergeant didn't talk much about what he had seen in his secret war, but he loved to tell the story about how his team had ambushed a Chinese bandit general in Laos. Porters had carried the general on a sedan chair surrounded by a ring of bodyguards. The team had killed the general quickly, then lost three men trying to get close enough to the body to capture his fancy hat.

To know someone who had wrestled with the same problems I had, and made the same decisions, made me feel less alone. We waited together for the flight across the Pacific. The Special Forces sergeant and I spent our last evening in Oakland with the unpleasant duty of roster NCOs. We had to take roll every hour and then every half hour to make certain that none of the draftees had deserted. In 1965, soldiers had actually bribed replacement center personnel to be called for Vietnam more quickly.

I said good-bye to the Special Forces sergeant at Tan Son Nhut Air Base outside Saigon. The air base was bigger than I remembered it from 1965 and was now the busiest airport in the world. Instead of climbing aboard big Army transport trucks, we were taken to the new Camp Alpha in air-conditioned buses. The road to Alpha was lined with tanks and APCs. The crews sported mustaches and sideburns and wore peace symbols around their necks. They flashed the "V for victory" sign as our buses drove by them. Nine months before, the greeting had been a thumbs-up signal. The new sign meant "stay high," not "victory." I knew something was different about those tank soldiers. I didn't understand what that difference was, but the discipline and confidence I had grown accustomed to seeing in Vietnam seemed to be gone.

I returned to An Khe over the same jungle ridges that had so impressed me three years before. At least the war hadn't changed the mountains. The airstrip at An Khe was now heavily protected with barbed wire and infantry bunkers. Knots of soldiers, most of them wearing Marine Corps fatigue caps and carrying K-Bar knives, rested in the shade of the wooden terminal building. A soldier beside me pointed to a dusty infantry patrol returning through the barbed wire.

"The VC set up a machine gun on the edge of the airstrip last summer. Killed some guys going home to the World. Gooks got away scot-free." How horrible it must have been to spend a year in Vietnam and to die waiting for the plane that would take you home.

Brown Army buses took us to the main camp. The bus windows were covered with chicken wire to keep out terrorist grenades. The drivers wore starched jungle uniforms and neat baseball caps. The sandbagged dump trucks and their ragged drivers had disappeared long before. An Khe had blossomed into a prosperous town, teeming with children and crowded with souvenir shops, laundries, massage parlors, and restaurants. It had grown fat on GI dollars. The replacement center was now a complex of wooden buildings equipped with electric fans, lights, and office machines. Once the whole place had consisted of three small tents and a grassy field. Instead of sleeping on the elephant grass, I slept that night on a steel bunk that had a firm mattress, blankets, and two pillows.

I received the news about my assignment the following morning. The new pilots were receiving artillery training in night school, so the 9th Cav wasn't using FOs anymore. I was assigned to an artillery battalion, either as an FO or as an operations sergeant. The second job would be the same thing I had done at the command post, but on a lower level.

A slick took me and two other men on the 230-mile trip north to Evans. The door gunner told us that we were riding on a new model of helicopter, fitted with a more powerful engine than the slicks that had carried the Blues on so many landings. We passed west of Hue and followed the coastal road north to a sprawling military camp. Evans was several times larger than it had been in March. Most of the inhabitants lived in large bunkers reinforced with steel plates and thick wooden crossbeams. The place bristled with howitzers and helicopters and seemed much safer than the surrounded camp that I remembered from the days of Tet.

The clerk at the 21st Artillery Battalion was sympathetic. He offered to send me to a Cav grunt company as a forward observer. I asked him whether a request to transfer to the 9th Cav as a Blue infantry sergeant would be approved. A young major had overheard the conversation from the next room. He stuck his head through the doorway and nodded to me.

"The transfer will be approved. You're too highly trained to be an infantryman, but requests for the infantry have the highest priority. Why don't you go over and ask them for a transfer? Bravo Troop's where it's always been."

"Thanks, sir. I'll do that right now."

I found the Blues living in the tents we had erected in January. I walked around the tent where I had watched the C-4 dancers and the gross-out sessions and touched the mortar holes in the canvas. I remembered how each tear had been made. I tried all

193

four tents before I found someone I recognized. It was Doc Mitchell, the man who had replaced Hippie Doc, and he didn't seem surprised to see me back in Vietnam. He led me to his cot, and we sat down to the Vietnam ritual of telling the one who had been away what had happened while he was gone.

Doc told me that some of the old Blues had gone home, and others had been hit in an ambush on May thirty-first. The Blues had made landings around Khe Sanh in March, but most of the NVA had fled before the Cav arrived. The Troop had also been the first Americans into the Lang Vei Special Forces Camp, which had been overrun by NVA tanks in February. Doc said that Khe Sanh had looked like a huge garbage dump after the siege, filled with trash and demoralized, shell-shocked Marines. He said the way you could spot the newly arrived cavalrymen at Khe Sanh was by the way they behaved during rocket attacks. The cavalrymen would wait for the black explosions and snap pictures. The Marines would dive for the nearest foxhole or ditch.

Bravo Troop had reconned the A Shau Valley in April. The Cav and the 101st Airborne had found tons of weapons and supplies, but had lost 138 choppers. The NVA used radar-controlled antiaircraft cannon in the A Shau. The pilots quickly learned to recognize the lock-on signal by a beep over their intercoms. If they didn't take sharp evasive action by the third beep, it was all over. The Blues were kept busy rescuing downed crews. The most frightening time for Blue was the three days they spent guarding an airstrip on the western edge of the valley. They were one of the last units in the A Shau Valley, and the strip was being used to evacuate the heavy equipment and supplies. The landing strip was under sporadic shelling from NVA 130mm artillery in Laos. None of the Blues was hurt, but it scared the hell out of all of them. The Blues were now mostly used to secure downed helicopters. Their reconnaissance operations had largely ceased after the ambush on May thirty-first.

We talked for a while longer, then Doc stopped and pointed to a tall man walking along the barbed wire. "First sergeant's back, if you still want to talk to him about coming back to the Blues. It's a lot safer where you are.''

"Thanks, Doc. I'll be seeing you.''

The first sergeant was a new man. He saw me walking toward him from the Blue tents and gave me a suspicious look. "What can I do for you?''

"Top? My name is Brennan. I was an FO with the Blues for sixteen months.''

He nodded. "I've heard about you, Brennan. The old first sergeant said you had one hell of a lot of air assaults under your belt. You probably know by now that we don't use FOs anymore. The pilots bring in their own artillery if it's needed.''

"Since you don't need an FO, could you use an infantry sergeant? I spent most of my time playing infantry, anyway.''

His eyes lit up. "We can use all the experienced sergeants we can beg, borrow, or steal." Top lowered his voice. "Right now we have a bunch of Shake and Bakes. Most of them can't lead a horse to water. What unit are you with?''

"The Twenty-First Artillery. I'm putting in for a transfer here as a grunt.''

"Okay, Sergeant. When it gets here, it'll be approved. You'll be doing us a favor.''

"Thanks, Top.''

I returned for a last look at the Blues. These men were different from what I had expected. The platoon sergeant and all the squad leaders were products of the Army's new ninety-day NCO course. They were called "Shake and Bakes" or "instant NCOs." It was now possible to join the Army and be a staff sergeant seven months later. I had been a private in the pre-Vietnam Army for eighteen months. There were two volunteers in the platoon. Everyone else, including all the sergeants, were draftees. The Blue platoon was composed of a batch of the new long-faced replacements. The toughness and aggressiveness of a year before were gone. What would Hippie Doc or Hill have thought of the platoon?

I began to realize what was different about the Vietnam Army

195

of late 1968. Something had happened to the Army's spirit after the Tet Offensive. The confident soldiers of 1967 and before had been replaced by an Army of draftee officers, sergeants, and enlisted men. The old NCOs and volunteers had either already served their time in Vietnam or were dead.

I returned to the 21st Artillery and began completing the transfer request forms. The young major wished me good luck, then told me that I would be a liaison NCO with the Army of Vietnam until the paperwork had gone through channels. I was the only experienced operations sergeant that the battalion had available for the position, but I had no idea what a liaison NCO was supposed to do.

Two days later, the Cav moved over 350 miles to the south, to positions northwest of Saigon. We were going to the aid of the 1st Infantry Division, the "Big Red One," whose artillery bases were being overrun along the Cambodian border. The artillery headquarters loaded its equipment on trucks and drove down the road toward Hue. A short distance south of Evans, the convoy passed the dead and twisted trees where Delta Troop had fought its daily battles during Tet. I wondered how many men's bones rested there.

The road was safe by then, and security precautions were lax. We passed companies of ARVN infantry armed with M-16s and AK-47s, and everyone smiled and waved. We drove through Hue, past the modern apartment buildings that had been gutted by the bombs of February. All that remained were blackened concrete shells. Then we arrived at the port of Hue and watched Korean stevedores hoisting our vehicles aboard a fleet of LSTs.

A convoy of LSTs was at sea by evening, heading south along the coast of Vietnam. I spent the next few days on deck. It was covered with an array of dirty brown vehicles, each flying a rebel flag or a pirate flag from its radio antenna. Between them were shelters made from ponchos and canvas tent halves. It looked like a seagoing gypsy camp. Below the top deck was a nightmare of sick men and slippery vomit. At night I would sleep on the bow, enjoying the sea breezes and sometimes seeing the lights of a port city gliding by off the starboard.

The LSTs approached Saigon down a winding river through the Rung Sat Special Zone. I had heard many stories of the bitter fighting and ambushes there from a friend who had fought in the Rung Sat with a Navy seal team, but there was no trouble that day. Ninth Cav pink teams patrolled the banks. *Rung Sat* means "killer swamp." It's a flat sea of perpetual mud, covered with scattered bushes and twisted trees. It was the ugliest place I ever saw in Vietnam.

Hoists unloaded the headquarters trucks at New Port, outside Saigon, and we prepared to spend the night in squad tents a short distance from the docks. I had never seen Saigon and thought that our night in New Port would give me that opportunity. I was walking through the New Port gate when a spotlessly dressed MP grabbed my arm.

"Where do you think you're going, Sarge?"

"For a walk. I want to see Saigon."

He shook his head. "Nobody from the Cav's permitted off base."

Fucking MP. "I'm a big boy. I'll be back in a few hours."

The young MP wasn't very good at being hard-nosed. "I can't let you through here, but there's a hole in the wire about fifty yards from here. If I wasn't looking . . ."

I headed in the direction he pointed, but he wanted to talk. "I always wanted to go to the Cav MPs. The Cav's a tough unit."

"Yeah, but MPs have the same job all over. You'd just be directing traffic and kicking people out of bars." His hurt expression made me quickly regret my nasty comment. "Maybe not. The Cav MPs do make combat assaults." I didn't tell him that Cav MP landings were usually made in secure areas to search for black market goods and deserters. "What's duty like around here?"

He was smiling again. "It's pretty good since the attacks in May. Saigon hasn't been rocketed in months." A jeep

197

with an MP sergeant and driver pulled up to the gate, and my new friend pointed to the rear seat. "Still want to see Saigon?"

"Sure."

"Why don't you go on patrol with my buddies? They're going right through the city."

The jeep crossed the New Port Bridge and headed down a modern highway toward Saigon. I bounced along in the backseat with a grenade launcher across my lap. The MP sergeant who had handed it to me turned around in his seat.

"You know how to use that thing, Sarge?"

"I shot one once or twice." I slid a grenade into the chamber.

The MP sergeant jumped, twisted completely around, and snatched away the elephant gun. "Heh! We'd better unload this thing. It might go off if we hit a bump." I thought of new names for rear echelon MPs.

The sergeant told me that we were going to cruise down Tu Do Street. That was wonderful. Every soldier in Vietnam had heard about Saigon's red-light district, and I had wanted to see it for years. My only regret was that the tour would be from the backseat of an MP jeep. We had reached the business district when a building ahead of us lit up for an instant and a shock wave hit the jeep. Those thunderclaps were my first experience with 122mm rockets. We raced down Tu Do Street, passing flashing neon signs and a milling crowd of painted girls in miniskirts, drunken GIs and Vietnamese pimps. The driver turned a corner and inched the jeep around a bucket brigade throwing water on a burning building. More thunder rolled across the jeep, and a building in the next block caught fire. The MP sergeant hunched down in his seat and pulled his steel helmet over his ears with both hands. The driver hit the accelerator and raced the jeep all the way back to New Port through dark, suddenly deserted streets. My only tour of Saigon was over.

The artillery headquarters convoyed to the northwest at dawn. The first few miles were on a four-lane highway that would have put America's interstate road system to shame. Army

bulldozers and road-graders were at work making more inter-
changes. Then we turned onto a narrow highway that had once
been paved but was now a crumbling patchwork of asphalt
chunks and red mud. Several hours into the journey, at about
9:00 A.M., we heard President Johnson announce another
bombing halt over North Vietnam. He said it was in the interest
of peace, but peace means different things in different places.
The soldiers on my truck were angry. They were convinced
that the bombing halt would only bring more 122mm rockets
raining down around them.

The convoy arrived at a base called Quan Loi, located a few
miles from the Cambodian border, in the late afternoon. The
countryside around Quan Loi was stunning. It consisted of rolling
red earth hills covered with well-tended rubber plantations. The
plantations were cut by straight roads and villages laid out in
carefully planned squares. This symmetrical world had nothing in
common with the mountain forests and populated coastal plains
of the northern provinces. Quan Loi was more beautiful than the
Bong Son Plains from the ground, but couldn't equal their splen-
dor from the air. The long rows of rubber trees were too regular,
too artificial. As we entered the gates of Quan Loi, an infantry
patrol from the Big Red One returned from the rubber plantations
that surrounded the base. They wore custom baseball caps, black
scarves, and too-neat jungle uniforms, and they reminded me of
Boy Scouts.

The headquarters slept that night in tattered, long-unused tents.
I was awakened at dawn by the crash I had been subconsciously
hearing for seven months now. An NVA 82mm mortar had fired
a single shell. The artillery headquarters moved to the other side
of the Quan Loi base that same day. I listened from another tent
as a long mortar barrage destroyed our tents of the night before.
The NVA were using forward observers around Quan Loi. They
had fired a marking shell, made the corrections, and then waited
for darkness to kill us in our sleep. The tents were empty when
the mortars exploded.

I became a liaison NCO in An Loc, about three miles down
the road from Quan Loi. An Loc was a sleepy little provincial

town, very pleasant and charming. It had schools and children on bicycles, girls in the traditional flowing dresses, and an excellent Chinese restaurant. Marks of the colonial past were everywhere. The brown stucco architecture was French Colonial, and the signs over the shops were printed in both Vietnamese and French. The entire local economy was based on the French-owned rubber plantations.

The French around An Loc and Quan Loi were supposed to be neutral, but they were on good terms with the Viet Cong. A favorite game at Quan Loi was to ambush NVA patrols visiting a certain Frenchman's home. The NVA used the plantations as sites for their mortars and rocket launchers, but we seldom got permission to shoot back. When we did attack the enemy weapons, the French were reimbursed for every damaged or destroyed rubber tree. The French in Vietnam had fought their own war with the Indochinese Communists. They knew who would win this one. They took what our side offered while remaining on good terms with their future masters.

I worked in the ARVN compound at An Loc, reviewing intelligence reports and sending the best targets to the gun crews. The reports gave me quick notice of what had changed since I had left in March. There were entire NVA divisions across the border in Cambodia, some with tanks and all armed to the teeth with artillery, multiple rocket launchers, and heavy mortars. The Cav was facing five separate divisions. To make matters worse, the NVA were re-arming the local Viet Cong with the latest weapons of all sizes. They were preparing for another Tet.

On my off-duty nights, I sat in the bar at the An Loc Compound and talked with an ex-sergeant of my age. He was an officer in a guerrilla force called the Green Lizards. They assassinated Viet Cong village chiefs and made hit-and-run attacks to capture prisoners. The Green Lizards were a strange crew of Vietnamese, Germans, French, Americans, and Cambodians, all of whom kept a very low profile. I never saw more than two of them at one time, and they never spoke to the regular troops. They were probably some sort of CIA mercenary unit.

One evening in the bar, the "officer" told me how they had killed a village chief that morning. They had been chased down the road by the village Viet Cong unit, and he had destroyed the place with artillery shells. I asked him what good it did to shoot the chief and then destroy the village. He couldn't answer that. The talk stopped when 82mm mortars exploded nearby, and we crawled under a heavy oak table.

The mortars were the bitter side of An Loc. They had become a daily menace since the arrival of the Cav. The 1st Cav was again destroying an armed truce like the one that had existed in the Chu Lai area before our arrival there. The shells crashed across the compound every day. Sometimes they landed on the lawn of the province chief's mansion, and other times they sprayed an ugly statue of a South Vietnamese infantryman with fragments. The NVA were after that statue. Once a schoolgirl at recess was killed. The school yard was in a direct path from the statue, and I'm sure the child's death was an accident. One of the shells exploded too far off target. The statue and the compound would be mortared again each night.

Two nights before I left An Loc, the NVA blew off the town gate with an antitank rocket and held a propaganda rally in the town square. The government garrison locked themselves in their homes until they left at dawn. The next evening I listened to Quan Loi being shelled by rockets, mortars, and recoilless rifles. The barrage was bigger than anything I had ever heard. On my last day in An Loc, I sat breathlessly once again as the mortars crashed across our compound, then gathered my small bag of belongings for a jeep trip to Bravo Troop.

I had already suffered through more shellings at An Loc than I had experienced during my first twenty-five months in Vietnam. The enemy no longer had a shortage of equipment and were bold enough to fire long barrages in broad daylight. I laughed at the thought of the familiar dawn crowds of soldiers in 1966 and 1967. The morning after each mortar attack, there had been a rush of people to the impact area to pry out the tail fins for souvenirs. It was not uncommon to see a full colonel and a private running for the same tiny crater to get a souvenir paperweight. Nobody bothered to collect such toys after the Tet Offensive. They were too common.

We had seen the beginning of this buildup a year earlier at Bong Son when the 9th Cav gunships had slaughtered those groups of lost but heavily armed replacements. No one had drawn any long-range conclusions in those days. We had believed that the war was almost over.

CHAPTER 15

The Mountain of the Old Man

(November 1968–February 1969)

I became a team leader in the Blues and was soon learning firsthand how things had changed. The old Huey gunships were being replaced with Cobra gunships. We called them "snakes." The Cobras were faster and carried more weapons, but they didn't have door gunners or fly at low level like the Huey gunships. Most of the Vietnamese killed by gunships in Vietnam had been hit by door gunners. The fancy miniguns, rockets, and 40mm cannon made impressive fireworks, but only rarely did they do more than force the enemy soldiers to keep their heads down. When they looked up, they were staring at a door gunner's machine gun. Snakes were "area suppression" weapons that were too sophisticated for guerrilla war. They became flying gun platforms to support the scout choppers, and the number of dead enemy soldiers dropped to about a third of what it had been. That third was mainly the work of the brave scout pilots and gunners.

The old H-13 scout choppers, the bubbles, had been replaced by the more maneuverable Hughes LOHs (light observation helicopters). LOHs look like brown eggs with four stubby rotor blades on top. They were easier to shoot down than the bubbles, and too often they exploded when they crashed. The pink teams of one scout chopper and one gunship were now standard throughout the 9th Cav and throughout Vietnam. Other units called them "hunter-killer teams," but we still called them pink teams. This arrangement, with the snake flying high and the LOH flying low, made scout pilots and gunners a very expendable commodity. They died quickly.

Some frustrated military genius had developed a rescue concept called "pile on," and it was now a standard procedure in the 9th Cav. The idea was to impress the enemy with your strength by rapidly increasing the number of helicopters over the danger point until their presence was overwhelming and frightening. In practice, the result was an aerial circus. If a chopper was shot down, pink teams in the area would fly to its location. Helicopters from the base camp were scrambled. Each chopper left as its crew arrived and its engine was brought up to proper RPMs. The result was usually a staggered line of choppers stretching over many miles. The rescue area gradually became a confusion of orbiting snakes, scouts, and slicks. The coordination of former 9th Cav landings was lost in a whirling insect cloud of different types of helicopters.

It was common for the first slick-load of Blues to arrive at a crash site fifteen or more minutes before the last one. If someone misjudged the situation, a squad or a single team of soldiers might find themselves landed in hell. I saw it happen several times. The 9th Cav rescue operations of earlier years had involved a formation of slicks escorted by a minimum of four gunships. We would roar into an area at high speed and land with a suddenness and a calculated violence that almost always disorganized the enemy. "Pile on" made ours the only confusion in 1969.

The generals were now worried about public opinion and casualties, and the Blues were often not landed where they formerly would have been. But the defensive tactics were a mistake. The NVA built enormous jungle ammunition depots. They shelled the Americans in their bases and trained sappers to breach the wire and destroy lives and equipment. The war became an impersonal affair. NVA were killed by scouts and snakes or by artillery and B-52s. Americans were killed by rockets and mortars or by infantry attacks and suicidal sappers. The big battles in 1969 were fought at the defensive wire of the Cav bases, not deep in the jungle, where the enemy had once been hunted and attacked. Landings were often left to LRRP teams, who usually had orders to report on NVA activities or on the locations of ammunition dumps, but not to start fights.

An army on the defensive has serious problems. Discipline begins to disintegrate. Our already demoralized soldiers, feeling impotence at the constant rain of high explosives, turned on each other. Men of color against the whites, blacks and hippies against the juicers (men who drank), officers and NCOs against the enlisted men, violent addicts of the false-power drug, Binoctal, against everyone else. The changes were starting in the rear areas in 1968–69, but they would sweep through the entire Vietnam Army and Marine Corps by the early 1970s. Even the Cav would have its mutinies.

My squad had nine soldiers. The squad leader was a draftee, like six of the others. The exception was Private Krueger, a German who had volunteered for duty in Vietnam. Krueger had come a long way to fight, and he was disappointed that the Blues didn't make many landings. He would have loved the Blues of 1967. My main headache was Private Granite. He was a draftee from the hills of Tennessee and recognized no authority from anyone born north of the Mason-Dixon line. Granite's best quality was his love of a good fight, even if it was for an army he detested. His most common profanities were "nigger" and "Yankee." He was in my squad because there weren't any niggers. There was at least one Yankee.

My first landing with the Blues was a frightening experience. The slicks carried us over the B-52 crater fields that marked the Cambodian border, and we jumped into the moonscape. The NVA were living there by digging spider holes into the sides and bottoms of the craters. We ran toward the leafless white trees of a defoliated forest. It was my first experience with the effects of Agent Orange. We found bunkers in the dead forest, but the NVA had retreated across the border into Cambodia. It was an alarming patrol. Two squad leaders conducted all the reconnaissance activities, and the platoon sergeant walked point. The rest of the Blues wandered aimlessly behind the platoon sergeant, crowded together for protection. I knew after that one landing that I had returned to a shadow of the former platoon.

The Blues sat by the choppers for several more days, and then Dusty Delta moved in down the road from us. I wondered what the jeep soldiers would be like now, so I walked over to their tent camp. I found Pete leaning against my old artillery jeep.

"Peterson! You're still around!"

"Brennan, what in the hell are you doing back?"

"I was bored. How are things with Dusty Delta?"

He frowned. Still didn't like that name. "Good. The troop's a lot tougher than it used to be."

"Pete, I thought there weren't any FOs with the Ninth Cav."

"There aren't. I'm the last one. They let me stay until I got tired of it, and I've about had it. I'm going home in two weeks. Been here twenty-nine months now."

Pete told me that Dusty Delta had left its jeeps behind and operated as an infantry company in the mountains around Khe Sanh. He thought the tea plantation country was the most beautiful place he had ever seen. Later, the Delta company walked into the A Shau Valley with the 101st Airborne. Their biggest day came in August, when they helped kill 140 NVA in the coastal village near Evans that the Marine pilots had refused to fly over. The survivors of the NVA garrison had been sealed in their bunkers by bulldozers.

Pete invited me to join Dusty Delta on patrol through the rubber plantations. I spent six days on patrols around Quan Loi. The jeeps would drive down the straight red earth roads, then we would park them along the road shoulders and walk through the rubber trees. We ate our C-rations in the little villages laid out in squares surrounded by the plantations. The villagers always gave us gifts of armfuls of bananas and breadfruit. The breadfruit tasted like a cross between bananas and oranges, and it was delicious. One day a sniper shot at us from deeper inside the plantation. We charged past rubber trees bleeding sticky white sap from our bullets, only to find cartridge cases and a Viet Cong bush hat in the mud of a shallow trench. The sniper had escaped down a fire lane through the trees. Dusty Delta was acting more like a Blue platoon than a bunch of jeep soldiers.

On my seventh day with Delta Troop, we convoyed north to the town of Loc Ninh, through a hot scrub country of brush and dead trees. About a mile outside the town, we passed the twisted wreckage of a line of APCs. Several of them had gaping holes in their armor, and the lead vehicle had been reduced to massive chunks of metal by a powerful land mine. The town of Loc Ninh was scarred and half-ruined from the pre-Tet battles of a year before. Some of the buildings had been demolished by antitank rockets, and many of the stucco walls had disintegrated under machine gun fire. The burned-out APCs had been part of an ambushed rescue force. We turned the jeeps around on the manicured lawn of a big French villa and headed back toward Quan Loi. The villa was apparently undamaged from the fierce battles that had raged only two hundred yards away.

Pete said his good-byes that night at Quan Loi. "I'm leaving because my mother's afraid I'll get shot. I promised her I wouldn't extend again."

"That's a good enough reason. Just don't give up like I did. You've been here too long already."

"Maybe. I might be seeing you in a few months. Take care of Combat Bolten for me. I'm concerned about the little squirt."

"Bolten?"

"Didn't you know? He's a scout gunner over at B Troop now. Crazy as a loon. He's got some kind of super–death wish. He has three Silver Stars now, but his luck's not going to hold out forever."

"So, sad little Bolten is still around. I'll probably see him after you're gone, but we were never friends."

"Just tell him to go home, Matt."

"All right, Pete. If I see him." Then Pete was gone. I returned to a Blue platoon that had been sitting by the slicks for seven days.

* * *

The slicks took us over a region of tall grass and hedgerows to the place where oily black smoke rose from the edge of a dead wood. A Charlie Troop scout chopper had exploded and burned. We jumped into a grassy clearing and Charlie Blues landed behind us. I didn't recognize a single man. Brave Fighter Blues left to find the scouts' bodies, but our platoon made no effort to protect the clearing. The Blues stood around in small clusters and posed for pictures. The platoon sergeant and all the squad leaders gathered in front of a hedgerow for a group shot. One well-aimed burst from an AK-47 would have wiped out the platoon's leaders.

Charlie Blues returned dragging two body bags and were extracted by their choppers. Our choppers followed. As the slicks lifted us out of the clearing, I saw the hedgerow where the sergeants had been posing for pictures. Behind it was a bunker in the grass, and crumpled in front of the bunker were two bodies in green uniforms and pith helmets. Their AKs were lying beside them.

The air rattled with the sound of a heavy machine gun, and I saw two barrels flashing in the shade of some trees below us. I emptied three magazines at the flashes and shook the frightened man next to me until he started shooting. Our tracers disappeared into the trees around the barrels, and the twin machine gun stopped firing.

A familiar face appeared in the doorway of my tent that evening. Private Page hadn't changed much, except that now he was a specialist and sported a big handlebar mustache. "Page? I don't believe it. Did you extend?"

"Yeah, Sarge. I heard you're back. Brought you some news."

"What news?"

"I work over at troop operations now. Anyway, Charlie Troop called a couple of hours ago and said you guys killed an NVA this morning. I checked around and found out that you were the one who did the shooting."

"You mean the twin twelve-seven?"

"That's it. They said to tell you it was good shooting." He

remained standing in the doorway. He needed something else. "Sarge, would you do me a big favor?"

"Sure."

"Come here a second." He led me to a tent occupied by a small group of enlisted men from the operations section. He pointed to the upturned faces. "They don't believe me. Tell them I got a Distinguished Flying Cross and killed ninety-eight NVA in those first days at Evans."

I looked at the man who had called me a baby-killer in 1967 and nodded. "It's true. He did it." They looked at Page with new respect.

Blue was in the body business for the next six weeks. The scouts would fly out day after day, each time killing more NVA. Then one inevitable day we would have to go out and bring back the charred remains of the scouts. This was heavy lowland jungle, and if a chopper went down, it usually exploded and burned. I couldn't enjoy the smell of a wiener roast for years after those horrible landings around Quan Loi.

New LOHs with miniguns arrived, but the guns were removed because they added too much weight and their vibrations shortened engine life. In the last days of 1968, a new LOH strayed about a thousand yards into Cambodia. The pilot came in over tall jungle trees and saw a group of seated NVA receiving a lecture from a man on a podium. The pilot sprayed the assembly with his minigun, and then the snake dived. Before the fireworks were over, forty-one NVA were dead in their jungle classroom.

Once a scout chopper left Quan Loi at dawn and flew toward Cambodia over a field of old B-52 craters. The gunner watched a man in green come out of a wood, yawn and stretch, and walk over to a crater. When the LOH got back to him, he was pissing in the muddy hole. He was dead before he could finish.

Another LOH surprised a column of NVA resting beside a bulldozer near the abandoned Bu Dop Special Forces Camp. The gunner killed eighteen men on the first pass, then snakes and bombers finished the work. The scouts were the most exposed

Americans in this new style of war. It was fast becoming a remote control affair, fought with machines and steel rather than with flesh and blood.

The scouts never knew what they might find. Once at Chu Lai, a scout chopper surprised a young Viet Cong with his pants down. He had a carbine strapped across his back and was screwing a village maiden on top of a haystack. The gunner had spotted him because of the sunlight reflecting off his naked ass. The gunner expertly shot him off her and watched the girl scream and hide her eyes. When she finally looked, he waved and the chopper flew away.

We were after the crew of a downed LOH from an artillery unit. It had been hit by a heavy machine gun in a place we called

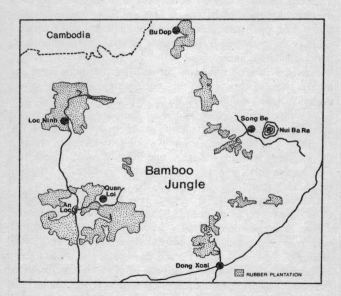

210

the "bamboo jungle." Agent Orange had destroyed the leaves of many of the jungle trees, and the sudden flood of sunlight had made the normally small clumps of bamboo grow into a tangled jungle of giant green and yellow stalks. Scientists now call it hypergrowth.

The slicks hovered down between the tall white trees, one ship at a time. We hung from the skids and dropped into the clearing created by an old bomb crater. We crossed a trail and stepped around a bunker where someone had been eating C-rations minutes before. The juice was still dripping from a can of ham and lima beans. If the NVA wanted to eat that meal, they could have it. A man ran to us from behind a clump of bamboo, and the squad leader on point almost shot him. He was the artillery observer from the downed LOH, and he was crying.

"God damn! Am I glad you guys got here! The pilot's hurt real bad!"

The injured pilot was lying on a bed of red jungle flowers only a few feet from where the LOH burned on its side in a clump of the giant bamboo. Doc Mitchell dragged him farther away from the flames and spread ointment over his burned chest, face, and arms. We strapped the pilot to a jungle penetrator stretcher, and he was pulled up through the trees by a medevac helicopter. It was time for us to get out, but the bomb crater clearings were too small for the slicks to use as "hover holes."

The circling pilots sounded hysterical over the radio. "Blue Mike, this is Saber Red. Move to the yellow smoke and prepare for extraction! Move to the yellow smoke! Move quickly! I say again, move quickly!"

We reached one of the bomb craters and an LOH dropped chain saws and axes. Two squads worked like demons to cut down small trees and bamboo, while my squad searched the jungle around the crater. The bomb blast and the hypergrowth had created a solid wall of vines and bamboo. It was impossible to find anything. When the clearing was big enough for a hover hole, the slicks pulled us out. Their blades chopped bamboo all the way in and out.

We had just reached Quan Loi when the jungle erupted with a string of black explosions, and the rumbling thunder of a B-52 strike swept past us. The bamboo jungle had been declared a "No Fly Zone" the day before, but the artillery LOH had flown over anyway. B-52 strikes were computer controlled, and once the big jets left Guam, they couldn't be turned back easily. We had been extracted just in time.

Page visited me again that evening. We had been best of friends since I had confirmed his war stories. I could tell he had some interesting news by the way he was grinning. "You boys had a close call this morning."

"That's putting it mildly."

"Hey, Sarge. Guess what the scouts found after the strike."

"Let's see. Craters?"

A sadistic grin. "Oh, better than that. They found five smashed twelve-sevens in the area where the LOH went down. They were all around you in the bamboo. Oh, yeah. I almost forgot. There was a dead gook ten meters from your hover hole."

Page, the bearer of ill tidings. "Thanks, Page."

The next afternoon, we were landed for a rare recon mission in an abandoned rubber plantation. Our point squad leader came face to face with an NVA on a narrow trail. Both of them fired until their rifles were empty, missing completely, then turned and ran. As the squad leader ran past me, the fear on his face reminded me of Patterson's expression the day his rifle had jammed in the Suoi Ca. The difference was that Patterson had been in Vietnam two weeks. The squad leader had been with the Blues for eight months.

On another day, we were taken to one of the few unbombed regions along the Cambodian border. The Air Force had dropped electronic movement sensors there, and the sensors had detected something. Our target was an open field of elephant grass sandwiched between heavy jungle on the north and south. I wondered why the camouflage-crazy NVA would infiltrate through elephant grass instead of jungle.

We jumped into the chest-high grass and carefully approached a trail the LOHs had discovered. The trail was made by wild water buffalo. There was not a single human footprint among the hundreds of hoofprints. Then we found a movement sensor. It was camouflaged to look like a green metal tree but was out of place in the light brown grass. The story of the "infiltrating water buffalo" circulated throughout the troop for months afterward.

Then the scouts found another "mortar." The Blues walked for hours through rubber trees that had been heavily shelled years before. At the edge of the old plantation in a jumble of rotting trees was the red marking smoke. A scout chopper hovered there, firing tracers into the plantation. Among the branches was the upturned tail section of a 500-pound bomb, rusty with age and looking for all the world like a mortar tube. Krueger had been watching me. He was curious.

"You don't look surprised like the others, Sergeant."

"It's happened twice before."

"Where?"

"In 1966 and 1967, when the Blues were at Bong Son."

"Oh. Where's Bong Son?"

What was the use of explaining? The events had happened a million years ago. "We'll talk about it sometime, okay?"

"Yes, Sergeant." Krueger was a good soldier. He asked only the proper questions.

We spent the nights in January and February guarding a mountaintop in War Zone D. Its Vietnamese name was Nui Ba Ra, but we used our translation, "The Mountain of the Old Man." It was the highest point in the province, and from the top we could see for miles in all directions. The slicks would come in over the limestone cliffs and clinging jungle, deposit us on the summit, and return to Quan Loi.

There was a small ARVN infantry unit and a radio relay station already there, so the defenses were prepared. There were bunkers, several rows of barbed wire, and a ring of deep trenches. The sleeping quarters were sandbagged steel "conex" shipping containers. The circular position was about fifty yards across, and we could easily defeat a large force from behind the closeknit defenses, but the ARVNs didn't want us to prove it. Some of them glared at us, and others cursed when we test-fired our weapons into the trees below. When Blues lobbed grenades far down the steep sides of the mountain, the ARVNs would put their index fingers to their lips to tell us to be quiet. Their expression would say, "Don't piss off the Viet Cong who own this mountain. They might think it's us making the noise."

The place was very rocky, and I knew that mortar shells could turn rock splinters into deadly shrapnel. I was in charge of the squad, so I called my men together. "I want everyone to sleep in the conex containers, not on top of them. If mortars ever hit this place, they'll get everyone who's not under cover."

Granite objected, as usual. "Aw, Sarge. The conexes are hot. The other squad leaders aren't making their men sleep inside. The guys on the relay station say this place hasn't been mortared since September."

"Granite, if you only knew how many times I've heard that. Now we're here. The gooks hate the Cav, and I promise you we'll be mortared. You have to sleep inside the conex containers or you'll be hit by flying pieces of rock."

Krueger backed my judgment. "I think the sergeant is right. It would be safer."

The other men nodded in agreement. After all, it was their lives I was talking about, and I was going to sleep in a conex container even if no one else in the platoon did. Granite walked away from us, muttering under his breath about "that brown-nosing kraut." Krueger stared after him in hurt silence.

Nui Ba Ra was a place with a reputation. A 101st Airborne platoon had been overrun there over three years before, and the story had passed to each new unit that occupied the summit. The Viet Cong had left the heads on stakes along the barbed wire. There had been repeated attacks since then, but the Blues got off lightly. The outpost was mortared several times during the Tet attacks of 1969, and the NVA infantry tried to capture the place one night in late February. The Blues stopped them at the wire. But there was a more frightening thing. Dawn once revealed a Viet Cong flag flying from a pole outside the barbed wire. It was booby-trapped with a Chinese claymore mine. That claymore is what the Blues remembered about Nui Ba Ra. Let me tell you why.

Claymores are mines that blast out hundreds of fragments in an arc. The American claymore is a marvel of engineering. It is an outwardly curved rectangle of high impact plastic backed by a steel plate. On the front of this little gem are the words FRONT TOWARD ENEMY. This contraption is placed against a boulder or a tree to protect the firer from the blast. The explosion follows the line of least resistance, hurling out a lethal shower of ball bearings.

The Chinese varieties came in several sizes, for revolutionaries of all ages, but were all brown and bowl-shaped. They were hung in trees on a nice steel handle provided for the purpose. And no ball bearings for the Chinese! A hinged door on the front opened to allow the mine to be filled with nails, pieces of rusty metal, bolts, glass, or sharp rocks. I once visited one of my soldiers, who had been hit by a Chinese claymore. His souvenir was a steel nut removed from within an inch of his spine.

Claymores were usually detonated by a man hiding somewhere and waiting for other men to walk in front of his mine. It was the most brutal weapon used by both sides in the war, partly because of its effectiveness and partly because of the way it was fired. In 1966, a 9th Cav ambush used claymores to wipe out an entire group of fourteen NVA along a mountain trail. They had been trying to escape a battle behind them in Happy Valley. In 1966, a soldier from the 173d Airborne Brigade told me how every other man in his squad had been killed by a Chinese claymore ambush. His effectiveness as an infantryman was over. He could only think about dying. The very word *claymore* could produce fear in men who knew what the mine could do.

The first night on Nui Ba Ra, we watched artillery and flares over the war zone below. Many miles to the east was a sea of light. Perhaps it was Saigon. At about 4:00 A.M., a B-52 strike tore apart the dark jungle to the west of the mountain. The strikes were called "arc lights," and for the first time, I realized how they were named. For a long instant, the area looked as if an intensely hot electric light were burning over the jungle. Toward dawn, a firefight erupted to the southeast. Red, white, and green tracer streams crossed and flickered out. It was a typical night on the mountain. The slicks came for us at dawn.

The scouts were enjoying "good hunting." The Communist divisions were massing northwest of Saigon for another Tet offensive, but this time the big bombers would crush them before they left their jungle camps. One morning, a scout chopper surprised a long column of NVA coming out of the jungle, walking along a streambed, and re-entering the jungle farther ahead. The LOH hovered over the streambed and the gunner shot a number of NVA; he wasn't sure how many. Then the little chopper landed while the gunner loaded aboard a 57mm recoilless rifle, a .30 caliber machine gun, and some rifles. They were put on display at Quan Loi. I was looking at the weapons when Bolten walked up. It was the first time I had seen him at close range in twelve months, and he looked ten years older.

He looked fondly at the trophies. "Aren't they something, Sarge?"

"Yeah. Did you have anything to do with getting them?"

"Of course. The gooks never knew what hit them." He had made the proper impression, so he turned to leave.

"Bolten? Can I talk to you for a minute?"

He looked like a caged cat. "Why?"

"You've been here a long time. You know, the first time I ever saw you was the day you killed that tax collector near Bong Son."

"I remember. He was my first gook. The lieutenant kept the money for the squadron orphanage, right?"

"Right. I know it's none of my business, but what I was wondering is, are you ever going home?"

I got a quick answer. "No! The Cav's my home. I don't want to leave."

"What about your family. Don't they miss you?"

A look of pure hate and venom. What did I say wrong? "You're right, Sarge. It's none of your business, but I'll tell you anyway. I don't have a family, just foster homes growing up. The state pays some greedy bitch to feed you. Where else can I walk into a club where there's a Ninth Cav guy and have him always buy me a drink? These people here really care." Another cat-eyed look. "What about your family? You've been here forever, too."

"I know. They think I'm crazy, but they're willing to let me make my own mistakes. I guess the difference is that they'll be there when I get back."

"Well, I'm not leaving! My main problem is trying to figure out what to do when the war's over. Maybe they'll need mercenaries in Africa again." Bolten ended our awkward conversation by walking away. He never gave me the opportunity to question him again, but I knew he was there only to die.

The little recoilless rifle meant something special. Headquarters units carried them. Rear echelon dudes. That was why it had been so easy for the scouts to land in the middle of an enemy column and gather trophies. Intelligence received a report that a scout helicopter had shot a North Vietnamese command group in a streambed. One of the dead NVA was a general. The scouts celebrated the news with an orgy of steaks and beer.

It was February twelfth. It was our turn. Two LOHs were burning in the rubber trees. The first one was shot down over some big rubber log bunkers. The second one had "piled on" to rescue the crew and had been shot out of the sky. Red smoke marked our landing zone beside old French plantation buildings in a big rectangular clearing. The main building looked like a brown tropical copy of a Southern mansion. The four slicks dropped toward the clearing, and hell broke loose.

The rubber trees were blinking like Christmas tree lights from the flashes of rifles. A machine gun fired white tracers from an upstairs window of the mansion. My slick came in fast along a ditch on the edge of the clearing, and the men on my side jumped.

217

The clacking roar of AKs continued until the slick was out of sight above the rubber trees, then there was silence. The four of us stared at each other. We were alone in the clearing. Three of the slicks had been driven off by the intense fire. The Blues on the other side of my slick had refused to jump. Two of them had already been shot.

With me were Doc Mitchell, a rifleman, and a new sergeant with a radio. That radio saved our lives. We belly-crawled along the ditch as a brushfire ate its way toward us. A single AK fired into the air, and it was joined by dozens more as a snake dived for a rocket run. The rockets hit the stucco front of the mansion, raising clouds of brown and gray dust. The machine gun still fired upward from a shuttered window on the second floor.

I shouted to the others, "Hit that window! They've got a thirty caliber up there!"

Plaster and paint flew around the window, and the barrel swung in our direction. They couldn't aim well because of our fire. Ruby, the new sergeant, radioed the snakes about our problem. He got a quick response.

Ruby pulled a smoke grenade from his harness. "Pop smoke! The gunships are making a run on the building!"

The smoke marked our location. A snake roared across the plantation at treetop level and hovered long enough to fire a salvo of rockets at the mansion. The wall around the window disintegrated and the machine gun was silent. A dazed soldier stumbled through the front door and ran in our direction. He didn't see us. Doc shot him.

Doc sucked in a deep breath and shook his head. "He was heading right at us! Man, I got him!"

The brushfire was getting closer. We lay in the ditch with our feet almost touching and faced in four different directions. I was watching the rubber plantation that began about thirty yards away. Something brown was moving there. I focused on a man in a khaki uniform and jungle hat, pack and AK, motioning on a line of other soldiers behind him. Brand-new troops, still wearing khaki uniforms!

The NVA dodged from tree to tree like Indians. The leader

ran straight at us in a crouch, firing short bursts from his AK. I took careful aim and squeezed off a five-round burst. The leader flopped on his back beside a rubber tree, legs kicking and jerking. The soldiers behind him dived for cover, so I emptied the rest of the magazine into the rubber trees at ground level. I had learned a hard lesson from the NVA. Always shoot the leader.

Ruby told the gunship pilots that the rubber trees were full of NVA. We popped more smoke, then two snakes came over, filling the air with the buzzing crack of flechette rockets. The NVA were hit by a whirring volley of thousands of steel darts. Clack-clack-clack. Bullets dug up the edge of the ditch beside me. The ditch was on fire, and the NVA in the trees were dodging rockets, so the bullets had to be coming from the neat piles of rubber branches about halfway between us and the trees. I raised my head and looked at the nearest pile. Clack-clack-clack. The burst kicked dirt in my face and eyes. I rubbed my eyes until I could see clearly out of one, pulled the pin on a TNT concussion grenade, and waited. When another team of snakes dived, I tossed the grenade. A black explosion scattered the branches. Somewhere among them was a dead man. The other Blues cringed from the unexpected blast.

"Hey! Everyone take one of these concussion grenades. We can use them on those branch piles if they try to use them for cover." I passed out three of my five remaining TNT grenades.

Ruby grabbed a concussion grenade, listened to his handset, and pulled the pin on another smoke. "Pop smoke! Gunships are making a minigun run on the edge of the rubber!"

I saw the snake dive, then the whole world was roaring. We were lost in a cloud of dust and flying dirt. Doc Mitchell rolled over on his back and groaned. Ruby gaped at him. The snake circled back for another run. I shook Ruby like a rag doll. "Tell them they were shooting at us! Quick, man, before that snake makes another run!" Ruby started to say something. "Don't fuck around! Do it!"

He fumbled with his handset and found his voice again. "Red.

Red. That smoke marked our location. I repeat, that smoke marked our location. Call off the snake! The medic got hit by that run. The medic got hit by that run." No snake pilot would ever remember hearing that message. None would ever admit that he might have been shooting a little off target. It was always the same reply: "The VC shot him."

Doc used his teeth to tighten a field dressing around his upper arm, and then he looked at the rest of us. "It's okay. I know how bad a wound is. It's just a flesh wound." He made a weak smile to show us that the wound didn't hurt.

Ruby finally got the merciful message. "They're going to try to get us out. They want us to throw all our smoke grenades at the woods for a smoke screen."

The rifleman laughed. "Yeah. Let's throw all two of them."

The brushfire was only a few yards away, but to run would have been suicidal. We crawled farther down the ditch. Ruby and the rifleman threw two red smoke grenades at the rubber trees, and I lobbed my last two concussion grenades into more wood-piles. A slick dropped into the clearing, flanked on each side by a rocket-firing snake. It landed just behind us, and we ran to board it. Two of us ran backward, spraying the rubber trees, and the other two triggered bursts at the mansion and outbuildings. A line of bullets kicked up dirt in front of the slick's nose as I scrambled aboard. It lifted out over the brushfire, and the rubber trees started flashing again.

Something slammed into my boot. I felt the foot go numb as we climbed away from the clearing. When I stepped off the slick at Quan Loi, I had trouble walking. The grass was bloody every time I put my left foot down. I sat down in the grass, pulled off the boot, and stared at the hole in my precious big toe. It was the one place I didn't want to be shot. I had heard of soldiers who shot themselves there to get out of combat. I was determined to prove that it wasn't self-inflicted.

I had the wound dressed at an aid station. A doctor stuck a wire completely through my toe and twirled it around inside the hole. It hurt like hell. I was tagged for medical evacuation but sneaked out of the tent and hitched a jeep ride back to Bravo

Troop. I wanted another crack at the NVA in the rubber trees. The bodies of one LOH crew had not been rescued.

It didn't work the way I had planned. The entire leg was swollen and painfully throbbing by the next morning. I limped to the headquarters tent and begged for a ride back to the aid station. Two days later, I arrived in Japan. My companions were Doc Mitchell, two other Blues, a scout pilot, and a scout gunner. The gunner had earned the name Crazy Man a few days before. His LOH was shot at from a maze of bunkers in War Zone D. It had been shot at mainly because the pilot had hovered there while Crazy Man stood on the skids and pissed on the bunkers. Now he had a bowl full of Darvon begged from sympathetic nurses and was intent on staying high until he was healed and could piss on some more VC.

The hospital in Japan was a turning point in my life, but in those first hours I was only angry that the Army had sent me so far from the fighting for such a little wound.

The man in the next bed was a Special Forces staff sergeant. A bullet had shattered his femur. His team had ambushed a trail in Laos and caught the NVA in a claymore and machine gun cross fire. Instead of waiting to die, the NVA had charged the machine guns. One of them shot the sergeant as he was being killed. The sergeant was tired.

"I've been in the Nam for thirty-five months, and I've never seen men like that. Each year they get harder and better armed. Those dudes wouldn't die out there. We kept hitting them and they just kept coming. I'm glad this happened to me. They're getting too much heart. Just too much heart."

I saw him leave for home one day, leaning on a cane and smiling. He said he hoped some "good guys" would need a mercenary in a few years. He preferred Asia to Africa, but he would take what he could get.

The bed on the other side of me held a Marine Corps platoon sergeant. He had been wounded by mortars in the northern part of the A Shau Valley and was afraid his missing eye would force him out of his beloved corps. Beside him was a teenage paratrooper who had been riddled from neck to feet by a Chinese claymore. And so it went.

I rolled my wheelchair to the mess hall one day and heard the grating voice of Private Granite. I figured I had to be mistaken, but Granite was there, wrapped in bandages and trying to bully another soldier out of beer money. I couldn't escape from that hillbilly, not even in Japan. His eyes lit up when he saw me.

"Granite, how did you get here? Did you get hit on February twelfth, too?"

"Naw, Sarge. They mortared Nui Ba Ra."

"Were you inside the conexes like I told you?"

"Nope. We was sleeping on top of them." As if to justify his own actions, he added, "They got the Kraut, too. Through the eyes."

"I warned you guys. That should leave about one man in second squad. Maybe we should have a squad reunion while we're here."

Granite became the motor for my wheelchair. We had a few good days of wheelchair races and wheelchair snowball fights, and then one day I could hobble. One of my first walks took me by the camp library, and I was hungry for books. I stayed in the library from morning to late afternoon. It had a well-stocked section on Southeast Asia, and it fascinated me. After scarcely two weeks, I had read every book on the shelves on Vietnamese history and politics, the French war and the American war. Then I read them again.

The war was very wrong after all. I read the books by Bernard Fall for the third time and realized only too well that our war was an extension of a war against foreigners that the Vietnamese had been waging for over a thousand years. I thought of the wasted bravery and suffering and wondered if America knew what it was doing to itself and to the Vietnamese by continuing that insanity. I had been so blind.

Combat had always been antiseptic in Vietnam. A man would be hit, and the helicopters would whisk him away to be repaired. Dead men were different. They were beyond being helped. But there in Japan, the horrors were piled up for all eyes to see. Head wounds that made vegetables out of strong young men, soldiers with their intestines in clear plastic bags, leg wounds, amputees, and men who shit into bags beneath their shirts. I watched wounds drain and young bodies trying to heal themselves, and I was appalled at the meatgrinder Vietnam had become. In the chaos of 1969, draftees were killing other draftees. Better that they all return to their farms and rice paddies. If we were fighting an aberrant strain of nationalism, and not world Communism or Chinese expansionism, then I had wasted the last three years. I had been convinced of the justice of America's presence in Vietnam. Now I was confused. If the Vietnamese killed me now, I couldn't blame them, because I would be fighting with the terrible knowledge that they would probably win the war.

A Marine staff sergeant of about my age joined me on the bench outside the camp beer hall one cold day in March. We exchanged war stories for a while, then he pointed to a group of young Marines and soldiers who were waiting for the movie house to open.

"Did you notice how much they look alike? The only way you can tell which ones are Marines is by their khaki belts. My first tour was in 1965 at Da Nang. Every one of us a Marine volunteer. Now there's more draftees in the line units than anything else. They fight well when they haven't got a choice, but it's not the same. You know?"

I knew. I had decided to be more concerned with keeping my draftees alive in the months ahead, rather than fighting for the love of fighting. That would be hard enough, because they had to be passable soldiers just to survive. There would be no more war for me after my tour was through. I would try to get out of Vietnam with as much as possible of my mind intact.

CHAPTER 16

Sky Pilot

(March–May 1969)

The troop was now at Redcatcher, the base camp of the 199th Light Infantry Brigade. We lived in modern two-story wooden barracks and slept on steel bunks with springs and mattresses. Redcatcher was part of the sprawling American command and supply center around Saigon that was affectionately referred to as Disneyland East. The accommodations were luxurious. Most of the buildings had air conditioning, and the asphalt roads were lined with hot dog stands, ice cream parlors, clubs, and swimming pools. The Saigon Army knew how to fight a war.

The lost Blues of February twelfth and Nui Ba Ra had been replaced in my absence. The platoon sergeant and three other instant NCOs had gone home. The new lieutenant was still around, and we had a new platoon sergeant, Bigelow. He was a tall, nervous black man in his forties who had spent the last four years in Italy, doing everything in his power to stay out of Vietnam. He wouldn't have made a good pimple on Sergeant Samuel's ass. Doc Mitchell's replacement, Doc Ring, had already been with the Blues for five weeks. He was plump and pink-faced and looked more like a cherub than a medic. The only old NCO was Ruby. He was a fine-featured, olive-skinned Italian from Oregon who was cool in any situation. The fight on February twelfth had been a good crucible.

Only Granite remained in my squad. He had been promoted to specialist, so I made him a team leader, over his bitching and

224

objections. The other team leader was Spear, a lanky paratroop sergeant. Spear had been with the LRRPs for six months, and a new policy allowed him to request a different assignment for the second half of his tour. He had chosen the Blues because he thought they were safer.

The platoon had made a few landings east of Saigon. They had surprised and killed five NVA on the first day at Redcatcher but had seen no combat since then. The five NVA had been deep inside one of the least militarized areas of Vietnam and had apparently been returning from R&R along the beach of the South China Sea. The platoon's longest day had been spent in the blasted wilderness that was the Ho Bo Woods. The Ho Bo Woods had been a dagger aimed at Saigon during the French war and the early days of the American war. B-52s and artillery had reduced it to an emptiness of collapsed tunnels and rotting corpses. That is what the Blues found there. They brought back three decaying heads for souvenirs.

The troop discovered Binoctal at Redcatcher. It could be bought over the counter at Vietnamese pharmacies, and it gave men a sense of general well-being and a false feeling of strength and courage. One Blue was stopped by two MPs after they had watched him walk into a deep ditch. He beat them senseless. On another night, a group of Blues tore up an NCO club and put a lot of rear echelon types in the hospital. Another Blue attacked a mess hall with a white phosphorous grenade because he didn't like the cook. The MPs could never prove that the platoon was responsible for these incidents, but they knew. Late night lineups in front of the Blue barracks became a familiar ritual. Binoctal was addicting. I spent months watching soldiers shaking and sweating as they went through the painful withdrawal.

Our vacation at Redcatcher was mercifully short. We made several more landings in an arid region of red earth and jagged boulders and secured a few downed choppers. Then one sunny morning in April, we loaded the troop's equipment on the slicks and were carried back to Quan Loi. I was glad to be leaving. Binoctal would be harder to get at Quan Loi.

The rubber plantation country was different when we returned.

The NVA had used the Cav's absence to move up 107mm rocket launchers, and these were hitting the base day and night. The Chinese rockets were usually fired in pairs, but sometimes a salvo of twelve would roar in and smash a tent area. I learned to eat Quan Loi's red dust and enjoy it on our first day back. By the second day, we could detect the boom they made when they were fired and use the five to seven seconds before they exploded to run for cover. The fronts of our uniforms were soon the rusty red color of the Quan Loi dust.

The Cav fought back when it could. Once the snakes rocketed the bamboo jungle for an entire afternoon. That stopped the 107s for two glorious days. One day, the Blues were landed at a rocket launching site. All that remained were long detonating wires and blackened patches where the rockets had been leaned against termite hills and fired. The twelve-barreled launchers were heavy and couldn't be moved around easily, so they fired from the untouchable rubber trees. But all the NVA needed to fire a 107 was a rise in the ground and a fair idea of how far it would travel. The constant rocketing became another routine. The boom, the run for cover, the roar, the crash, all were facts of life, like sleep or the rain.

Blue was still "Rescue, Incorporated." It was nearly dusk when the slicks carried us on a thirty-minute ride to the northwest. We passed the abandoned Bu Dop Special Forces Camp and circled over a wild region of massive jungle hills and valleys untouched by bombs or Agent Orange. Below us was primary growth, triple-canopy jungle, and those ugly hills were excellent sites for heavy machine guns. A slick hovered into a jungle valley far below us, and I silently prayed, "Thank God. They're sending in someone else."

The door gunner beside me leaned over and shouted in my ear, "Rappel! Medevac ship shot down by twelve-seven, extracting Special Forces team! Other bird's ropes are too short!" He pointed down. "We're going in!"

Our slick dropped straight down past those ominous hills, then crossed over a camouflaged road. The branches above the flat surface were tied together with vines. We hovered over 120-foot-tall trees. Directly below us was the smashed helicopter, lying on its side in clumps of bamboo. The white background of the red cross was clearly visible in the failing light. The gunner threw down a rope. The specialist sitting in front of it looked at me with pleading eyes.

"I can't do it, Sarge! You go first!"

I was numb with fear. "I'm scared, too! Go! God dammit! Go!"

He hooked his D-ring through the rope, leaned back on the skids, and disappeared. My turn. I hooked up, took a deep breath and jumped backward, riding down the rope in fifteen- to twenty-foot drops. The slick hit an air pocket, the rope tangled in the bamboo, and I was flipped upside down, suspended thirty feet in the air. Now every movement of the slick slammed my back against a jungle tree. It hurt, but the adrenaline dulled the pain. As I hit the tree again, I saw huge burlap sacks of rice beside the road, somewhere beyond the wreck.

The specialist untangled the ropes, and I lowered myself to the ground. We were followed by another rifleman and Sergeant Bigelow with a radio. The slick left us in that terrifying place. The specialist climbed over the belly of the medevac chopper and smashed the lock on the medicine chest with a short fire axe. He stuffed the Methedrine bottles into his leg pockets as the other rifleman gaped at him. Bigelow was hiding under the tail boom, shaking and talking to himself. I ran over to him.

"Is the radio on the right frequency?"

He looked up with a dazed expression. "I can't remember." He picked up the radio and handed it to me. "Here, you take it."

I remembered the right frequency for ground-to-air communications. I don't know how to this day, because no one had given it to me. That frequency was only used by the platoon sergeant. I clicked the dial to a set of numbers, and wondered what I was supposed to say. "Birds. This is Blue Three-Two. We're on the ground." Obviously, you idiot.

"Roger that, Blue."

"Ah, Birds. Do you have any instructions? Over."

"Roger, Blue. Check the downed bird for wounded. We have a medevac on the way to your location. Over."

"Blue Three-Two, roger wait."

I found three men in the wreckage. They were Vietnamese trail watchers in tiger stripe jungle uniforms. One was crushed beneath the side of the chopper and was already dead. Another was pinned in the wreckage and couldn't be freed without a cutting torch. The third man was lying free inside the ship. He was the only one we could hope to save, but save is the wrong word. The two living men had been shot through the head after the chopper had crashed. I knew in that instant that we had a hidden audience.

A medevac chopper hovered over and dropped a stretcher to us. It almost hit Bigelow, and he crawled away to hide beside a clump of bamboo. I gave the trail watcher first aid, trying to keep his brains inside his skull with a field dressing. We strapped him into the stretcher, attached a cable, and watched him hoisted up through the trees. It was dark and raining when I radioed the LOH hovering over us.

"Birds, this is Blue Three-Two. Over."

"White One-One, go."

"Blue Three-Two. How are we gonna get out of here?"

"Roger that, Blue. Medevac will hoist you out. Destroy what you can't salvage from the downed bird and prepare for extraction."

I told the specialist to kill the pinned trail watcher. It was an act of mercy. We riddled the instrument panel and radios with volleys of rifle fire. The NVA had already taken the door guns and the trail watchers' weapons. The jungle penetrator snaked down through the trees. The rifleman went up first, and I followed on the second hoist. The trip up through the trees lasted an eternity. A snake hovered over the medevac ship, firing rockets into a hilltop hundreds of feet above us. I was watching the white flashes of the exploding rockets when four hands grabbed my harness and pulled me aboard.

The specialist was thirty feet in the air when the cable broke and snapped back through the door. He landed in a sitting position on the wrecked chopper, with enough force to break the tail boom away from the rest of it, but that cushion had saved his life. I wondered if he had broken any of his Methedrine bottles. He and Bigelow were hoisted out by a backup medevac chopper.

I rode back to Quan Loi with the worst backache of my life. I tried to help carry the wounded trail watcher to a tent operating room, but the sudden weight doubled me over. I walked behind the stretcher bearers and explained what had happened to a waiting team of three doctors. Then I walked to another tent and sat in the red dust, trying to sort out the events of the past two hours.

When my eyes focused, I saw five more Vietnamese in tiger stripe uniforms. At first I thought it was a hallucination. I came to my senses and made motions of rappelling and bandaging, then pointed to the operating room tent. They thanked me with bows and the Vietnamese folded-hand gesture of submission and left to see their friend. A medevac gunner walked into the tent.

"Hi, Sarge. We got your buddies out. They were dropped off over at Bravo Troop. I'll take you home in a jeep."

"Thanks. I'll walk over. I need the air right now."

He sat down beside me. "That took a lot of balls what you guys did. I've seen a bunch of people leave Fifteenth Med alive because you guys got to them before the gooks did. We think a lot of the Blue platoons."

"Thanks. I was scared. All that kept going through my mind was, 'This is a green hell, this is a green hell.' I hope I'm not going crazy."

He shook his head. "Don't worry about it. That was a bad place. You'll be able to tell people back in the World that you got to see one of the meanest parts of Cambodia close up."

"Thanks."

The green hell was in my dreams for weeks. The mission had been the last straw in many ways. After that, whenever the Blues made a landing, my stomach churned and my heart pounded wildly. It wasn't the fear of dying, which I had conquered long before, but a horror of what we might see or have to do. The awful experiences of the past years were creeping back into my mind. My dreams were filled with exploding rockets and burned scout corpses and charging NVA, dying by the hundreds but always being replaced by more of their brothers.

Spear and I were on duty at the gate bunker to Quan Loi. An APC unit was parked in the rubber trees behind us, and one of the crewmen ran over to our bunker to warn us to stay under cover. Mortars had killed three of his friends the night before. They had been sleeping in pup tents between the armored tracks.

Quan Loi shook with the rapid thunderclaps of Russian and Chinese rockets and the sharp crashes of mortars and recoilless rifle shells. The explosions had a strobe light effect through the rubber trees. The barbed wire about a hundred yards away echoed with the roar of antitank rockets and the firing of massed rifles. Shouts of *"Tien lien! Tien lien!* [Forward, charge! Forward, charge!]" floated across to our bunker on the night air. Spear laid grenades in a row along the sandbags while I rechecked the bunker machine gun.

The shelling continued for hours. Two NVA companies had cut through the barbed wire, swarmed around the defensive bunkers, and turned back two rescue columns. Stray AK bullets smacked into the sandbags around us all night long. The NVA retreated shortly before dawn.

The Blues were sent to patrol the attack area in the early morning half-light. Evidence of the battle was everywhere. We passed a smoking APC and the burning wreckage of a big truck. The truck had been the first vehicle to arrive with reinforcements. The APC had been the lead track of an armored counterattack. Both had been stopped by antitank rockets. Two bunkers had been completely destroyed by antitank rockets in the first minutes of the battle. Other bunkers were blackened, collapsing shells.

Twenty Americans had been killed, and only one NVA body remained. He was a teenage boy, lying next to an equally young blond GI. In an accident of death, their hands were touching. Both the corpses wore green uniforms and similar jungle boots. One of the Blues kicked the American corpse, thinking that it was a dead NVA. He recoiled in horror when another Blue pointed to the blond hair.

The grassy slope leading up to the rubber plantation was littered with bloody bandages, AKs, packs, rocket launchers, satchel charges, grenades, and long green wire cutters. If only those NVA who had left their weapons behind had been hit, at least thirty of them were out of action for a while. A last 107mm rocket roared in as we tossed armloads of enemy equipment in a jeep trailer. It blew apart a squad tent about forty yards behind me.

Smoke rose above the rubber trees throughout the day. APCs from the 11th Armored Cavalry Regiment had trapped some of the retreating NVA. Jets dropped bombs in strike after strike, and snakes dived into the smoke on long rocket runs. The noise was deafening, even over the several miles that separated us from the action.

Because of that attack, the platoon spent most of the next two weeks filling sandbags, laying barbed wire, and erecting anti-rocket screens of cyclone fence. My squad was riding in the back of a truck filled with sandbags when a black cloud erupted behind us. Mortar shells walked down the road after us. The driver floored the accelerator and raced the truck over ruts and potholes. The seventh mortar was the last one. It landed a few feet behind the tailgate.

Granite pushed aside the sandbags that he had been feverishly pulling on top of himself. "Those gooks are using us for target practice."

"Yeah. I know. Tell me what we can do about it."

He threw up his arms in a helpless gesture. "Not a thing, Sarge. Not a nigger lovin' thing."

The convoy is burning. Two more weeks must have passed. A convoy of fuel tankers and ammunition trucks drives up the road from Saigon every two weeks. In the early afternoon, columns of black smoke rise above the rubber trees to the west, and the pink teams roar off. We gather around the radios and listen to the LOHs and APCs searching for the attackers. They usually get away. We are too close to Cambodia here. It has become a costly effort just to keep us supplied. That's the slow horror of Quan

Loi. The North Vietnamese ambush the convoys more violently each time.

Our LOH had crashed and burned. We were trapped in a large clearing in a defoliated jungle only a few hundred yards from Cambodia. Air strikes had not fazed the NVA around us. Spear had been hit by a machine gun as he jumped off the slick. One moment he was beside me, and then he was sprawled facedown, bleeding into the grass.

A squad of Blues was pinned down by a machine gun in the trees. They jumped up and rushed at the gun, shouting at the top of their lungs. One last burst from the RPD, then silence. The NVA ran away, leaving behind his green pith helmet. That display of bravery from the normally listless draftees stunned me. An LOH hovered over the white trees where the NVA had disappeared. Da-da-da-da-da. A twelve-seven fired from the bamboo jungle a few yards ahead of us. We pulled back to the clearing. Camouflage-painted Australian Canberra bombers streaked across the clearing at treetop level, dropping CBUs on the twelve-seven positions.

As the CBUs exploded with a continuous crackle, Granite rose to his knees and shook a fist at the dead trees. "Love thy neighbor, but bomb the fucking Cong!" He looked so ridiculous—a skinny hillbilly shouting at the jungle.

We ran alongside the burning bamboo jungle, heading north toward the greasy black smoke column from our downed LOH. Another LOH hovered over the crash site, and AKs opened fire. Then the NVA turned their assault rifles on us. I dived for cover when bullets kicked up clods of grass and dirt in front of me. I wondered if Blue would ever get off that clearing.

Bigelow received a message that the pilots would fire 155mm artillery along the northern edge of the clearing. We crawled into old artillery craters for cover. The first shells were too close, sending fragments smacking into the ground around us. Granite and I hugged each other in the bottom of our crater as the next four shells whistled in. Crump! Crump! Crump! Crump! The hot concussion sucked the air out of the crater and bounced us off the bottom. Two men in the next crater started screaming.

Granite whispered across the inches separating our faces, "It doesn't look like our day, Sarge."

An LOH flew over the north trees until a burst of AK fire tore up the floor beside the gunner's feet. The chopper veered sharply to one side and raced back over the craters. Another NVA machine gun clattered from the north, showering us with rocks and pieces of dirt. A snake hovered over us and sprayed the area with its minigun. Four thousand rounds a minute chopped down the giant stalks of bamboo. Granite and I took turns slapping red-hot shell casings off each other's uniforms. Our commander radioed for us to wait in the craters for reinforcements. A slick landed behind us and four Blues heaved the wounded men aboard like two heavy sacks of grain. The pilots swung the tail boom around and flew over the south edge of the clearing, over more AKs. I listened on my squad radio as an infantry battalion commander talked with our major.

"Saber Six, this is Golden Lion Six. Over."

"Saber Six, go."

"Golden Lion Six. We have an element of one-one bravos on the way to your location in two lifts. Have your element mark their positions with smoke."

"Roger that, Golden Lion. White will mark lima zulu with red smoke. Over."

"Ah, roger. How big is your element? Over."

"About one eight. Over." Actually, there were only fifteen of us left.

"One eight? Those boys down there have a lot of balls." Maybe we had a lot of balls rolling around in our heads.

The NVA stopped their target practice when twelve slicks came in, followed by twelve more. More than a hundred grunts ran to the north end of the clearing and threw themselves down around us. Four snakes roared overhead to rocket the trees, and the grunts led us into the bamboo jungle. The NVA had fled. A grunt sergeant walked back down the line to our lieutenant.

"The wreckage is up front, sir. We found the bunker that probably got them. They left these behind." He held out a pair of Chinese binoculars, an officer's belt with a pistol, and an AK. "They killed some gooks before they bought it. Looks like a lot of gooks were watching this landing zone."

We gathered the burned pieces of the pilot and gunner and left the grunts in that loathsome place. Later at Quan Loi, Doc Ring and I were sitting inside a bunker, talking about the day's events.

"Do you think Spear made it, Doc?"

"I don't think so, Matt. He looked pretty white when I put him on the slick."

"Just once, I'd like to see a decent man live through this. He went through enough shit with the Lurps."

Granite stuck his head through the entrance and shouted in his grating voice, "Hey, Sarge! Spear's dead!"

It felt like he had hit me with a baseball bat. "Get out of here!"

"Don't come down on me, you fucking Yankee!"

"Get out of here, asshole!"

Granite left and then Doc left, and I sat alone in the bunker for hours, crying. It wasn't only for Spear, but for the wife and two little girls he had loved so much. Tomorrow a man in uniform would knock on their door.

One of the Blues had kept the NVA machine gunner's pith helmet. It had a slogan penned on its side, and we asked Con, our new interpreter, to translate. Con read the words and spat.

"What's it say, Con?"

Con, himself an ex–Viet Cong, spat again into the red dust. "It says he has come South to kill Americans. He prays that he has the chance."

"That son of a bitch! I hope he's dead now, too. Maybe the CBUs got his ass."

I passed a Blue tent later that night. A squad was singing the favorite song of the past few months.

> Sky pilot!
> How high can you fly?
> You'll al-ways, al-ways, al-ways
> Crash and die!

They had never heard of "One Keg of Beer." All they knew were wrecked helicopters and burned bodies.

Morale was nonexistent by late May. The Blues were being used mostly for guard duty or construction. Sometimes a few of us could fly on Nighthawk missions. A Nighthawk was a slick outfitted with four machine guns and a powerful searchlight, followed by a snake. The slick was blacked out, while the snake had all lights on and flashing. The idea was to get the enemy to fire at the snake and then attack them with the four machine guns. It worked very well for a few weeks. The Nighthawks sank supply sampans and attacked jungle rest stations that usually had campfires blazing to heaven to mark their locations.

The Blues waited in line for a chance to fly on the Nighthawk missions. It wasn't much, but it allowed one or two infantrymen to escape the rockets for a couple of hours and fight back. Other Blues occupied their spare time making powerful C-4 bombs for the scouts. We had a real bomb assembly operation going for about a month. We stopped making them when one of my bigger bombs almost blew an LOH out of the sky. When the Nighthawk missions were stopped because a slick got riddled with antiaircraft fire, there was nothing left for us to do but continue waiting for the rockets.

The nights at Quan Loi became grotesque. The sutures on the inside of the Ho Bo Woods skulls were coated with wax, and Blues sipped their beer through the foramen magnums in the bases of the skulls. The platoon splintered into an all-black squad and a Southern white squad. I had one of two neutral squads, but most of the men leaned one way or the other. The tents reeked from vomit and marijuana smoke. Those who didn't drink or smoke popped speed. They had discovered speed on Nui Ba Ra when Doc passed out some big orange tablets to keep us awake at night. Dawn often revealed two or three passed-out Blues, lying in the red dirt between our tents. Sergeant Bigelow was too worried about his own skin to notice that there was a problem. The young lieutenant was more afraid of his platoon than the Viet Cong. We saw him only on the disgusting body landings. He never walked among our tents at night.

It might have become the pattern if Bigelow hadn't spilled a pail of boiling water on himself. A lot of people thought the accident wasn't really an accident. Bigelow's departure made both him and the Blues very happy. Something had to change. Our new platoon sergeant reported to the lieutenant that same night. He was Terry, formerly scout gunner Terry, smiling a boyish smile that hid a fearsome reputation.

Terry was a man in his late twenties who smiled too much. He seemed like a nice person, with that Alfred E. Neuman smile, until you got to know him a little better. I had first heard of him at Redcatcher, where he spent a lot of time bitching about the lack of VC. But such impressions aren't much to go on. He was probably a new dude who wanted to see some action.

But Terry wasn't new. He had been a squad leader with Bravo Blues in 1965, when they started the battle of the Ia Drang Valley and won their first Presidential Unit Citation. That was during Terry's third tour in Vietnam. He had stayed with the Blues until an AK stitched his chest in October 1966. His squad had been crossing a vine bridge in the Suoi Ca. The doctors told Terry he could never return to combat because of his injuries, so he went home to Georgia to be discharged. By then he had spent forty-one months in Vietnam as a Special Forces sergeant, an ARVN advisor, and a Blue squad leader.

Terry might have remained a civilian if his brother hadn't been killed in the 1st Cav. He swore a vendetta with the Communists. He re-enlisted for noncombat training, spent a year in the United States learning how to repair helicopters, then talked a clerk into fixing his records so he could return to the 1st Cav. Terry returned to a Bravo troop where no one knew him. He started as a mechanic, begged his way into gunning a scout chopper, and was finally back with the Blues. All that scheming and planning had been aimed at returning to a platoon he remembered as an elite fighting machine. Other gunners said that Terry didn't know fear. When a man tried to bully him at Redcatcher, Terry pulled out a pistol, held it to the man's temple, smiled, and asked him to reconsider. He did.

Terry called a meeting of the squad leaders his first morning as platoon sergeant. He was smiling as we filed into his cramped room. A smile for each of us. "Okay. This will only take a minute. The major wants the Blues to start going out more, so tell your men to get their gear squared away. We're going to be bopping down trails, so emphasize silent movement and security."

He paused for a moment, thinking of events that had happened long before. "The Blues aren't what they used to be, but that's going to change. This platoon that you are honored to be serving with used to kill more gooks than the infantry battalions. We were called the Headhunters. It was different then." The other squad leaders had no idea what Terry was talking about. They stared at him with blank faces.

The changes were swift. Blue squads were reintegrated and the white and black troublemakers were sent away. The platoon began to practice ambushes and patrolling in the fields of Quan Loi. At night, they'd be called from deep sleep to run through counterattack drills. There wasn't time to sit and wait for the rockets. Soon the new Blues, the long-faced draftees, were wearing the blue bandannas that had been our trademark since 1965. No one told them to do it.

CHAPTER 17

The Highly Decorated Rat

(June–July 1969)

The first landing of the "new Blues" was near the vast Michelin rubber plantation. It was not a complete success. The slicks came in over a field of old bomb craters baked cement-hard under the tropical sun. My slick had a new pilot. He was flying too fast and dumped some of us into the deep craters. I fractured my ankle on the rocky lip of a crater and fell in. The wobbling slick caused the door gunner to lose control of his machine gun. His bullets sent the rest of my squad scrambling into the craters and destroyed a rifle and a grenade launcher that were left behind when two Blues dived for cover. Another slick returned for a man with a dislocated knee, then we finally began the patrol.

My squad led the way down a wide trail toward the NVA camp. We stopped when we reached a four-foot-high earth bank, the outer wall of a large camp. The wall was overgrown with grass and nearly invisible from the air. Inside it was more bamboo jungle with firing slits peeking out under clumps of bamboo. An LOH flew over the wall. Clack-clack-clack-clack. AK fire from a clump of bamboo at the base of a dead tree. The gunner poured down a stream of solid tracers, and the chopper suddenly banked away. The gunner had been shot through the leg. The lieutenant told our grenadiers to hit the firing slits with their grenades. I was listening to the steady Blam! Blam! Blam! reports of the elephant guns when Terry ran over in a crouch.

238

He sat with his back against the earth wall and smiled. "It's not like the old Cav is it?"

"Hell, no. We would have gone in under the scout's fire and grenaded the bunker. The gunner wouldn't have been hit that way."

Terry nodded in agreement. "And that's not half of it. Those chunkers will tell the gooks we're here and give them plenty of time to *Di-di* out of here."

He was right. The only things left in the bunkers were a few items of NVA equipment and one bloody shirt. The camp was a maze of long connected tunnels with firing ports concealed under the clumps of bamboo. The platoon carefully searched the tunnels while LOHs shot NVA climbing over the far wall of the camp. I grenaded one large living bunker and walked down the wooden staircase to have a look.

It was a big room, complete with bunk beds, pinups of Vietnamese swimsuit beauties, a Big Ben alarm clock, and the latest edition of the NLF newspaper. The newspaper had a feature article on how to shoot down 1st Cav helicopters. The front page had a drawing of men in jungle hats firing a machine gun at a slick with the crossed sabers of the 9th Cav. That drawing sent a shiver down my spine. They had precisely identified the 9th Cav as the enemy. There was also a photograph section. It had pictures of peace demonstrations in America, a cluster of NVA infantrymen overrunning a Marine position, and a row of dead GIs. They were typical young Americans with mustaches and sideburns and long hair, lying in the grass along a trail somewhere. One of them had a peace symbol dangling around his neck.

The camp had been a comfortable place to live. In an open pit were a table, chairs, a little potbellied stove, and a sea chest full of china and chopsticks. The pit was covered with a canopy of camouflaged parachute silk. Everywhere were crates of canned fish, sacks of rice, baskets of fresh vegetables, and enough new equipment to outfit several companies of infantry. Boxes of explosives and ammunition were hidden all over the camp. They could easily have stayed and fought, but these

239

were supply depot personnel, the NVA equivalent of our truck drivers and typists.

We took what we could carry and set demolition charges to the stacks of boxes left behind. On the way back to the crater field, Ruby's squad found a park of bicycles painted green, each loaded with more supplies. We took a few of them back to Quan Loi for souvenirs and blew up the rest of them. The scout pilots and gunners were soon using the green bicycles for trips between our tents and the LOHs.

Bicycles were the way the NVA moved their supplies down jungle trails. There were thousands of them northwest of Saigon. A bicycle could be loaded with five hundred pounds of supplies and pushed along the trails to the various camps. The LOHs found entire convoys of them loaded with rice, tires for Ho Chi Minh sandals, ammunition, and replacement weapons. There was seldom a day when at least a few of the bicycles and their porters weren't destroyed. For some reason, the porters always hid behind the bicycles rather than seeking cover in the surrounding jungle. This stupid habit made the supply trains easy targets for the experienced killers in the scouts.

The doctors put a plaster cast on my ankle. I spent the days digging a deep bunker in the ground beside my cot. I put an air mattress in the bottom so I could roll into the bunker when the rockets hit our tent area. The other Blues made daily patrols around Quan Loi. At night I would listen to their war stories and watch them start acting like soldiers again.

One afternoon they were landed near Nui Ba Ra and found a division supply depot with hundreds of cases of mortar shells and rifles. Granite swaggered into my tent that evening wearing a leather NVA belt, now a rare souvenir. He refused to believe me when I told him that the entire Blue platoon had once worn those belts. Con walked past my tent with two AKs strapped across his back. Two NVA guards had made the mistake of shooting at him. Con had crept up behind their bunker and dropped in a grenade. Con was a dangerous man. He had been a loyal Viet Cong until a North Vietnamese squad made a mistake and killed his wife and children. Now he loved to run ahead of the Americans, hunting for NVA. His eyes would become harder than any eyes I have ever seen as he silently ran through the jungle like a hard-muscled cat. I hoped his former comrades were not as brutal and efficient as Con. He called the Communists gooks, just as we did, and one night I asked him why.

"Con, do you think it's right to call the VC gooks and dinks?"

He shrugged. "It makes no difference to me. Everything has a name. Do you think the Americans are the only ones who do that?"

"I don't know. I suppose not. I never really thought about it."

His eyes glassed over for a moment, and he smiled his hard smile. "My company in the jungle"—he swept the countryside around Quan Loi with his arm—"called you Big Hairy Monkeys. We kill monkeys, and"—he hesitated for an instant—"we eat them."

Today the lieutenant was killed. A night patrol of snakes had shot up an NVA truck convoy on the border, and the Blues were landed at a deserted American artillery base nearby. The scouts had flown over the base for hours, dropping tear gas and white phosphorus to flush any NVA, but it looked empty. The platoon was ambushed as soon as they jumped from the slicks. The North Vietnamese had dug spider holes in the corners of the big artillery bunkers and waited for the helicopters to arrive. That's been their favorite trick lately.

The lieutenant ran straight into a machine gun. It happened so quickly that the Blues are split on how he died. Some say he was attacking the machine gun. Others say he was running toward the bunker for cover. In any case, he went down shooting. The Blues killed about twenty NVA in the bunkers or between them and then were pinned down by AK fire from the jungle around the base. The pilots say it could only have been NVA companies waiting to spring a trap. The quick victory at the bunkers confused the NVA, and they fired too soon. Artillery and gunships chased them away.

Terry saved the day. He killed a lot of NVA with grenades and gave me a detailed description of how each of them had died. He especially liked the one who had squealed like a pig until a white phosphorous grenade turned his spider hole into a crematory oven. Terry's story included the squeal. He says the Blues acted like they were running through another drill at Quan Loi. If Bigelow was still here, the platoon would have been lost.

Morale is higher than I have seen it this tour. Most of the draftees are just happy to be fighting back, and other men in the troop are already volunteering for the Blues. We'll miss the lieutenant. He was starting to visit our tents again.

Clashes with NVA scouts and patrols had become a nightly occurrence. It surprised no one when they finally attacked Quan Loi in force. The attack was aimed at Bravo Troop's tents and our flight line along the southern perimeter. Mortars and rockets crashed around the helicopters in a steady drumbeat. The Blues were defending the choppers, and five sappers were already dead. The NVA had mistaken the field hospital beside us for our tent area. The medics and doctors were using their sandbagged hospital tents as fortresses. The sappers used satchel charges and antitank rockets on the medical tents. Flashes and sparks.

Snakes rocketed the bamboo jungle between our flight line and the rubber plantation. Aerial rockets exploded in the bamboo, and AKs fired green tracers at crazy angles. Sappers were being hit and were firing by reflex. Twelve-sevens damaged blacked-out snakes by firing tracers along the streaks from their miniguns. A snake limped back to Phouc Vinh with a wounded pilot. Then Puff the Magic Dragon, a big Air Force transport plane refitted with three miniguns, attacked the twelve-sevens. The tracers from Puff's miniguns looked like flowing pencils of thick red light. One of the red pencils found a twelve-seven, and fat tracers from the big machine gun stitched an arc across the night sky. The machine gunner had continued squeezing the trigger after he was shot. We found his bloodstained pit a few days later. The dueling lasted until dawn.

Twenty dead sappers had been counted inside the wire by the

time I hobbled out to the flight line to help search for survivors. These sweeps were deadly serious. After the last attack, two NVA hid in a drainage pipe for two days. They finally surrendered to a surprised truck driver. If two regular NVA grunts could hide for that long, the sappers could pull off an even better disappearing act.

The flight line was pitted and scarred with rocket and mortar craters. Several of the choppers were smoking wrecks. The bodies of three sappers were sprawled beside a slick and more were lying facedown along the barbed wire. They had been elite soldiers, volunteers with over a year of tough commando training. Each of them wore only green boxer underwear with the fly sewn shut and Ho Chi Minh sandals. They carried wide leather belts with thick brass buckles, hung all around with NVA concussion grenades and demolition charges. One of the belts had been taken from a French Foreign Legionnaire. The inscription on the buckle read *Legio Patria Nostra*. Bandoliers of AK magazines were strapped across the sappers' chests and backs, and their assault rifles had commando-style telescoping metal stocks. They had come to teach the 9th Cav a lesson.

A sapper had died cross-eyed from a painful groin wound. He was on his back with clenched hands stretched above his head. One Blue pried the hands open and put a Pabst Blue Ribbon can in each of them. Another man stomped on the forehead, leaving a clear bootprint above the crossed eyes. A chaplain walked onto the flight line, seeking to comfort the wounded or whatever else a military chaplain is supposed to do. A rocket roared in and exploded beside an LOH, riddling it with fragments. The LOH mechanic was furious.

He jumped up from the oil-stained dirt and cursed. "Those fucking bastards! I just spent three days getting that chopper fixed and they got to fire a fucking one-oh-seven! Fucking gooks!"

The chaplain tried to calm him. "It's all right, son. The important thing is that no one was killed."

The mechanic grinned maliciously at the chaplain and pointed at the three dead sappers. "They were killed, sir."

The chaplain saw the cross-eyed body for the first time and took in the bootprint and beer cans with one long stare. He gaped for a moment, then uttered three words—"Oh, my God!" He sat down in the dirt beside a blackened bunker and started crying. A group of us stood around for a moment, trying to think of something to say, then we left him there. I hope I never again see a man of God sobbing. It makes you wonder where your tears have gone.

Smoke columns rose above the rubber trees until darkness. APCs had cornered the retreating sappers. It had been an attack by a sapper battalion from Tay Ninh Province. They had force-marched through the jungles of War Zone C to attack Quan Loi and were supported by the NVA artillery units and heavy machine guns that were always around us. A wounded sapper said that his battalion wasn't given enough time to study Quan Loi's defenses and had suffered heavily as a result. He didn't apologize for the attack, just for the lack of proper preparations. The ending might have been different.

The shelling intensified each day. Much of it was directed at our helicopters, and the flight line began to look from the air as if a miniature B-52 strike had hit there. Several times in broad daylight, choppers exploded and burned from direct hits. One mortar shell hit a parked gunship and simultaneously set off a volley from its rocket pods. The rockets hit a stucco French building inside the wire with a broadside. A stream of frightened staff officers boiled out of the front door and ran into their small bunkers around the building. After that incident, the staff decided to leave the French building and build a deep underground bunker instead. Engineers labored for several weeks behind our flight line, excavating the hole, reinforcing the sides and top with cross-beams and steel plates, and trucking in sandbags. The day before the staff was scheduled to occupy their new quarters, a direct hit from a 122mm rocket collapsed the bunker. Life at Quan Loi was a continuously frustrating experience.

Once, a string of mortar shells hit the tents, filling them with holes above the sandbags. We rolled over and went back to sleep.

The troop began going to eat in small groups to avoid needless casualties. One afternoon a 107mm rocket hit beside the mess tent, killing the mess officer and wounding the people in line for food. We were too numb to care anymore. Those of us who weren't hurt continued eating lunch.

One dark night, a big 120mm mortar pounded the troop area for several hours. The distant boom, the twenty-second wait, the screaming of the shell, the crash, and the shaking earth terrified all of us. Granite, Doc, and I huddled in a small bunker while people around us were being wounded. A shell erupted behind our bunker, and a gunner started moaning. Doc ran to help him, and I grabbed a compass and ran to a place where I could get a clear view. I saw the flash as the mortar was fired, sighted down the compass, and ran back to the bunker before the shell hit. The next time the mortar fired, I estimated the distance by the time it took the boom to reach me.

I plotted the location on a map of Quan Loi and took it to the troop operations bunker. The duty officer greeted my data with skepticism. Where would a Blue learn how to plot a mortar location? I explained to him that I had once been an artilleryman. The pilot told me to take the information to the base defense headquarters. I walked to the base defense bunker over a carpet of broken rubber branches and plowed earth from the big mortar. A smart-assed young captain there told me to leave the mortar siting to them. My plot was in the rubber trees, and they couldn't shell there anyway. I went away mad. The mortar hadn't been firing at his friends.

I found five Blues who had been trained on mortars. We drove a truck over to the rear area of an infantry battalion, and I talked the supply officer into lending me an 81mm mortar. He said we could have it "off the books" for three days. We picked up some unauthorized crates of mortar shells at the base ammo dump. We set up the mortar behind the flight line, dry-fired it until we could do it in our sleep, and waited. If the NVA mortared us again, we would shell the rubber trees; permission to fire be damned! I sat by the mortar for three unusually quiet nights. The rocketing continued, but there were no mortar attacks. Late in the third afternoon, I repacked the tube and base plate in Cosmoline and returned them to the supply officer. We were mortared again that night.

I chipped off the cast when I couldn't stand the itching anymore. We spent that night on alert for a snake that had crashed in the rubber trees less than a mile from Quan Loi. At dawn, we patrolled through a tiny rubber village. I remembered its friendly villagers from the jeep patrols with Dusty Delta. Terry found the village elder and brought him over to Con for questioning.

"Con, ask him if there are any VC around here."

The two Vietnamese talked for a moment, then Con looked at Terry. "He says there are many. They come each night in small groups to watch Quan Loi."

"Does he know the VC shot down a helicopter last night?"

"Yes, he saw them do it." Terry's mouth popped open. "He says they set up a big machine gun in the rubber trees every night and wait for the helicopters to fly over. The VC put it near the village because they know the people are afraid, and the Americans won't fire artillery in the rubber trees."

The elder looked at Terry with a frightened expression. He didn't know how his news would be received. Terry smiled at him. "Thank him, Con. Thank him for being honest with us."

We found the antiaircraft site and returned to Quan Loi. There was nothing left of the snake. It had buried itself in the ground and exploded. Two more pilots were dead. We tried to sleep that day, but the shelling was too intense. Blue made a collection of the ruptured 107mm rocket mortars instead.

The day's patrol through the rubber trees had exhausted me. It was more of the same—disarming booby traps, collecting abandoned enemy equipment from the sapper attack, chasing another NVA scout through the woods. All I wanted to do was sleep, but first I had to find out why Terry was visiting, smiling as usual.

"Well, Matt. I hope you like being platoon sergeant."

"Platoon sergeant? What are you talking about?"

"I'm going on a thirty-day leave to Europe, starting tomorrow. You won't have all the responsibility. A captain from the lift ships is going to be platoon leader." Another smile.

"Terry, you're dropping this in my lap and giving me a slick pilot as a platoon leader?"

"Right on. Just pretend he's not there. Nobody's got any doubt that you can handle it. The major recommended you for the job."

"Do I have a choice?"

"No." Now I couldn't sleep. I never thought that I would fill the boots of leaders like Sergeants Sam and Billy. I didn't want the responsibility.

But nothing changed. Blue continued patrols and landings, and the captain left the decisions to me. At night, the captain and I attended the troop briefings. The pilots were proud of the troop's record. The major told us that Bravo Troop was killing more NVA than any other Cav unit, including the battalions. He said that 126 had died during the previous month. I thought back to the months when 200 or 300 Communists were about average and didn't know whether to laugh or cry at our most recent body count.

Another LOH was burning in the bamboo jungle. The NVA who had hit it were several hundred yards away, pinned in their bunkers by a snake's minigun. Four of us hung from the skids of a slick and dropped. Another of those ten-foot drops into bamboo, stumps, and logs. I left two men at the LZ to wait for fire extinguishers and body bags and cut a path to the wreckage with a machete. The captain followed me.

The LOH had burst into flame and dropped like a rock. It had burned a hole straight down through tree limbs, bamboo, and jungle vines, and somehow landed on its skids. A new warrant officer had been aboard for his orientation flight. Three smoldering bodies sat upright in their seats, staring straight ahead through hollow sockets. The pilot's jaws were frozen open in a final prayer or a cry for help. The captain stumbled into the burn zone, saw the awful scene, mumbled, "I'm sorry.

I can't take this,'' and ran back to the others. He had been the scout pilot's friend.

The afternoon was a horror. Extinguishing burning bodies with fire extinguishers and choking on the thick smoke, trying to drag bodies out of their seats and having the arms rip away instead, pulling red-hot grenades and belts of machine gun ammunition from the flames. I had to do it all alone. When the bodies were finally free of the wreckage, we carried them back to the LZ. As slick crewmen pulled a body bag up on ropes, the scout gunner's hot skull and rib cage burned through the rubberized canvas and crashed at my feet. The crewmen's shouts had saved me from being killed by a corpse. We had to wait until the thing cooled down.

I returned to Quan Loi and drank myself into a stupor in an empty tent. Granite walked in, watched me add another beer can to a pile on the table, and started counting them to get my attention. I knew he was standing there but hoped that he would go away if I ignored him.

"Hey, Sarge? Hey, Sarge!"

"What?"

"Know who the gunner was you pulled out today?"

"No. Couldn't tell. They were burned too bad."

"They say you knew him for a long time."

"Knew who?"

"It was Bolten."

I wanted to hit Granite, wanted to shut that whining mouth forever. "Would you please get the hell away from here and leave me alone?"

He always thought that I needed to know. He always said the wrong thing at the wrong time. "Sorry, Sarge. I really am."

It was another example of the disorganization of 1969 that the first slick to pile on dropped four Blues into an unknown situation deep inside an enemy sanctuary. Two of the four had been the platoon leader and the platoon sergeant, a concentration of leadership that violated every rule. We survived many such landings only because of our speed and good fortune.

* * *

We extracted an ambushed LRRP team on the Cambodian border one day, and when we returned to Quan Loi, a new lieutenant was waiting for me. He was Kelly, a West Point officer who didn't act like one, a cavalryman, and a compassionate and friendly person. The soldiers liked him instinctively. He was one of the few officers of any brand who really cared about his enlisted men, and the Blues sensed it immediately. He was also a bit chubby and boyish-looking at first, and this made him slightly less fearsome to those whose lives depended on his whim.

My first landing with Kelly was not a textbook affair. I was supposed to be training him, and I tried too hard. Blue was landed beside a muddy stream in the bamboo jungle. The scouts had spotted bunkers to the northeast, so I glanced at my compass and moved the platoon down a trail—to the southwest. It was my mistake, but no one stopped us.

We followed a silent trail for hours, picking up NVA concussion grenades and heavy belts of twelve-seven ammo. This was the trail that the sappers used to retreat from Quan Loi. They must have been demoralized and running, or they wouldn't have thrown away so much equipment. We eventually arrived at a clearing, found another pack full of demolition charges in the bushes, and were extracted by the slicks.

The major was impressed by all the ammunition we had brought back. He commented to the seated officers at the briefing, "That's the way we should use the Blues, as a separate recon force. If they find something interesting on the ground, they should go after it and not always follow the directions of the scouts."

I wondered what he was talking about for a moment and then realized what had happened in the clearing. I avoided the major's eyes as he continued with the briefing. Kelly jabbed me with his elbow. "I thought we went the wrong way."

I replied in my lowest whisper, "You should have said something, sir."

* * *

In late July, the Blues were assailed from other quarters. One of the squad tents had been claimed by a big rat as its territory. The rat would help itself to packages from home, nibble through packs of cigarettes, and hurl itself through the air at night, landing on blankets and mosquito nets and scaring people half to death. The rat was getting bolder each night, and the squad decided that enough was enough.

For three nights in a row, they stayed awake after the lights were out, hoping to ambush the rat as it went about its mischief. The rat didn't show. On the fourth night, a Blue looked under his cot and saw the rat chewing on a pack of Winstons. I was startled by his shouts. I arrived at the tent to find an enormous rat backed into a corner on its hind feet, clutching a pack of cigarettes and baring its teeth. Granite was aiming his .45 automatic. I grabbed the pistol. The rat darted between Granite's legs.

We chased the marauder from cot to cot for the next fifteen minutes. The chase ended when I pinned it to the plank floor with a bayonet. Although it was sad that the rat had died, the Blues wanted to make an example of it for all other rats to heed. Someone hung the rat by the neck in the doorway of the tent, using twine from a package it had gnawed through.

Granite had another idea. "We can't leave him like that. He was a brave rat. Why don't we give him a medal?"

"Got any suggestions?"

Doc Ring volunteered. "I've got one. Hold on a minute." He dug a National Defense Medal from his duffel bag and pinned it on the rat's chest. We hoped that a Vietnamese rat wouldn't be offended by an American decoration. Eventually, I went to bed.

Granite shook me awake the next morning. "Sarge, wake up. The new rear area captain wants to see you."

I looked up at the bedraggled hillbilly. Granite was worried. "What's it about?"

"He's over at third squad's tent. He said to get your ass over there."

"Okay. I'm coming."

The captain's shaven head was glistening in the morning sunlight. He was looking up at the rat. A Bronze Star and an Air Medal had been added to its chest. I tried to sound as cheerful as possible. "Good morning, sir. What can I do for you?"

He looked at me as though I had come for his garbage. "Are you the platoon sergeant?"

"Yes, sir. That's me."

He pointed a stubby finger at the highly decorated rat. "Do you think this is funny, Sergeant?"

"No, sir!" I think it's hilarious.

"It's unsanitary; rats spread disease, in case you didn't know. Have one of your comedians cut it down." Now the threat. "I'll hold you personally responsible if something like this happens again."

"Yes, sir." Fuck you, sir. "Okay, Granite. Cut this thing down and bury it with full military honors." The captain winced.

Granite snapped a mock British salute. "Right, Sarge."

There had been a feature story in the *Stars and Stripes* for several days about the road east of Nui Ba Ra. The road was supposed to be rebuilt and secure for the first time in years. "The pacification of Blank-Blank Province continues on schedule," et cetera. After three years of reading such propaganda, I wasn't surprised to learn that a Lurp team had made contact almost as soon as they landed beside the road. Blue was being sent to reinforce them. I wished that some howitzers were within range of the "safe" road.

The four slicks landed in a line along the road. The place didn't look at all dangerous. The road surface was graded and well banked, and bulldozers had leveled the jungle for one hundred yards on either side. We walked toward a wall of bamboo on the west, stumbling over rotting trees and branches. Clack-clack-clack-clack. I fell backward and wriggled under a big tree limb. A string of bullets snapped through the limb, stinging my face with tiny wood splinters. The first line of Blues fired into the bamboo until a snake made a long rocket run across our front. Silence.

We reached the bamboo and headed north, firing bursts at

small groups of NVA walking parallel to us about thirty yards inside the jungle. They would drop out of sight when we fired, then pop up again a few yards ahead. I couldn't decide whether it was the same group or relays of NVA. Red smoke blossomed on the edge of the bamboo, and a man in a camouflaged jungle uniform stood up from a branch pile beside me. He had hidden himself well. The Lurp jerked his thumb in the direction of the smoke.

"Red smoke marks the team's location. Where's your platoon sergeant?"

"That's me. What've we got here?"

"I'm not sure. We were inserted on the road and set up an ambush about fifty meters inside the bamboo. About twenty minutes later, I saw what I thought was another Lurp team ahead of us. They had camouflage fatigues and flop hats, and their faces were painted with battle grease, just like us. Then I noticed they were carrying AKs and I shot the point man. I'll show you where it happened." He led me to a pool of blood at the base of a tree.

The scouts wanted us to check a ridge farther north, so we continued the strange walk beside the wall of bamboo. We climbed a gentle slope to the place where red smoke marked bunkers. Wham! Wham! Wham! The NVA stopped the point with Chinese grenades, then opened up with their AKs. Wham! Wham! The man beside me had the leg blown off his trousers. I caught a fragment just above the elbow. I cursed myself for raising the arm off the ground. Wham! Wham! An LOH flew over our heads with its gunner firing like crazy. It reached the bunkers, spun around, and shot back over us. The gunner had taken a bullet in the ass. So much for the safe road.

Four snakes rocketed the bunkers with big seventeen-pound warheads. The detonations shook the ground around us. I had already watched those new warheads break thick rubber trees like matchsticks. As the last snake climbed away, the point squad rushed the bunkers. There was nothing left but a few bloodstains. The bunkers stretched back into the jungle as far as we could see.

The pilots told us to return south to another ridge, past the place where the LRRPs had been ambushed. An LOH hovered there, dropping white phosphorous grenades into the bamboo. We headed in that direction, firing at more NVA beside us in the jungle. They continued their game of disappearing and reappearing.

On the south ridge, overlooking the road, were new recoilless rifle and machine gun pits, all concealed by dead branches. They were invisible from the air. There were marks in the hard earth where weapons had been sited along the road. Fields of fire for the ambush were marked by branches stuck innocently among the other scrap wood. A big NVA unit was waiting for the first convoy to pass. The unit was large enough to occupy every rise along the road and could send out a specialized recon patrol on short notice to attack our LRRPs. It also had soldiers who liked to play chicken with M-16s.

The scouts radioed that the bunkers behind the weapons pits were empty. I sent Henry, a black squad leader, to find out for certain. As Henry's squad entered the bamboo, Granite and I made our own recon about forty yards to the south. I saw three firing slits not ten yards inside the bamboo. A roar of rifles and machine guns swept over Henry's squad, and we sprayed the firing slits. At least five AKs shot back at us. Bullets cut the bamboo stalks inches above my head. We turned around and executed what may have been the fastest ground-hugging bellycrawl in military history. I tumbled into one of the NVA recoilless rifle pits with Granite hard on my heels.

He huddled in the corner, gasping for air. "I thought they had us dead to rights, Sarge."

"Me, too. I ain't never moved that fast."

I told the black machine gunner in the pit to fire bursts at the place we had just left. I was watching the bullets snap the bamboo when Henry ran out of the jungle, leaped a series of branch piles, and dropped into the pit beside me. He was bleeding from a deep bullet wound in his shoulder.

"They've got bunkers everywhere up there. Two of my men were hit by a gook machine gun. I'll need another machine gun to lay down a covering fire and get them out."

"Where's your machine gun?"

"Gunner's shot. They won't let us get close to him." He turned to the machine gunner in my pit. "Want to play hero?"

I waited for his answer and hoped that I wouldn't have to make him go. This fellow called himself Panther. He called Sergeant Henry an Oreo (black on the outside, white on the inside) for being a sergeant in the white man's war. Panther spat. "What are we waiting for? The pinned man's a brother."

I tied a field dressing around Henry's wound, and seconds later he, Granite, and Panther were running back into the echoing bamboo. I was afraid to go along but told myself I was staying behind because a platoon sergeant should remain with the majority of his men. A long, hammering volley from Panther's machine gun, and then the squad came backing out of the bamboo, dragging the two wounded men and firing as they walked. Bullets snapped the bamboo all around them. It was a miracle more of them weren't hit. More bullets clacked over the pits that the rest of us were using for shelter. The only time the NVA firing stopped was when the snakes rocketed the bamboo. The NVA turned their guns on them.

Granite was carrying the wounded man's machine gun. When a slick landed for the casualties, he jumped from my pit and ran back along the bamboo, firing belt after belt of ammo at the bunkers. He was the last man to board a slick, still firing. In his insane rage, he had covered our entire withdrawal without even knowing it. The slicks lifted directly over the bunkers. Every weapon we had blasted down at them, and then we were safe. There would be no ambush along the "safe" road. The B-52s struck a few hours later.

I stepped off the slick at Quan Loi, and a scout gunner told me that a rocket had blown apart the supply room while we were away. It had been another typical afternoon at the base. I was writing commendations for Panther, Henry, and Granite when a clerk walked into my little room.

"The rear area captain wants to see you, on the double."

I found the captain seated at his desk in the orderly room tent, paging through a stack of reports. His eyes followed me through the door. "Well, Sergeant Brennan again."

"Yes, sir."

"Your report shows eight men wounded today. Four lightly wounded by grenades, three by bullets, one serious grenade wound. Is that correct?"

"Yes, sir. That's my after action report you're holding."

"We're trying to keep casualties down. Why so many?"

"We got in a firefight, sir. The major sent us in, not me!"

He hadn't forgotten the highly decorated rat. "This says that you were wounded, but here you are, standing in front of me. Let's see it."

I showed him the gash in my right arm. He had noticed the prick-marks on my face. "They're only little wounds."

Little wounds hurt, too. You bastard. "Sir, if an enemy action draws blood, that's a wound. That's what regulations say. I think what you're telling me is don't report wounds unless people are evacuated."

He looked down at the casualty report and then back to me. "Now, don't misinterpret, Mr. Platoon Sergeant. What I'm saying is that it's important to keep down casualties. Think about it, Sergeant. Think about it. That's all for now." He should have added "But don't leave town."

I left the tent wondering what I would do if we ever had to rescue his regulation ass in the real war. I would probably want to kill him.

I was at Bien Hoa Army Base, near Saigon. It was supposed to be a trip to check my pay records, but all I really wanted to do was give Kelly the full responsibility for a few hours and escape the rockets. I was there anyway, so I gave a clerk my name and waited. He couldn't find the pay records and walked into the next room for a conference with an administration officer. He was grinning like Santa Claus.

"Staff Sergeant Brennan? You're with Bravo, First of the Ninth?"

"The last time I heard I was."

"Well, sorry for the delay. We transferred your records to the officer section yesterday. You were a second lieutenant as of zero-zero-one hours this morning . . . sir."

"What?"

"Congratulations, sir."

"Yeah. Thanks."

They were turning a weary, frightened, homesick sergeant into a shiny new officer. I returned to Quan Loi that afternoon and was greeted by the senior NCO in my absence, new sergeant Granite. He was relieved to have me back until I told him that he was now the platoon sergeant. They probably heard his groan three miles down the road in An Loc. I was commissioned the next morning amid little speeches and ceremonies. It was the only time in twenty-six months that I had ever seen the Blues stand in a platoon formation. We were all tired. The rockets had crashed around us for most of the night. The rear area captain stood to one side, watching the whole show in stony silence. Fuck you again, sir.

I was leaving the Cav for the 199th Light Infantry Brigade. The news shocked me. The 199th was known as one of the poorest combat units in Vietnam, almost as bad as the raggedy-assed Americal Division. They were based in the luxury of Redcatcher. That was their nickname, The Redcatchers, but they didn't catch many Reds.

I spent my last night with the Cav at the officers' club in Bien Hoa. There I met a shaven-headed company commander who had been a police lieutenant in New York. We were scheduled to leave for home on the same day.

"What made you give up a reserve major's commission to come here, sir?"

"It's simple, Lieutenant. I got tired of those young punks on the street telling me what Vietnam was like and justifying their actions by it." He mimicked them. "It's the war, man. I get flashbacks." He paused. "When I go back, they won't be able to feed me any more of that crap."

We were joined by an infantry lieutenant from the 7th Cav, Custer's old outfit. He said I reminded him of his little brother

256

back in Virginia. The lieutenant was battle-crazed, talking only about his recent experiences in the jungles.

"Man, we're hurting Charlie out in those boonies. Finding big caches and blowing 'bushes on him every time he bops down the trails. But man, I'll tell you something. Charlie's been here a long time and this is mostly jungle. Not many places to land. We've been hit by one-twenty mortars in our last three lima zulus. I think they've got every clearing in War Zone D watched and zeroed in." He made a scream like a big mortar shell.

"I know. I know how you feel about those one-twenty mortars." I remembered the big mortar that had pounded our tents at Quan Loi. The mortar that no one wanted to bother with because it was in the rubber trees.

CHAPTER 18

Redcatchers

I was assigned to an infantry battalion of the 199th Light Infantry Brigade. A sharply dressed captain was waiting at the battalion headquarters to brief me. He led me into his large office, picked up a swagger stick from his desk, and paced back and forth in front of a large wall map. He would have made a smashing British colonel.

"The brigade is operating in the jungle for the first time in years. That's the reason you were sent here from the Cav. We need your knowledge of the jungle. The battalion is experiencing light contact around Zuan Loc,"—he rapped the map with his stick—"but Delta Company had a heavy contact last week. They were ambushed by claymores and machine guns here,"—he pointed to an area of low ridges and thick jungles—"and lost a lieutenant and nine men."

"What unit are we fighting here, sir?"

"Most of the contact has been with the Thirty-Third NVA Regiment. You've surely heard of them. They're supported by local Viet Cong battalions."

I had heard of them. The 33d NVA Regiment had started the battle in the Ia Drang Valley in 1965. In one of the great ironies of the war, it would be the first and the last unit the Cav would fight in Vietnam, across six bloody years. I nodded to the captain. "The Cav fought them in the Ia Drang."

"Well, they're still around." He smiled proudly. "It's a good feeling to be fighting NVA instead of local guerrillas and booby traps. The battalion commander is excited by the change. This has opened up a whole new set of options.''

Options? I had fought the NVA for more than two years, and I wasn't excited about seeing more of them. The captain told me that the battalion was experimenting with cardboard artillery cases as outer shells for dropping water in jungle resupply missions. The Cav had used them for four years now.

He returned to his desk. ''Do you have any preference of assignment, Lieutenant?''

How about Indiana? ''No. It makes no difference to me.''

''All right. We'll send you to a company that needs a lieutenant.''

I had returned to the Zuan Loc forward base from three days in the hills with my new company. It was commanded by a thin paratrooper captain, and I was the third platoon leader. The patrol had been an unpleasant experience. The soldiers were careless with their weapons and very noisy. The jeep soldiers of Dusty Delta had been a bunch of commandos compared to this company. Sergeant Bradley, the platoon sergeant, had told me that the company had been in action only once during the previous year. The rest of the time had been spent in a place called the Pineapple Forest, where they had found only booby traps and rare snipers. Two weeks before my arrival, the platoon had killed five Viet Cong on a jungle hill. Bradley was proud of their fight.

''Gooks opened up from a bunker and second squad was pinned. Then we got on line and charged the bunker.''

''Did they have a machine gun?''

''No, sir. Just rifles.''

''That charging on line is dangerous business, especially if the enemy has many automatic weapons. The safest thing is to work up from tree to tree with covering fire. That's how we'll do it from now on.''

He gave me a ''Goddamned meddling officer'' look. ''Okay, sir.''

The company was sent on another series of patrols in the rugged foothills around Zuan Loc. I soon discovered that no amount of badgering could make the platoon walk quietly. They refused to walk down trails, no matter how old they were, unless I took the point. It was better that way. The platoon was a crowd of scared draftees who wanted to go home, and they were not the Blues, not even the present Blues. They would cross the trails quickly, making brief inspections to the left and right, while I conducted the necessary reconnaissance. They were not the soldiers of 1967, not even the draftees of 1967, and I knew in my heart that they were no match for the NVA who lived in those hills.

On several occasions, we almost surprised groups of NVA eating rice or bamboo shoots. They would hear our noisy approach and run away. One day, the platoon crossed a trail where many people had been walking only minutes before. No one noticed. Once, a volley from a lone NVA sent the entire company into a panic. I gave my soldiers frequent lectures on silent movement, always greeted with "Stop hassling us or you'll be sorry" looks. When we returned to Zuan Loc, I called them together.

"Look, I've seen things out there that might get you in trouble if we make real contact. The most important thing is that everyone is too noisy. I'll say it over and over again. The jungle is silent. You guys have to be silent or the NVA will hear you coming a long way off. The little groups run away, but the heavies will stay and fight. If you are trying to scare them off by making a racket, forget it. Tie down your canteens; carry your rifles so they don't clank against grenades. Things like that can save your life."

Hastings, leader of the second squad, the heroes of the fight on the hill, interrupted. "But, sir. We did okay against those five VC. They even had a claymore."

"Let's talk about that hill. They had a claymore, but they didn't use it. You did fine, but you were fighting local yokels. That charging stuff doesn't work against automatic weapons. Another thing. The claymores you saw in the Pineapple Forest were booby traps. Up here, chances are that a claymore's going to have a man behind it, waiting to blow you away. If a lot of people expose themselves, Charlie's gonna take you out. You guys are here for one year. Those same Charlies have been fighting Americans for a hell of a lot longer.'' I wanted to add, ''and fighting a lot tougher Americans.''

The lecture was greeted with no enthusiasm. Most of them thought I was another lieutenant trying to make their lives harder than they already were. We sat together in a field and cleaned weapons, and I prayed that they wouldn't have to use them.

I met a new lieutenant at the officers' club that evening. A crisp young man with the shining eyes of a fanatic, wearing paratrooper wings and a ranger slash, pulled up a seat at my table. He had seen my Cav patch. He told me he had graduated from West Point and immediately volunteered for Vietnam. He had requested the 1st Air Cav, but they had assigned him to the 199th Light Infantry Brigade. He didn't want to miss the war.

I saw much of my former self in him—unquestioning loyalty, no good sense of danger, a craving for excitement. He wanted to know what medals I had gotten and I told him. He wanted to know about the 1st Cav, so I told him what he wanted to hear. I knew what the lieutenant would be like in the jungle, so I cautioned him to be careful at first and rely on the experience of his NCOs, if he was lucky enough to have experienced NCOs. I still felt that green lieutenants were as worthless as tits on a boar hog.

''Most of all, don't take chances with your life. You can only lead if you're still alive after the shooting starts.''

''Don't worry. I'll be okay.''

He was dead three weeks later. He had taken one man with him to search a jungle camp along a trail. A machine gun had killed them. I had known what the ending would be that night in the officers' club.

The company was in trouble five minutes after landing by the jungle road. An NVA had walked into the middle of another platoon, and thirty men had shouted *''Choi hoi!* [Open arms—surrender]'' at the tops of their lungs. He crawled between two of them and ran away. Now we would be watched.

We set up squad-sized night ambushes for 150 yards along the road. NVA moved around us for long hours, and none of the men with me slept. We were waiting for the clear target that never came. I had the misfortune of locating my ambush beside an anthill. At dawn, we were not only soaked from a night of rain, but covered by red welts from hundreds of insect bites. One of my squads had the wires to its claymore mines cut and didn't see a thing. A squad from another platoon watched a man walk up to a mine and piss on it. They thought he was an American.

I walked to the captain's position, passing a stream below the road. The banks were muddied with Ho Chi Minh sandal prints. On a rise above the other side of the road, I found a place where the NVA had hidden behind a tree stump. The impression of a rocket launcher was etched in the mud. No one had bothered to investigate those obvious ambush sites.

The captain sent out morning ambushes in both directions from the road. I remained with one squad at the far end of our road positions. About noon, there was a crash of a claymore mine followed by a short burst from a machine gun. One of the company's ambushes had made contact without killing any NVA. This was the signal for the ambush squads to retreat to the road in a disorderly mob. The soldiers who had fired the mine stumbled past me a few minutes later. One of them had an NVA bush hat. I was curious.

I grabbed his arm. "What happened up there?"

He blushed. "Sir, a patrol of about nine NVA walked down the trail where we had the 'bush."

"Why didn't you get any of them? Have the claymores pointed the wrong way?"

"Sir, the point man had a grenade launcher, and they looked like Arvins. I thought we should warn them."

"They all look alike. What were they wearing?"

"Brown uniforms and cloth hats."

It would have been funny if the game wasn't so deadly. He was lucky he didn't try to shake hands with them. "Next time, remember the Arvins wear green uniforms and steel helmets like we do."

Another blush. "I will, sir."

The company followed the road deeper into the jungle. One of my men left his rifle on the road and went into the woods to take a leak. When he looked up, he saw a man leaning against a tree and smiling, watching him piss. The NVA was gone by the time he found his rifle.

My platoon led the way until we were ordered to take a break. Sergeant Bradley, my radioman, and I went ahead about 150 yards while the rest of the company rested. We found another road with fresh tire tracks, leading up a hillside. The road junction was marked by a wooden sign nailed to a tree. It had a warning in Vietnamese beneath a five-pointed star and a skull and cross-bones. Bradley's whisper sounded like a cannon shot.

"What do you think, sir?"

"The hill is off limits for some reason. It's late afternoon. If we go up the hill, we're asking for a fight. I'm not risking it with guys who haven't fought in the jungle before."

Bradley nodded. "That's the way I feel. Besides, artillery might be hard to get."

I didn't need to make excuses. "Let's find a route around this hill."

We camped for the night on a hill that was covered with rotting leaves and branches. I was trying to sleep when an NVA mortar thudded from the next hill, shelling a target somewhere in the valleys below. I was lucky to be awake. A black scorpion, at least five inches long, was crawling across my chest. I threw the ugly thing off with one quick jerk and killed it with a loose canteen. Scorpions were everywhere on the hill. It was another night without sleep.

We left the hill at dawn and passed tiger traps and bees' nests on the border of a populated valley. Ancient logging trucks rumbled by our column. We waved to the drivers, but they acted like we didn't exist. Someone was watching them. They were vegetable farmers and loggers, at least during the daylight hours. The company rested among the hooches of their shabby village until a convoy of trucks arrived for us. I didn't feel tired or breathe easily again until we were being driven away.

* * *

We had been on patrol for two days. Around us were new jungle camps where the NVA had been eating mackerel from cans with Saigon labels. Coca-Cola bottles littered the camps. My platoon crossed a trail where men had passed so recently that grass was still snapping back from the direction they had taken. I showed my squad leaders a rest camp beside the trail, then took them aside.

"What does this grass tell you?"

Only blank looks and awkward silence.

"It's wet, so gooks can walk by and bend it without the stems breaking. It'll bend in the direction they're going and then snap back for about fifteen minutes. What about those Ho Chi Minh sandal prints in the mud?"

Hastings stepped forward. "Looks like maybe a squad came by." He looked again to be sure of his estimate.

"Three or four at most. The water is still seeping back, so they passed here quite recently. Most of our bootprints haven't started filling up yet. You can learn a lot from trails. What the Charlies are eating, what they're wearing, what kind of weapons they're carrying, how many there are, and where they're headed. You've got to know the signs and keep on your toes."

They began to look for the signs, and I felt that my nagging was finally reaching them.

The battalion's reconnaissance platoon was at Zuan Loc when we returned. They were volunteers and a different breed. Several days before, the recon platoon had ambushed a group of important NVA in the hills. They had found a personal letter of commendation from Ho Chi Minh on one of the bodies. Another NVA had been wearing a little star with a green background. It was the award given by the Viet Minh to the veterans of Dien Bien Phu. The star was now pinned to a soldier's jungle shirt. My company commander told me that the colonel wanted me as the next recon platoon leader. I told him, "No, thanks." I was going home soon, and my men were getting less careless.

There was a rubber plantation on the north side of our patrol base. A Frenchman and his Vietnamese cook lived there in a big stucco house. The old Frenchman was an ex-soldier with a crew cut and a barrel chest. He had fought the Japanese in 1945 and had fought for years against the Viet Minh. A sniper had shot off his arm. He pulled a tattered map from his teakwood desk and showed me where he had fought—An Khe, Pleiku, Kontum, An Lao. Yes, I knew about those places. He didn't speak English and I didn't speak French, but one of the other officers remembered his college French, and what was left unspoken was replaced with gestures.

We were talking one evening over glasses of his excellent wine when a report came over the radio. Another company was pinned down by machine guns. The old man grabbed a map of the Zuan Loc area and gestured for me to show him where the battle was taking place. Then I looked past his smile to his Vietnamese cook. She stood behind him so she couldn't be seen and was motioning violently with her head and arms for us not to show him. I understood and picked a location many miles from the contact. We never returned to the Frenchman's house. He had been using us to gather information for his Communist friends. Later, several Viet Cong visitors died in ambushes near the Frenchman's home.

We returned to Zuan Loc from another patrol in the jungle. I walked to the mess hall and loaded a tray with hot food and fresh bread. We lived for that delicious bread. The new battalion commander was seated by a window. He was a lean, muscular man with close-cropped hair and a deep tan. He looked every inch the professional soldier. The colonel gave me no smile or other greeting, just "Come over here, Lieutenant."

"Yes, sir."

"I'm Colonel Black. I don't believe we've met yet."

"No, sir. Lieutenant Brennan, ——— Company." We shook hands.

"What university did you attend, Lieutenant?"

He had hit a sore spot. I had spent most of the time since high school graduation in Vietnam, and I was embarrassed by my lack of education. "None, sir. I only have a high school education. I got a direct commission."

A condescending look. "Oh."

"Sir, I intend to go to college when I get back to the States."

He wasn't interested. He stared out of the window with the back of his head turned to me. "See that you do. It's very important."

"Yes sir. Thank you, sir." He didn't notice me leave the mess hall with my tray of food.

I was trying to relax for one evening at the officers' club. I had been listening to Judy Collins's song "Both Sides Now" when the young lieutenant walked over. He was a military history buff and wanted to talk about Verdun and Stalingrad and Dien Bien Phu. I had once been interested in such things, but then, all I wanted to do was hear Judy Collins. He tugged on my sleeve to get my attention, so I decided to let him know how I felt about the war.

"It all comes down in the end to the depressing business of scared men trying to kill other scared men."

He wasn't listening. "If the French only had more than four one-five-fives at Dien Bien Phu and hadn't left all those one-oh-fives sitting back at Hanoi, things would have been different. They should have reinforced the airhead, rather than launching that amphibious operation along the central coast. The addition of only . . ."

"What bullshit! My friend, what difference does it make how many one-five-fives the French had at Dien Bien Phu? The only thing that matters is that thousands of healthy men died like slaughterhouse pigs!"

That reached him. "That's a pretty speech, but we have to face reality. War will always be with us, at least in our lifetimes."

He had a good point and I knew it. The most effective politics are backed by steel. "But can't you see how insane this all is? We hunt each other from tree to tree, like game."

He shook his head. "No. It will always be that way." He left to find someone else to talk with about war.

We were in a rubber plantation, crossing parts of a bunker system that stretched for miles. This had been a regimental camp during the Tet Offensive of 1968 and had been used often since then. NVA were living in some parts of the bunker system even as we blew up some of the hundreds of deep log bunkers. It was a strange region. There were artillery-smashed bunkers and rows of graves in some places, Communists living in other places, and an American company destroying bunkers in still other places.

We were always followed. All the company had to do was pass a quiet rubber village. The smiling workers might be members of the local Viet Cong cell. I had spent years as a hunter of men; now we were the ones who were tracked and watched. We always ambushed the trails we had taken. One night, one of the trackers died. We found his pack hidden under a pile of rubber branches. Blood and drag marks. On another day, there was a skirmish in the rubber. One American was wounded, and the NVA abandoned their food, clothing, and supplies. There were constant patrols and more madness.

On our last night in the plantation, Bradley's ambush squad blew their claymores at rustling noises in the darkness. We found two dead wild boars at dawn. The Americans left the carcasses alone, but the Vietnamese scouts shoved each other and cursed, fighting over chunks of meat. The scouts hated each other. Both had been NVA soldiers, but one had been a private and the quieter one had been a lieutenant. They had a major point of disagreement that often ended in fist fights. The private had walked for three months down the Ho Chi Minh Trail, through Laos and Cambodia and American air strikes. The lieutenant had been flown to the border of South Vietnam by a Soviet helicopter. The private could never forgive the lieutenant for his easy trip south.

We left the plantation and cut a path across a series of deep bamboo-covered ravines. The NVA shadowed us all day. They were playing the game that I had first seen along the "safe" road. They would walk parallel to the company column until somebody fired. They would disappear for a moment, then reappear. The unnerved soldiers began shooting at shadows. The camps we found had been abandoned as the NVA heard us stumbling and shooting our way through the ravines.

We finally reached another plantation of young trees. I sent a squad under Wilson, a specialist, to ambush the trail we had made. It was almost dark when Wilson radioed to tell me that five Viet Cong, dressed in black pajamas and armed with carbines, had just climbed out of the last ravine. The captain broke into his transmission and told Wilson to shoot them. Wilson refused. He said his compass didn't work, and he wasn't certain where he was. I looked around to see a pissed-off captain beckoning for me.

"Lieutenant Brennan! Get the hell over here!"

"Yes, sir!"

I ran to the rubber tree where he had set up his command post. "Brennan, did you check your squad leader's compass before they went on ambush?"

"No, sir, I didn't."

"That's your job isn't it? Making sure your men are properly prepared for missions?"

"Yes, sir."

"From now on you will check all equipment before the ambush goes out. You will then make a report to me. Is that clear, Lieutenant?"

"Yes, sir. It won't happen again."

"You'd better be damned sure it doesn't."

The chewing-out was a farce, staged for the enlisted men who had heard Wilson's radio messages. The captain and I both knew that nine Americans, lavishly armed with two grenade launchers, a machine gun, claymore mines, and six automatic rifles, were refusing to engage a tiny VC patrol armed with World War II carbines. If we admitted the fact, we would have to report a mutiny.

The Viet Cong spotted Wilson's squad a little while later and faded back into the bamboo. The squad came dragging back to our camp shortly after dark. Wilson walked quickly by me and headed for the shelter of a rubber tree away from my line of sight.

"Wilson?"

He turned around slowly, not wanting to hear. "Yes, sir?"

"Let's see that compass." The compass worked perfectly. The fluorescent needle spun around and pointed in the right direction. "Why is it working now and didn't before?"

He shrugged and held out his hands in a helpless gesture. "I can't explain it, sir. Maybe it was magnetism or something."

"Yeah. Or something." He cringed at my words. "You're relieved as squad leader. Turn all your duties over to Flores. Don't go around the captain. He wants to bust you back to private."

"Yes, sir. I'm sorry."

The days in the young plantation were a pleasant time of patrols and long rests in the shade of tree lanes. Everything had a picnic atmosphere. I sat on a freshly mowed bank of grass one day and listened to snakes and Phantoms attacking a Viet Cong company only two miles away. Danger was that close, but for me the war was surely over. I had only a few days left in the field.

One afternoon at dusk, a column of APCs took us back to the patrol base. Sergeant Bradley left for home and his replacement returned in the same jeep. The new platoon sergeant was a veteran of a previous tour with the 199th, a fact that didn't recommend him highly to me. But I didn't have to know him for long. I only had eight days left in the "boonies."

The company returned to another part of the extensive bunker system in the plantation. As we walked for hours past the fortifications, I tried to imagine the time when thousands of NVA had swarmed there on the eve of Tet. We spent the night in a rubber log fortress. The irregular walls had been carefully constructed from interlocking trees to look like accidents of nature. In reality they were well-planned defensive positions.

The whine of jet engines and a whistle of bombs awoke me at dawn. A large B-52 strike thundered across the jungle a few miles away. The NVA scouts huddled together in tense silence, staring at each other with the haunted eyes of men who were remembering a terrible common experience. The private trembled each time a fresh string of bombs started their rumbling walk. I wondered how many times the big bombs had crashed around them.

We walked to the edge of the clearing and boarded a flight of about twenty slicks. Forty-five minutes later, we were cutting a path with machetes toward the B-52 strike zone. The rest of the

269

day was lost in a churned-up expanse of former jungle. We passed the familiar scenes of uprooted trees, dead snakes and parrots on the lips of giant craters, swarms of biting red ants that had been blasted out of the trees, boulders reduced to rubble, and streams that had changed their courses or been dammed by debris. We left the wasteland at dusk and prepared to spend the night in untouched jungle. The captain had told us nothing about our mission, but I knew that the bombs had missed their target.

We awoke to a cloudless sky and a beautiful sunrise. It was September fifth, my mother's birthday. I had spent 1160 days in Vietnam and had only 6 more left that mattered. My platoon led the company column, cutting a path over steep wooded hills. Once, there was a loud rustling in the trees ahead of us as we cut straight downslope, but it was only a troop of langur monkeys. We climbed a rocky ridge above a swamp and sat among the jagged boulders to eat our rations.

I sent a patrol to recon the ridge, but they soon returned, reporting nothing but more colonies of the black scorpions. Two resupply slicks hovered at the edge of the swamp while the gunners pushed out cases of rations, ammunition, and explosives. We would be in the jungle for at least three more days. My platoon remained on point, so I put my best squad, Hastings's men, in the lead. I could trust them to be careful. They led us off the ridge, along the edge of the swamp, and back into the jungle.

Hastings found a wide trail at the base of the next hill. When I saw it, I radioed the captain. "Six, this is Three-Six. Over."

"This is Six, go."

"Roger. We have a trail with fresh Ho Chi Minh prints and animal snares. Signs suggest base camp nearby. Request permission to recon the area before continuing."

"This is Six. Permission denied. We have another one thousand meters to go before dark. Keep moving. Over."

"Three-Six, roger that." I will never forgive myself for not following my instinct about that trail.

Hastings's squad began climbing the hill behind the trail. They stepped over a log about ten yards up the slope, then my radio squawked. My radioman shoved the handset at me. "They've got something, sir."

"This is Three-Six, go."

"Three-Two. We have a claymore hanging in a tree up here. We are investigating." They had gathered around the mine to have a look.

I knew in that instant that I was talking to a dead man. If they made any sudden movement, the NVA would trigger the ambush. I motioned for the men behind me to hit the ground—fast! As they disappeared into cover, I pressed the transmitting button. "Three-Two! Get down! Get down!"

Boom! The continuous roar of a machine gun was drowned by four more booms. The air around us was filled with screaming metal as the captain radioed, "Three-Six, this is Six. What have you got up there?"

I wanted to push his face into one of the mines. "Six, we're pinned down by motherfucking claymores!"

Two NVA machine guns and forty AKs turned the slope into a bloody nightmare. I had never seen such concentrated fire. I dropped my heavy pack and rolled onto my back in a shallow depression. The earth kicked up all around, and bullets clipped the grass and vines. White tracers streaked by only inches above my body. I noticed that every sapling along the trail had already been cut by claymores and bullets.

I silently prayed, "My God! Dear God! We're in the middle of a kill zone!"

Moans and screams filled the jungle around me. Everything I had done to keep them alive had been wasted. I rolled back to the log where I had been when the mines were fired. Everyone in front of it, my five best men, were surely dead or dying. A machine gun raked the log, tearing off chunks of bark in front of my face. Leaves were pushed aside by the muzzle blast as it fired. It was only ten yards from the log. My radioman and I emptied six magazines at the muzzle blast. The machine gun stopped firing, and the shouts of the crew echoed through the suddenly silent jungle.

Whoosh-whoosh. It happened three more times. Another

271

whoosh and an antitank rocket ricocheted off the log, hit a tree, and bounced along the ground behind me. The NVA were forgetting to pull the arming pins, and that was saving our lives. More shouts from above us, then the machine gun fired again. Another platoon crawled up the slope behind me, firing wildly at everything above them. Bullets were hitting both sides of my log. One round smacked my helmet and shoved my face into a pile of decaying leaves. I shouted for them to cease fire, and their platoon sergeant belly-crawled to my log.

"We're going after the wounded."

"Don't do it! They're dead for sure!"

"Captain's orders. Hang in there, sir."

They had seen no real combat. All they knew how to do was charge, like they had been taught in the infantry training camps. The line ran into a clacking roar of NVA fire. They stumbled back down the slope, dragging one dead man and four wounded. One of the wounded soldiers was from Hastings's squad. His face was covered with dirt, and he had a mouthful of leaves. He saw me leaning over him and spat out the leaves to say something. I looked into his eyes and they turned to glass. Dead.

The platoon sergeant looked at the corpse with bulging eyes. "They've got a lot of AKs up there! The rest of your men are fucked!" Dead.

I positioned what was left of the two platoons behind the trail and started evacuating the wounded toward the swamp. I saw a man with a gash across his shin and braced him with my arm. I wanted an excuse to go back to the swamp and hide. My radioman saw me leading the wounded man away. He knew that I wasn't coming back. "Sir! Where are you going? You can't leave us here!" I was ashamed and handed the wounded man to another soldier. If I ever left the trail, I wouldn't have the guts to return.

I placed a machine gun by a small tree in front of the trail and told them to fire bursts to keep the NVA under cover. The rest of us collected ammo belts to feed the gun. I sent another machine gun crew about twenty yards to the right front. They disappeared behind a clump of bamboo, then were chased back to me by long

272

.30 caliber machine gun bursts. They tore past me at a dead run, heading for the swamp.

The NVA were in bunkers. The only way to fight them was to pull the rest of us back to the edge of the swamp and crack the bunkers with delayed fuse artillery. I wanted to remain by the trail just long enough to cover the evacuation of all the wounded. Three men in green uniforms ran past the bamboo clump where the machine gun crew had been. They were headed for the swamp and the wounded. We killed them.

Two snakes circled far above the swamp. As our marking smoke drifted through the treetops, I directed their rockets. Each run was met by dozens of clacking AKs, not only from the hill above us, but from at least three others.

"Three-Six, this is Tiger Three-One. How was that last run?"

"Three-Six. Bring it in closer."

"Roger that, Three-Six. Rolling in hot." More rockets.

"Three-Six, this is Tiger Three-One, over."

"Tiger! We need it closer!"

"Roger that, Three-Six. Understand closer." More rockets.

"Three-Six, Tiger Three-One, over."

"This is Three-Six. Rockets are suppressing November Victor fire. Bring it closer, right in front of smoke, over."

"This is Tiger Three-One. Are you sure you want it there?"

"This is Three-Six, roger that. We're behind trees. That smoke is right in front of bunkers."

"Roger that you want it closer. Keep your heads down." This time the rockets burst where the first bunkers should be. Fragments smacked the tree trunk above my head. The second snake fired a salvo of flechette rockets. Branches and leaves rained down on us, but the NVA fire suddenly stopped.

"Three-Six, this is Tiger Three-One. That was the last of our rockets. We took hits on that last run. Can no longer assist. Pop smoke and my teammate will expend forty mike-mike and mini-gun."

"Roger that. Smoke popped."

They left after the second snake made two more passes. The jungle was silent for a long moment, then the AKs opened fire along the trail. I watched a man in a green uniform climb a tree on the slope a few yards above me.

"Shoot that tree! Spray it! Spray it!" He fell heavily through the branches, bounced once, and was still. I radioed the captain. "Six, this is Three-Six, over."

"This is Six."

"Three-Six. We just shot a sniper out of a tree. Have four confirmed NVA KIA. If we're going to stay here much longer, we need the FO. Over."

"This is Six. FO has first round on the way. You direct from there. Keep up the good work."

The FO had given the gun crews bad coordinates. The rounds exploded too far away for me to hear them. I started dropping the shells two hundred yards at a time. I heard the muffled crash of a shell about four hundred yards away and was preparing a new set of corrections when the captain told me to cease fire. An Air Force spotter plane wanted a target. I told the FAC that we were too close to the target for an air strike, but maybe his rockets could help. I knew how inaccurate spotter planes were for close support in thick jungle, so I instructed him to hit one of the hills from where the Vietnamese had been firing at the snakes.

I spotted a man running up our trail from the swamp. I thought the FO was finally coming forward to help us. But it wasn't the FO. Colonel Black flopped down beside me. "You call those rockets close, Lieutenant?"

"No, sir. That's a FAC and I wa . . ."

"Why haven't you got a position by that log in front of you?"

"Sir, there's a machine gun on the other side of it. I think they're in bunkers, and I'm planning to pull back about thirty meters and get some artillery in there. We're too close in to crack the bunkers."

"We don't know that they're in bunkers. You're not pulling out! Get your men back up past that machine gun!" His tone told me he thought he was talking to a coward. The pompous ass had nothing better to do than take over my two platoons in a battle he knew nothing about. I wondered what medal he was trying to win.

274

The colonel crawled up to the log, followed by the other platoon sergeant. I crawled forward with ten frightened men until we were against the bamboo where the antitank rockets had been striking. I could see the patterns on the soles of the dead sniper's jungle boots, about five yards in front of us. I guessed that there was a trench just behind his body. The colonel looked over at me and frowned. "Have all your men got grenades, Lieutenant?"

"I'll check."

"See that they do. Each man should have a grenade to throw when the NVA try to close with us."

Try to close with us? They weren't about to leave their bunkers and trenches when they were doing so much damage without exposing their asses. The colonel must have been in the open Mekong Delta, and he thought he was still there. Any grenades we threw would bounce back on us, so I passed out three of my four grenades, whispering to my men not to use them unless we pulled back from the bamboo. "Don't listen to that idiot colonel!"

The platoon sergeant and the colonel peeped over the top of their log. The machine gun opened up, and I watched the sergeant do a back-somersault down the slope. Two soldiers grabbed his arms and dragged him away toward the swamp. More pieces of bark flew off the log. I crawled over to the colonel.

"Sir, we had four men wounded by that fire. I think we should pull back and give the artillery a chance."

He gave me a look of pure hate and disgust. I was a piss-ant lieutenant, questioning a colonel's judgment. "We're staying here, Lieutenant. I've spotted a bunker on that hill, and we're waiting for LAWs to knock it out."

"Sir, that's just one bunker. Delayed fuse artillery would get more. I can bring it in."

"No! The LAWs will be here soon."

The firing along the bamboo was now a continuous roar. I could see a line of blinking muzzle flashes just behind the dead sniper. My seven surviving soldiers were lying facedown in the leaves, playing dead. When the NVA fire stopped for a moment, I pulled them all back behind the trail, leaving only the machine gun forward. The Vietnamese apparently couldn't see its location through the bamboo. We left the colonel and his radioman behind the log. I wasn't going to lose more men to get a crazy officer a medal.

The colonel directed another team of snakes at the hill, but the rockets exploded far behind the bunkers. As the choppers pulled away, another wall of bullets swept over us. The man beside me was shot through the ear from somewhere behind us. There were only a hole and bits of cartilage and skin left. I crawled back to the log. "Sir, we got three more men hit."

He looked around and saw my one-eared soldier. "How did the one by the tree get hit?"

"Sniper." You stupid son of a bitch.

I helped a gut-shot man back to the medical station on the edge of the swamp. It was still far forward of the captain, the FO, and a bunch of other frightened, cowardly soldiers. I saw my platoon sergeant for the first time since the mines had exploded. He was bleeding from a gaping back wound. He had run away and hid with the wounded as soon as the firing started. A ricochet had ripped open his back. Specialist Wilson crouched beside another stretcher. I patted him on the shoulder, trying to see how badly he was wounded.

"Where'd you get hit, Wilson? Is it bad?"

He stared at me in silence.

"Is it bad?"

He shook his head. "I'm not hit, sir."

I didn't understand. "Then why are you back here?"

"I don't know." He looked away for a moment. "I'm scared."

"Let's go back up there. We need all the rifles we can get."

He shook his head again. "No. Sir, I can't do it."

For the first time, I realized that he wasn't hurt. "Let's go!"

There was terror and shame in his eyes. "No!"

"Wilson, it's your ass. If we both get out of here . . ." I took his ammunition pouches and ran back toward the hill.

Another infantry company landed on the far side of the hill and were quickly pinned down. A medevac chopper picked up a load of wounded at the swamp and flew over our heads. NVA on four hills opened fire. Some of my wounded were hit another time. After an hour-long wait, a soldier ran up from the swamp with four LAWs (Light Anti-Tank Weapon). He fired where the colonel pointed. The first two LAWs thudded into the ground—duds. The next two exploded with deep crashes. Two direct hits on a dead tree. That was the colonel's bunker. It was almost dark when the colonel directed the last team of snakes. The 40mm cannon shells exploded in the treetops far above us.

He gave me a look of triumph. "Now, that scared them, Lieutenant."

"Yes, sir." And that was all it did. He was settling for scaring the NVA.

After one last gun battle with the NVA, we pulled back to the swamp. I was the last man in the file and carried four rifles, belts of machine gun ammo, and two packs. I tossed all of this garbage on a growing pile of discarded equipment in the muddy water.

The captain was sitting beside the pile. He caught my eye. "It doesn't mean much now, but you did a good job up there."

I remembered his absence during the battle and shouted one word, "Ha!" He looked away in embarrassed silence.

Jets dropped napalm bombs in the darkness and missed the hill. The FO finally stopped pissing in his pants and brought artillery shells around us until dawn. A fragment split open my skin to the tailbone, but I didn't care or feel anymore. I made a mud cake to stop the bleeding and sat in the swamp water with a machine gun across my lap, waiting for the attack that never came.

The captain sent the survivors of the two platoons away from the swamp at dawn. He wanted us to avoid seeing the bodies of our friends on the hill. I now commanded six men, instead of twenty-four, and what was left of the other platoon. The wait for the LAWs had cost us twelve more seriously injured soldiers. When we returned to the swamp, I saw the four twisted body bags and another pile of useless weapons. The soldiers from the other company were resting against their packs and smoking. I found one of their lieutenants seated on a mud mound in the swamp.

I pointed to the body bags. "Did they die quickly?"

He nodded. "A claymore messed them up real bad. The gooks didn't take their rifles or radio, so you must have scared them. There were some unexploded RPG rounds up there."

"Yeah. I'll bet we scared them. They didn't take the damned rifles because they don't need them. They don't have to capture stuff anymore."

He stroked his chin. "You may be right. Looks like the same bunch that wasted Delta Company two months ago. Did they get your lieutenant?"

"No. That's me. I stopped wearing my rank a long time ago. I'm interested to know what we were up against."

"Well, there were three trench lines with bunkers on them. They had a lot of cartridge cases in them. Looked like Sunday morning at a shooting gallery. There was one big bunker on the top of the hill. Looks like they used that for an aid station. We found some Chicom grenades and a lot of bloody bandages, no bodies. Does that sum it up?"

"Just about. Did the rockets do any damage?"

"No. They brought down some branches but didn't hurt the bunkers much. Sorry about that. Are you the guy who brought them in? The word's out that some platoon leader did some pretty fancy shooting."

"I brought in some of them. The ones closest to the kill zone. One last question. Was there a bunker next to the dead men, in front of that log?"

"Yes. It had hundreds of .30 caliber shell casings on top of it. A big trench running right behind it. We found a lot of dried blood. If you ask me, I'd say they changed crews a couple of times."

At least a few of our killers had been repayed. "Thanks."

The two-day walk out of the jungle was a horror for the Company. We found more NVA camps, and these were now terrifying places. At the site of our battle, the other company was discovering an underground hospital and a battalion base camp. An elite Viet Cong "guards" company had been holding the hill above us. Three other hills also had garrison companies.

We followed elephant trails through the jungle until we reached a series of banana and cassava plantations and finally the road. We waited for over an hour for the transport trucks to arrive. I climbed into the cab of a truck beside a smiling driver. He had no right to be grinning after the ordeal that we had just experienced. I glared at him and he crowded against the door.

"You guys had a hard time of it from what I hear."

"Yes. Why are you so damned happy?"

Now the big secret. "Sir, I've got some good news. Have you heard the latest?"

"We've been out of touch for a few days."

"Sir, Ho Chi Minh is dead! The war might be over in a few days."

I thought back across four years to the soldier who had hitched a ride in the dump truck in An Khe Village. We had all believed then that it was almost finished. There was always that hope among soldiers. I looked at the teenage driver. He was straining to catch my reply. "Don't count on it, partner." My answer disappointed him.

The trucks left us at an ARVN camp. Wilson was waiting for me as I stepped down from the cab. He looked tired and afraid. "What're you going to do to me, sir?"

"Nothing."

His eyes widened in disbelief. "Nothing?"

"Wilson, I don't condone what you did. You abandoned your platoon when they needed you most, but I've been doing a lot of thinking on the walk out. You weren't the only one who wasn't there. If somebody got called on the carpet for cowardice, they'd have to investigate the platoon sergeant, the company medics, the captain, the FO, and about twenty other men. None of them showed their smiling asses during the whole afternoon."

"I know that, sir, but thanks all the same. It means a lot to me."

"Wilson, you have to do one thing for me. Go back to Redcatcher and get a job driving a jeep or something. Tell the first sergeant you are one of only six men left out of a platoon. Tell him I sent you. I'll square it with the captain if he asks any questions. One more thing. When you're a civilian one day, think

279

about everything that happened and maybe think a kind thought about me.''

His expression was a mixture of gratitude and relief. He saluted like a recruit. ''Yes, sir!''

I spent the last night with the company on ambush with the two platoons. Wilson and I left for Redcatcher the next morning. There I met the new platoon sergeant and another batch of targets, more of the long-faced draftees. They would be luckier than most. Their platoon sergeant was a tough old veteran of both Korea and Vietnam. I arrived in time to hear Armed Forces Radio describe our battle—moderate American casualties near Zuan Loc, twenty to forty NVA dead. They were broadcasting trash. Later, President Nixon made a speech. He said that American troops had been engaged only in defensive operations for the past month. If that were true, my draftees would still be alive. Just more lies and trash. I wanted to be alive to vote for anyone but Nixon.

CHAPTER 19

Twilight

I had to make one last trip north, had to see the Blues one more time. They were playing volleyball between rows of rubber trees when I arrived. The few of them who recognized me shouted and waved. They were proud and professional once again, and Terry beamed over the quality of the soldiers he was leading. As far as he was concerned, the war would go on forever, and Americans weren't being withdrawn from the rice paddies and jungles.

"They're a fine bunch, Matt. We took on an NVA recon company on the border a couple of weeks ago. Greased fifteen before they turned and ran. The gooks weren't recruits, either. One of them came at me with a fixed bayonet. Blew him into a tree with a frag. Neatest somersault you ever saw. The snakes caught more of them carrying wounded across a clearing an hour later. Wiped out the whole gang."

"Sounds like the Blues I knew in the days of Bong Son and Chu Lai. In the Old Cav."

His eyes clouded over for a moment. "The Old Cav. They called the Blues the Headhunters in those days. I've found my home here."

"If that's what you want." It went unsaid between us that this platoon had many volunteers, that once any group of draftees could have fought as well. One face was missing, and I had to know. "Where's Granite?"

Terry hung his head. "We had to send him to a hospital for a while. There was a rocket attack. A one-twenty-two hit next to the bunker he was in, and he went crazy. Driving a truck up and down the flight line through the rockets. He never was the same after that."

Oh. That kind of hospital. "Sorry to hear it."

Kelly was excited about the missions the Blues were being given. They were chasing NVA down trails, taking prisoners, and searching base camps. He was surprised when I told him that the platoon had always done those things until the last horrible year. Everything was the same again, but nothing was really the same. The long patrols of the early years had been replaced by actions that stressed a short distance to the target area and little time on the ground. Instead of the gunships avoiding the area where the platoon was patrolling, so they wouldn't give away the Blues' location, they now flew as noisy gun platforms along the line of march. Minimum combat exposure and few casualties were the new yardsticks of success.

Kelly asked if I wanted to make one last landing with the Blues. I wanted to say yes and no at the same time. My war was officially over, but I had to do it. I had stopped counting combat assaults in the spring of that year, but this would make at least 419 landings with a Blue platoon.

The scouts had killed three NVA on an infiltration trail from Cambodia. The slicks carried us past Nui Ba Ra, over one of the "instant LZs." It had been blasted out of the jungle with a 10,000-pound butane bomb, and I could see howitzers and bunkers at the circular position below. The concussion from those bombs was supposed to kill everything above and below the ground in a radius of one thousand yards. I had talked to enough grunts to believe that claim. Butane bombs reduced triple-canopy jungle to a clearing of ankle-high stubble and created an additional nine-hundred-yard zone of death. Ants, beetles, snakes, birds, monkeys, tigers, and always a few unlucky NVA would die in one roaring instant.

When the slicks dropped toward a grassy swamp, I fought the urge not to jump. I understood a little of what Ray must have felt at Chu Lai. We landed in the swamp and followed a trail into the jungle. The trail was a well-engineered affair, camouflaged by branches tied together with vines and floored with woven bamboo mats. Along both sides were pieces of uniforms, torn NVA jungle boots, bits of plastic ponchos, rotting packs, and the remains of Vietnamese and American rations. The trail had been used for years.

After spending fifty days with a noisy, clanking infantry company, I found it hard to believe how silently the Blues moved. For the first time in many days, I wasn't alone when I walked down a trail. It was good to be back with them. A squad patrolled to the place where the bodies had been, but their comrades had already dragged them away. We stopped by a muddy stream, listening to snakes firing flechette rockets into a rest camp ahead of us.

Kelly motioned for Terry. "Those hooches are inside Cambodia. Take a patrol there and return."

Terry smiled. "Right, sir."

Fifteen minutes later, American rifles fired long bursts into Cambodian woods. Terry burned the hooches and returned. The Blues would be among the first Americans into Cambodia in Nixon's 1970 invasion. When we returned to the swamp, a snake was hovering there, spraying its minigun at two NVA on the far side. The minigun stopped for a moment, and two green uniforms disappeared into the trees. Then the slicks were clattering above us and it was over.

Terry and I sat in his room at Quan Loi that night and talked about the past. He recited the familiar ritual, the brutal litany. Those who had been hit by bullets since I left, those who had been hit in the shellings, those who were burned alive, those who had broken under fire. He told me about a sapper attack in August, when forty of the tough NVA commandos had died. I told him about September fifth, when my platoon and my purpose had died. The next morning, I sadly headed to the flight line for the first leg of my long trip back to Redcatcher. I knew that I would probably never see any of the Blues again and would never again ride the skids into a landing zone. That had once been my life, but it was really over this time.

I was riding in a jeep toward the ARVN camp, delivering pay to the company. It was my last official duty. I had a pistol on my lap, and I constantly scanned the rubber trees and jungle. I remembered the frightened major at Mang Yang Pass on my first convoy, four long years before. Now I was the frightened officer, waiting for the unknown. There was only a half mile to go. Clack-clack-clack-clack. A bullet ricocheted off the hood, and the driver floored the accelerator. I emptied the .45 automatic at the trees, shoved in another magazine, and fired again.

I shouted at the stunned driver, "They're not going to kill me now!" Then we were at the camp.

The captain walked over as I stepped out of the jeep. "The VC have been sniping at vehicles. Did you hear any firing coming down the road?"

"Yeah. They put some rounds past us."

A slow nod. "We'll set up an ambush tonight. Maybe we'll get lucky and catch a couple of them."

"Good luck. 'Bush that finger of jungle about five hundred meters west of here." That was my last experience with an enemy I had fought for so long but could never understand.

The final days at Redcatcher were long and painful. I spent the days on minor duties and spent the nights drinking cheap Army champagne. I blamed myself for the six dead men in the last battle and relived the engagement over and over again. I should have ignored the captain and reconned that trail. I should have told my men more about claymore mines. I should have gone after the machine gun behind the log. I was bitter to the point of tears. It had been so stupid, trying to keep those bungling soldiers alive in the jungle. It hadn't been a fair fight—American college boys against Asian peasants. Even to know that I had killed more Vietnamese tore at my heart. But more than anything else, Colonel Black had finally and completely broken my spirit. He might as well have been blind and deaf. And so it went.

284

I began to find fault and see humor where there was none. I was drunk when a captain in a jeep wanted to tell me about the body of his Red Cross girl friend. "You've probably seen her around. She's a natural blond"—a wink—"and she has one of the nicest . . ."

"You rear echelon son of a bitch. You sit back here and plug your damned donut dolly while men are dying out in those hills. Goddamned coward!"

He reached for the notebook that all correct officers carry in their left breast pockets. "What's your unit, Lieutenant?" Some friends pulled me away before he could get my name and number and report me.

On another night I stood on a chair at the Senior NCO Club and challenged anyone in the place to a fight. A group of first sergeants and sergeant majors laughed me through the door. I was pissing one evening in a buried fifty-gallon oil drum painted with the words CLEAR ALL WEAPONS. I was thinking how funny it was when the company first sergeant walked up behind me.

"Clearing your weapon, Lieutenant?"

"You got it, Top."

He waited for me to finish, then put his hand on my shoulder. "Look, if you keep drinking like this, you're not going to have a liver left when you get home."

His concern irritated me. He should go away and leave me alone. "I got things to forget!"

He spat. "Stop feeling sorry for yourself, sir. Nobody's blaming you for what happened out there. The FO broke down one night and told me you carried the show. He said that everyone else was afraid to go forward. Hell, they put you in for a Silver Star."

"Fuck that piece of tin! They're only trying to cover their asses. Nobody came forward except the colonel, and he got a lot of men hurt. I was with a Blue platoon. They were a team. Then they sent me to this sorry outfit. Why can't the training camps send us men who can take orders and stay alive?"

He had listened to my babbling with patience, then he raised his voice. "I know about the Cav. I was with them in Korea. I

285

saw your Blues beat up a dozen MPs here one night in March. But you don't mean what you said about Bravo Company. It's people who make anything good or bad, not numbers. You know how the platoon was shaping up. Every enlisted man in the company wanted to be in your platoon, because if anyone could keep them alive, you could.''

"Yeah. But now they're all dead or wounded. I'm leaving the green machine.''

He was tired of my self-pity. His eyes were hard when he spoke again. "Six men are dead. It could have been a lot more. Look, Lieutenant. You've got a good career ahead of you, but what you do after you leave here is your business. You'll be going home in a few days. Try to cut down on the booze and pull yourself together.'' I thanked him in a sullen voice, and he was gone. Time to clear my weapon again.

I wanted to stay drunk until I boarded the jet for home. It seemed to be the only way to get through those last days. I was drinking more champagne in the officers' club when two muffled explosions came from the direction of a USO show. Officers, waitresses, and the bartender ran through the door and scurried into a bomb shelter outside. I was alone with my bottle.

I shouted to the empty tables. "Those idiots! Anyone can tell those were grenades and not mortars! What they need is a one-twenty-two to really scare them!''

As I sipped the champagne, I didn't question why someone would lob grenades in the middle of a sprawling American base. Two blacks had tossed grenades into a crowd of whites. Two GIs had killed two other GIs and wounded many more. I was witnessing the beginning of the disintegration of an army, once a truly formidable army. There was nothing left.

Only once did the problems of other men help me to forget my own. I read in the *Stars and Stripes* that a battalion of the 18th NVA Regiment, our old friends from the Suoi Ca, had tried to ambush a supply convoy in the Deo Mang Pass. I remembered the tough Koreans along the pass, doing martial arts training in their underwear. The article said that the Koreans had driven the

NVA back into the mountains with heavy losses. Martin was long since home, so I raised a silent glass and toasted those brave men of the Suoi Ca one last time. "To the Eighteenth NVA Regiment: may they sleep on firm straw pallets tonight and may their rice rolls be full."

The 1st Cav sniper found me at Tan Son Nhut terminal. I had known him at Quan Loi, and he wanted to recite his latest deeds. On his last mission in Vietnam, he had wanted to do everything right. He had broken the legs of a young NVA with his bullets and waited patiently all afternoon while the boy screamed for help. At dusk, two other Vietnamese had crawled out of the jungle. The sniper killed all three of them. "Only cost Uncle Sam thirty-five cents, Matt." Now he laughed.

I remembered the day in 1966 when a 1st Cav soldier carrying six rifles had told me a story. Four of his friends had tried to help the wounded man, and a sniper had killed them all. He had been afraid and didn't crawl out of the bushes like the others. He lay in the bushes throughout the night, with the bodies of his friends only a few feet away. In the morning, the sniper was gone. I took a gulp from my bottle and waited for the jet. The horror of the war was destroying me. Every story reminded me of other stories.

I boarded the plane for America with the police lieutenant from New York. Now he was going to tell the street punks what the war was really like. For my part, I was only confused and afraid. As the jet left the runway at Tan Son Nhut, I tensed for the twelve-seven fire that would surely come. After what I had done to their country, they would never let me leave. Only the roar of the jet engines. "They're letting me out alive!" As the jet crossed the Pacific, I swore that never again would I bitch at the thought of leading a quiet life. I should have died many times and hadn't; now I would use that gift of life. I silently prayed, "Dear God in heaven. It's finally over!"

The jet touched down in San Francisco on Moratorium Day, 1969. I walked through the terminal past people singing protest songs and others reading the lists of war dead. Were the 9th Cav's dead on the lists? The early ones who had loved the killing so much? Were my platoon's dead draftees yet among them? A long-

287

haired man in a cowhide coat handed me a pamphlet on the "immoral war in Southeast Asia." I had never seen such long hair on a man.

I caught another jet for home. Beside me was a Marine recruit, just out of boot camp, muttering about the damned hippies. I wasn't sure what they were, but I knew that much of what they were saying was true. The war was lost. Moral issues aside, the shameful quality of the new draftees led to that conclusion. I watched my country glide beneath the jet until the snow-capped mountains of Colorado were behind me. Then I opened Heinlein's new book, *Stranger in a Strange Land,* and began to read. It was a fitting title.

Epilogue

I told the officers at Fort Benning, Georgia, what they wanted to hear. "Yes. I'll go back to Vietnam when they need me." But I made a hard decision at Christmas in 1969 that I could no longer remain in the Army. I was proud of my years in the war, but the memories were too powerful. Even the sight of dead animals along the highway overwhelmed me.

I tried to resign my commission and was refused. Then I went through several difficult and draining months, awaiting discharge as a conscientious objector. One day in April, the nightmare was over. I walked into a field of flowers in Georgia and let the raindrops caress my face. There was only life ahead of me. Perhaps I could help to better a world that I had once helped to destroy.

The effects and memories of the war didn't vanish quickly, even after the troubled sleep was past. I have more than once driven my car off the road after a truck backfired. The Fourth of July is a night of uneasiness and drawn shades. A silent walk or an approach from behind is unsettling. I can see anything moving a long time before my friends can, although the survival value of such vision is only a memory. But the emotions and reflexes have dimmed.

Once, I saw the Blues at Quan Loi on the evening news. I didn't dare to watch the program again for weeks. They were doing helicopter rescues. I wanted to be with them. Later I saw the 18th NVA Regiment being hurt again. I toasted them from a small room in Boston where I was studying at the time. When the familiar provinces toppled in 1975, I buried myself deeper in my studies and stopped watching television altogether.

I was working in Washington, D.C., when the veterans marched in November 1982. For the first time in my life, people hugged me and welcomed me home from the war. We stood in front of the black granite memorial and cried for ourselves and the names on the wall. I returned home that night and found an unfinished manuscript that had gathered dust for ten years.

This book is as accurate as memory and notes allow. I changed the names and some of the personal characteristics of all the characters except John Martin and Sergeant Samuel. Both of them were special people in my early life. Some of the men who served in Vietnam with me will want to remain anonymous. Others would prefer to tell their own versions of what they experienced during the war.

I first wanted to write this book a decade ago to tell Americans who weren't there what Vietnam was like, without the exaggeration and distortion that comes with most war novels. As I put these words down on paper, however, I realized that the audience that really matters to me is the Marine and Army grunts who had to eat mud for twelve or thirteen months. America didn't want us when we returned, and I believe most combat veterans are now beyond caring what she thinks of us, or of our actions in her name. The wounds are deep, but by sharing our experiences, we can help each other to forget and be proud once again.

This was not an easy story to write. I had to drag out memories that I had spent years trying to forget. Now I know that some things cannot be forgotten. There was a story that wanted telling. Now it is told.